UNINSURED
IN AMERICA

UNINSURED IN AMERICA

LIFE AND DEATH IN THE LAND OF OPPORTUNITY

UPDATED WITH A NEW AFTERWORD

SUSAN STARR SERED AND RUSHIKA FERNANDOPULLE

UNIVERSITY OF CALIFORNIA PRESS
BERKELEY LOS ANGELES LONDON

University of California Press, one of the most distinguished
university presses in the United States, enriches lives around the
world by advancing scholarship in the humanities, social sciences,
and natural sciences. Its activities are supported by the UC Press
Foundation and by philanthropic contributions from individuals and
institutions. For more information, visit www.ucpress.edu.

University of California Press
Berkeley and Los Angeles, California

University of California Press, Ltd.
London, England

Library of Congress Cataloging-in-Publication Data

Sered, Susan, Starr.
  Uninsured in America : life and death in the land of
opportunity / Susan Starr Sered and Rushika Fernandopulle.
     p.   cm.
  "Updated with a new afterword."
  Includes bibliographical references and index.
  ISBN-13: 978-0-520-25006-2 (pbk. : alk. paper)
  ISBN-10: 0-520-25006-0 (pbk. : alk. paper)
    1. Medically uninsured persons—United States.   2. Insurance,
Health—Social aspects—United States.   3. Insurance,
Health—Economic aspects—United States.   4. Health
services accessibility—United States.   5. Right to health
care—United States.   6. Social classes—Health
aspects—United States.   7. Marginality, Social—Health
aspects—United States.   8. Working class—Health and
hygiene—United States.   I. Fernandopulle, Rushika J.
II. Title.

RA413.7.U53S47   2007
368.38′200973—dc22   2006044487

Manufactured in the United States of America

15   14   13   12   11   10   09   08   07

10   9   8   7   6   5   4   3   2   1

We dedicate this book to the uninsured women and men who shared their experiences with us and trusted us to do our best to make sure that their voices are heard.

The initial interviews that inform this book were conducted during the years 2003–04.
Many of the people we met at that time kindly agreed to stay in touch and share with us the challenges—and triumphs—that they face.
In 2005 we carried out a set of follow-up interviews in order better to understand the ongoing meaning of being uninsured in America.
These updates, together with comments on recent health care policy trends, are in the new Afterword.

CONTENTS

ACKNOWLEDGMENTS \ ix

Prologue: Loretta and Greg's Story \ xv

Introduction: The Death Spiral \ 1

1. From Working Class to Working Poor:
The Death of Industry in America's Heartland \ 21

2. Medicaid, Welfare Reform, and Low-Wage Work
in the New Economy \ 40

3. Family Matters: Divorce and Domestic Violence \ 57

4. Who Cares for the Caregivers?
Love as a Portal into the Death Spiral \ 72

5. The Fox Guarding the Henhouse:
Work-Related Injuries and the Vagaries
of Workers' Compensation \ 86

6. Risky Business: The Self-Employed, Small Business
Owners, and Other American Entrepreneurs \ 107

7. Young, Sick, and Part-Time: The Vulnerability
of Youth and the New American Job Market \ 122

8. Mental Health Matters: A Mexican Immigrant Hits
the Bureaucratic Wall \ 140

9. Race Matters: Health Care Stories
from Black America \ 152

10. Descent through the Death Spiral \ 163

11: Moving Forward \ 184

Afterword: Several Years Later \ 195

Appendix 1: A Primer on the U.S. Health Care System
and the Safety Net \ 217

Appendix 2: Resources for Health Care \ 227

NOTES \ 229
BIBLIOGRAPHY \ 239
INDEX \ 257

ACKNOWLEDGMENTS

This book was jointly conceived by Susan Sered and Rushika Fernandopulle. Susan conducted most of the fieldwork on which the book is
based and is the primary author of chapters 1 through 10 as well as the
introduction. Rushika is the primary author of chapter 11 and appendix
1 and has contributed medical and policy expertise at each stage of this
project. John Mihelich co-authored chapters 1 and 5.

SUSAN SERED WRITES   This book was truly a collaborative effort.
   At each fieldwork site, local scholars and activists worked with me to
identify interviewees, understand local variations and conditions, and
make sense of the huge amount of information gathered. Many of these
local research associates became fast friends over the course of this project, and for that I am truly grateful.
   In Idaho, Debbie Storrs and John Mihelich, professors at the University of Idaho, were my guides to Idaho culture, society, and economics. (We also had a lot of fun visiting local bars together!) John was kind
enough to read numerous drafts of the manuscript and spent countless
hours brainstorming with me. His insights into the restructuring of the
American economy and the changing nature of blue-collar work appear
throughout this book. Working with Debbie and John has been one of
the very best parts of this project. I also wish to thank Sharon Connors,

director of Social Services for Shoshone County, for her clear explanations of the county public aid system; Terri Sterling of the Idaho Community Action Network for her important insights into what it means to scrape by in Idaho; Dale Bates of the Benewah Medical and Wellness Center in Plummer for his hospitality; Frankie Yockey and Ila Burch for helping us network in Troy and Orofino; and members of the Read to Me Coalition in Orofino for their open, honest, informative, and enthusiastic conversations.

In Mississippi, Lynne Cossman, professor at Mississippi State University, and Melody Burrage, a graduate student at MSU, traveled with me through the Delta, Meridian, and Starkville regions. Their deep knowledge of southern society, together with their patience and good humor, was indispensable. Lynne helped me work through repeated drafts of the manuscript, providing sociological insight and close attention to details. Thank you! I also wish to thank Robert Cadenhead, chief executive officer of Kings Daughters Hospital; Robert Bell, executive director of Delta Health Ventures; George Scheiderman at Deporres Delta Ministries; Bishop Dennis E. Huggins Jr., senior pastor of the First Apostolic Church of West Meridian; and Kathy Tentinto at the Good Samaritan Medical Center in Columbus for taking the time to share their thoughts and experiences.

In Texas, Maria Luisa Urdaneta, a nurse and professor of anthropology at the University of Texas in San Antonio, served as tour guide, culture broker, interpreter, colleague, and friend in the Rio Grande Valley. Her hospitality, encouragement, and vast knowledge of Mexican American experience have been vital to this project. I particularly want to thank the wonderful women of ARISE (A Resource in Serving Equality) who introduced me to their community and to their important work on behalf of Mexican Americans in south Texas. I also wish to thank Carmen Boudreau at the Brady Green and Yolanda Santos at the Good Samaritan Center for sharing their keen knowledge of health care issues in San Antonio.

In Illinois, Claudia Lennhoff and the Champaign County Health Care

Consumers were my hosts. It was a privilege to see the work of this dedicated, grassroots community organization. In Decatur, a large group of individuals offered their expertise, extensive knowledge of the community, and personal and professional networks: thanks go to Stu Ellis, Mildred Warren, Rexlyn Nicole, Diana Lading, Judy Gibbs, Hugh Phillips, and Karen Schneller as well as to Ken Smithmier, chief executive officer of the Decatur Memorial Hospital; and Barbara Dunn, director of the Community Health Improvement Center. In Danville, Cheryl Rome, Pam Burgoyne, Jonathan Jett, Robert Frazer, and the staff of the Vermillion Area Community Health Center shed light on the economic and health issues of the community. I thank Allison Jones for being my patient and good-humored guide and companion in Decatur.

In Massachusetts, Rob Restuccia and his colleagues at Health Care for All helped us network with uninsured Massachusetts residents and gain a clearer understanding of state policies that affect the uninsured. Rob's encouragement from the start of this project has been an ongoing inspiration. Pazit Aviv at Jewish Family and Children's Services generously assisted me in making connections in the Boston Jewish community. Phyllis Howard, long-time volunteer at the Worcester Evening Free Medical Services Program held at the Epworth and Wesley United Methodist Churches, explained the challenges faced by volunteer and faith-based clinics.

George Sheth, senior director at Trianz Inc., patiently read and commented on several versions of chapter 6, which focuses on small business owners. We are in awe of both the breadth of his knowledge and his generosity.

Marty Malin, Martha McCluskey, Mark Zientz, Lisa Cullen, and Linda Landry patiently walked us through the health care maze of workers' compensation and disability. Susan Stefan helped me make sense of the legal issues surrounding psychiatric disabilities.

Frank Furstenberg offered important insights into the experiences of young adults, and his input was crucial in developing the ideas in chapter 7.

Lynn Davidman, colleague and dear friend, offered support, encouragement, and sociological insights during every stage of this project.

Susan Lloyd McGarry, my colleague at the Center for the Study of World Religions, tracked down references, edited the manuscript, sorted out travel receipts, and kept a steady supply of tapes on hand, in addition to taking charge of countless other critical tasks.

Sharon Kivenko served as the primary research assistant on this project. Thank you, Sharon! We are very lucky indeed to have had her on the project team.

Debra Cash and Bill Novak were kind enough to (repeatedly) share their expertise regarding the world of publishing, and Julie Arnow helped to pick a title for the book.

We particularly thank Larry Sullivan for making the funding and time for this project possible.

Naomi Schneider, our editor and friend, shepherded the book through the publishing process at truly incredible speed, offering insightful suggestions along the way. We also wish to thank Mary Renaud and Dore Brown for their exceptionally dedicated and professional editing of this book.

My son, Barak Sered, and my father, Robert Starr, served as sounding boards for ideas, read drafts of the manuscript, and helped identify the core themes that are developed in this book. Thank you!

My family—Yishai, Yoav, Asher, Shifra, and Barak—have kept me company, kept me sane, kept me grounded, and enveloped me with love and support.

RUSHIKA FERNANDOPULLE WRITES   In addition to the people mentioned above, a number of others helped us understand what it means to be uninsured in the places we visited, what services are available, and how the current policy climate affects their particular states and localities. Many are front-line workers or advocates, asked to do much with very few resources, and their generosity with their time and wisdom is especially appreciated.

In Jackson, Mississippi, Roy Mitchell, from the Mississippi Health Advocacy Program; Teresa Hanna, from the State Department of Insurance; and Rica Lewis-Payton, executive director of the Division of Medicaid, explained policy questions regarding the state's uninsured. For pointing out issues that especially affect some of the poorest Americans living in the Delta, we thank Sister Anne Brooks from the Tutwiler Clinic; Hugh Gamble, a surgeon in Greenville; Tim Alford, past president of the Mississippi Academy of Family Physicians; and Robert Bell, executive director of Delta Health Ventures.

In Texas, Eliot Shapleigh, Texas state senator, and Anne Dunkelberg, from the Center for Public Policy Priorities, offered their perspectives on the plight of the uninsured in Texas. Ileana Hinojosa spent many hours speaking candidly to us about her years of experience in serving uninsured individuals along the Mexican border; and Pete Duarte, administrator of Thomason Hospital in El Paso, described the difficulties in running the area's provider of last resort. Mary Helen Mays, executive director of Community Voices, recounted the effects of budget crises on the operation of nonprofit, advocacy, and service groups dedicated to the uninsured.

In Idaho, Michelle Britton was kind enough to set up a focus group in Coeur D'Alene that allowed us to meet consumers, providers, and administrators and hear their viewpoints. Laura Rowan, from the Office of Rural Health; Mike Wilson, from the business community; and LeeAnn Hall and Jessica Fry of the Idaho Community Action Network helped us identify contacts and understand the politics in the state. Alan Conilogue taught us about Idaho's workers' compensation system, and Bill Foxcroft from the Idaho Primary Care Association explained the challenges faced by federally qualified health centers in rural parts of the state.

Here in Massachusetts, Mark Rukavina, executive director of the Access Project, was extremely helpful in identifying important issues, people, and areas of focus.

David Cutler, professor of economics and assistant dean of the Faculty of Arts and Sciences at Harvard, helped to sponsor us through the

Institutional Review Board process. Amy Trenkle and Hyunsook Ryu Song assisted with research and logistics for our fieldwork. Liza Rudell, my research assistant, did background work on each of the states we targeted.

David Blumenthal, director of the Harvard Interfaculty Program for Health Systems Improvement and of the Institute for Health Policy at Partners HealthCare, deserves special recognition for having faith in me and in this project and for making the funding and my time available to allow us to complete this work.

Finally, and most important, I would like to thank my wife, Maria, and my daughters, Gabrielle, Serena, and Kathryn (who was born in the middle of our research). Their support has been invaluable, and I hope that any positive impact this book may have on helping those who are uninsured makes up for the many evenings, weekends, and weeks I was absent while working on this project.

Funding for the fieldwork and tape transcriptions was provided by Harvard Divinity School's Center for the Study of World Religions and by Harvard University's Interfaculty Program for Health Systems Improvement. Opinions stated in this book are those of the authors and not necessarily those of either of these research centers or of Harvard University.

LORETTA AND GREG'S STORY

Walking up to Loretta's front door on the outskirts of a midsized town in Mississippi presents something of a challenge. Her neighborhood was built on a swamp, and the developer has not planted lawns or put in proper drainage. After a few rainy days, the ground between the street and her door is inches deep in slushy Mississippi mud.

The chaotic signs of poverty that mark her neighborhood—rusting cars in driveways, a broken washing machine in front of a house, muddy and cluttered lawns—are a far cry from the orderly military-base housing in which Loretta, the blue-eyed daughter of a career army man, grew up. With a love of literature and hopes of becoming a veterinarian, Loretta believed in the American dream. Her father was securely employed in a setting that guaranteed good health care and other benefits for his family. Loretta, with her long hair, bright eyes, and glowing complexion, fit in well in the stable working-class communities where she spent her youth. In 1990, she married Greg, a self-employed flooring subcontractor dedicated to precision in his craft, and envisioned a comfortable life with a chance to move up the ladder of opportunity.

But times changed, and life, as Loretta reiterates, doesn't always turn out the way you planned.

In early 2003, she heard through a friend at her job at Mississippi State University that some visiting professors were interested in hearing how families without health insurance try to scrape by. Loretta signed up right away.

And that is how we found ourselves gingerly navigating our way from the curb to Loretta's front door, as she called out instructions about how to step down in the few spots where it was possible to walk without mucking up our shoes too badly.

PHYSICAL CUES

Loretta welcomes us warmly, offering us seats on a torn couch and an unsteady chair in the room that serves as entrance hall, living room, dining room, and play room. She apologizes for the blotches of mud that her five children (ages one to eleven), several cats, three dogs, and various other assorted pets have tracked into the house.

It is hard to piece together the physical cues that would allow us to guess Loretta's age. Her white skin is smooth and unwrinkled, and her long hair has no gray; but her sagging breasts and belly seem to belong to a much older woman. Her eyes are clear and animated, but she squints to see us—she needs glasses, "but they charge an arm and a leg for them." She had a pair of glasses when she was on Medicaid during her last pregnancy, but the kids broke them. She tells us that she manages okay without them, except when she drives. She is wearing an oversized t-shirt, somewhat faded and stained, and no shoes ("too much mud, it's not worth it"). Her hair is mussed up by the baby and a toddler, who take turns sitting on her lap.

But the most striking aspect of her appearance is her teeth, or, to be more accurate, the absence of most of her teeth. She tells us, "I've gotten toothaches so bad, so that I just literally pull my own teeth. They'll break off after a while, and then you just grab ahold of them, and they work their way out."

We ask how she can face the pain of pulling out her own teeth.

"It actually feels—it hurts so bad, because the tooth aches. Then it's a relief just to get it out of there. The hole closes up itself anyway. So it's so much better."

Loretta tells us that if President Bush were to change his mind and make health care available to all Americans, the first thing she would do is go to the dentist. "I've gone two weeks with being able to eat just soup, because my teeth just hurt so bad."

HUSBANDS, BABIES, AND TEMPORARY EMPLOYMENT

Loretta has not had adequate health care since she married her husband thirteen years ago. Because Greg is a construction specialist, he and the family move frequently, going "wherever they are doing a lot of building." His work tends to be seasonal, and the winter months are difficult for the family. In good months, he might earn as much as $2,500; in other months, he brings in as little as $1,000; and in some months, nothing at all. Like many self-employed Americans, Greg cannot afford to carry health insurance for himself, much less for his family.

Loretta has begun to work nights at a university research center, making calls for a telephone survey lab. She loves the work and enjoys getting out of the house and talking to people. Unfortunately, the work is temporary, only part-time, and does not offer health insurance.

"My husband is one of those [who has], I think, a real macho attitude, where the woman is supposed to stay at home and take care of the children and clean the house and cook the food. And he's going to go out and work. This last year, he's finally started to realize that it does help a little bit if I go out and work."

Loretta, a devoted mother, feels stretched to her limit with five children, but Greg is a member of the Church of Jesus Christ of Latter Day Saints (Mormons) and won't hear of a tubal ligation. "I tried very hard after this last one to convince him to let me have my tubes tied, but he was adamant that this is just not happening. His way of thinking—for religious reasons, he doesn't want it done. Because it's just not natural for a woman to have her tubes tied. And, you know, if God wants you to have babies, then you're going to have one. If He doesn't want you to have it, you're not going to have it. Okay! Well, but it's me that has to carry it for the nine months, you know, with the morning sickness all day long through the whole nine months!"

Though their family income would seem to be low enough to qualify her for Medicaid during her pregnancies, she has had trouble with the enrollment process. She applied during her first pregnancy but was turned down because she did not have a proper U.S. birth certificate. (She was born in Germany when her father was serving there in the U.S. Army.) She wrote to the U.S. State Department, paid $40, and received a birth certificate signed by Madeleine Albright in time for her second pregnancy. But in the many moves the family has made to follow construction booms around the country, Loretta misplaced the birth certificate and thus had no Medicaid coverage or prenatal care for her third pregnancy. By the time of her last pregnancy, she had written again to Washington, this time receiving a certificate signed by Colin Powell. Loretta playfully describes herself as a friend of not one but "two secretaries of state!"

Loretta was given birth control pills after her first two "back-to-back" babies. Six months later, she had a heart attack, which the doctor seems to have attributed to the pills. She has not had an EKG or any follow-up care since. She is hesitant about using birth control pills again, especially in the absence of ongoing supervision by a physician whom she can get to know and trust. Dependent on free family-planning services, she rarely sees the same provider twice.

SCRAPING BY ON MOLOTOV COCKTAILS

Six weeks after the birth of her fifth child, Loretta was again taken off the Medicaid rolls. "I refuse to get sick. And, like all mothers, you just can't afford to be sick anyway. And if I get sick, I mainly go and do. When I can afford over-the-counter medication, I'll buy everything I can get my hands on. Just a 'Molotov cocktail' of everything, you know. NyQuil is really good. The Vick's cough syrup. We keep stock in BC powders [a popular over-the-counter headache remedy in the South] and Advil, the liquid gels. Cough drops, cough syrup." Loretta estimates that she spends about $150 a month on over-the-counter medicines.

Fortunately, her children are covered by Medicaid, which in most states has more liberal income limits for children than for their parents. "As a matter of fact, if it weren't for Medicaid for the kids, I couldn't even tell what I would do. Because they've been, oh, they stay constantly sick. You know, with a cold. Last year, I caught pneumonia with the three-year-old, and I've been fighting bronchitis with my one-year-old. My oldest one has allergies that are so severe that if he doesn't take his medication, he'll walk around with a bloody nose constantly. This is only since we moved here to Mississippi."

The reasons they are sick so often, Loretta explains, have to do with the living conditions and the absence of good public services. The nearest supermarket is a Wal-Mart four miles away. To reach the food department, Loretta has to walk with her kids through the clothing and toy departments, a route that makes each trip an adventure in patience. More often, she uses the convenience store located two and a half miles away, which unfortunately does not carry much in the way of fresh food.

Loretta tells us that she and her neighbors are worried about the swamp right in the middle of the neighborhood. "It's breeding territory for mosquitoes, and last year I know [the city government] didn't come out and spray."

Women in the neighborhood further attribute their children's poor health to the mediocre quality of the available medical care. Loretta introduces us to her closest friend, Robin, whose children were turned down for Medicaid. Robin recalls, "I took my son and our neighbor's son in to the hospital because they'd gotten into a whole bunch of pesticide. He was eating it off his fingers, and it was on the mouth of the neighbor's child. The first thing it says on the bag is to induce vomiting. But the doctor looked at me and said, 'Okay, he's fine. Sign those papers, and you can go home.' The doctor didn't [examine the kids or] come to me and explain nothing. He didn't even follow the prescribed guidelines. I mean, that was just totally outrageous in my eyes."

Loretta confirms that the care at the local emergency room often is less than optimal, at least for uninsured patients. "I had to go to the emergency room just last week. I had a sinus infection, and it was so bad that the side of my face was swollen. And the doctor just came in and looked at me and said, 'Oh, you've got a sinus infection.' I mean, did he bother? He didn't do any [tests or exam]. . . . I thought to myself, 'I hope that's what it is. And I'm glad you're giving me the antibiotics.' But what if something else were the problem?"

Loretta has not yet received the bill for her last emergency room visit, but the antibiotics alone cost her $100. She knows that she will not be able to pay the bill when it arrives, and she knows that it will go to a collection agency. The debt will go on her credit record and cause problems later if she wants to get a credit card, lease a vehicle, or rent an apartment.

While Loretta considers herself reasonably healthy, she does suffer from frequent migraines accompanied by violent vomiting. We ask whether she has seen a doctor about the migraines.

"The one time I went to see a doctor with them, the doctor looked at me—and this was really years before they realized that migraines are an actual thing—the doctor looked at me and told me it was my imagination. And I asked him, I said, 'Well, don't you think if my imagination was that good that I would have imagined something a little bit better than a migraine headache?' And he did not appreciate me being flip. He just kind of looked at me and said, 'Well, there's nothing wrong with you. You need to leave.' And I'm like, 'Okay.'"

Greg has some health problems of his own. He was injured when another car smashed into his, and he suffers from chronic elbow inflammation. At the time of his elbow surgery, his blood pressure was high. "And it's probably something that he needs to have medication for, but even if we could afford to go to the doctor for it, I know we couldn't afford the medication." He suffers from constant headaches, which Loretta suspects are linked to the high blood pressure.

Greg also has ulcers, diagnosed when he was a teenager, but he has not been examined by a doctor for nearly thirteen years. "He keeps stock in Rolaids and Tums and Pepcid AC and Zantac," Loretta jokes. Over the past few months, his stomach troubles have become worse: "He throws up whatever he eats. He just—he gets cranky." The large hole he punched in the living room wall when a customer didn't pay him for his work attests to his crankiness.

Over the course of several conversations, Loretta spoke at length about the stress of choosing between buying food and buying medicine, the stress of working in temporary and seasonal jobs, the stress of feeling trapped in circumstances of poverty that she cannot control, the stress of living with a man who is often angry and frustrated that he cannot provide for his family, and, above all, the stress of living with chronic illnesses and chronic pain that she does not have the resources to remedy.

Loretta is brilliant at scraping by. We ask her how the cost of medicine fits into her very tight household budget.

"You just find a way. Say, for instance, I need a bag of diapers and cough syrup. Instead of buying the big bag of diapers, you buy the smaller, and you're able to afford the one bottle of cough syrup." What she does when the small bag of diapers runs out, we don't have the courage to ask.

THE CASTE OF THE WORKING POOR

Loretta is illustrative of many of the people we met on our travels across America. Although she grew up in an economically stable working-class family, she now teeters on the brink of economic destitution. She is married to a man who opposes birth control for religious reasons and who works at seasonal jobs that do not provide health benefits. Despite her disagreements with her husband, Loretta is committed to the marriage and to raising the children with their father, and she has no immediate plans to leave him.

Greg is self-employed in an occupation that, while necessary—we all enjoy having houses with floors—has frequent economic ups and downs. As a result, Loretta has not had consistent health care for fifteen years. During those years, her status has shifted: once a member of the working class, she is now a member of the caste of the ill, the infirm, and the marginally employed—a group often called by the more palatable name *working poor*.

Her physical appearance (missing and rotten teeth, a nearsighted squint, and her generally unkempt self-presentation) makes it unlikely that she can fulfill her dream of a job in a veterinarian's office, where she would be dealing with the public. She is more likely to be steered toward jobs like the one she found shortly before we met her—conducting a phone survey during the evening hours at the local university. In other words, Loretta is bright enough to participate in a university research project, but she is not considered presentable enough to work in an office where she would meet clients or research subjects face to face.

Loretta's work at the university is temporary, part-time, and dead-end. Because she is a "temp," the university does not provide health insurance. Thus, she finds herself in a bind: as long as her only job opportunities result in dead-end positions (across the nation, telemarketing—where the employee is invisible—is one of the mainstays of the working poor, but such jobs rarely offer health insurance), she cannot access the health care she needs in order to make herself more presentable and pursue a better job with benefits.

Within the current social and health care framework, what are Loretta's options? The first is that she could leave her husband. Then, as a single mother with no income (without Greg to take care of the children in the evening, she would have to quit her job at the university), she would be eligible for welfare and Medicaid. But this choice would offer only temporary relief. Under the welfare reform legislation of the 1990s, her lifetime eligibility for public aid is limited to a set number of years, after which she would be back where she started, but without the income (however sporadic) provided by her husband. And, of course, this option involves breaking up a family—not exactly the intended goal of either the health care system or the current system of public aid.

The second option is to have another child in order to be eligible for Medicaid during the pregnancy. The downside here is that once a woman gives birth, her Medicaid coverage ends. Also, because Medicaid during pregnancy does not cover many nonpregnancy health problems, on balance another pregnancy (Loretta's sixth) would probably do more harm than good to her overall health. While this option certainly sounds foolish to us, we were told by a number of women we interviewed that this is precisely what the clerk or caseworker at the public aid office suggested when they applied for help with medical expenses.

Loretta's third option might be to pack up the family and try to move to a state that has more liberal cut-offs for Medicaid eligibility. But the family could face serious obstacles if they made a decision to move based on Medicaid benefits rather than on where Greg could most easily find work. If the family moved to an area without a good amount of available construction work, there is no guarantee that Greg would earn enough to pay the rent, which could leave them vulnerable to homelessness (a situation Loretta fears above all others). Small businesses like Greg's are notoriously difficult to start, and it would certainly take a while until he could generate enough business to support the family. They have no savings to get them through a slow start-up period, and Loretta, who is only marginally employable, probably could not earn enough to carry the burden.

We will never know which option she chose. A few months after we first met her, we went back to see how Loretta was doing. Her house was empty, the family had moved, and none of the neighbors knew where they had gone. At this time, we suspect, they are either camping out with relatives somewhere in the country, living in a homeless shelter, or about to be evicted from another house or apartment.

THE DEATH SPIRAL

This book was born at a Harvard health care symposium when Rushika, a physician specializing in health policy, met Susan, an anthropologist who recently had returned to the United States after living for two decades in Israel and Japan, countries that have national health care programs. With the fresh eyes that an outsider sometimes can bring to a situation most of us take for granted, Susan asked Rushika: "Where are the bodies? If forty million Americans don't have health insurance, there must be a lot of bodies. I would think that American cities would look like Delhi or Calcutta, where trucks collect corpses from the streets each morning. Where is America hiding its uninsured sick and dying citizens?"

Rushika initially responded with standard answers: We have government programs such as Medicaid and Medicare. Many counties run clinics with sliding-scale fees. Our hospitals offer charity care to indigent patients. And, with the support of the Bush administration, churches have opened up faith-based clinics.

Yet, when the two of us began to look more closely at the statistics, we saw that these responses did not speak to the actual experiences of many people in our country. In 2003, Medicaid covered only slightly more than half of Americans whose family income was below 200 percent of the poverty line (that is, below $36,800 for a family of four). Public clinics typically are so overwhelmed that the wait for an appointment can be several months. Hospitals often fail to inform patients that charity programs exist, instead simply billing their uninsured patients and turning their accounts over to collection agencies. In fact, although the government requires not-for-profit hospitals to offer charity care, many hospitals avoid doing so by redefining the uncollectable debt as "charity care." And faith-based clinics, which were touted as a compassionate safety net to take the place of big government bureaucracies, usually seem to flounder, seeing patients only a few evenings each week and relying on volunteer physicians to squeeze in a couple of clinic hours a month on top of their already overflowing private practices.

So, we asked each other, where are the uninsured? Who are they? Why are they uninsured, and how do they scrape by? What does the absence of consistent access to medical care mean in their lives? What is its impact on their jobs, their families, their aspirations? And, equally important, what does the fact that more than forty million Americans lack reasonable access to health care mean for our country as a whole? How does the divide between the health care "haves" and "have-nots" reflect or contribute to other painful social and economic ills?

THE JOURNEY

Combining a medical perspective with the tools of anthropology—in-depth interviews and extensive "hanging around" with uninsured individuals and families (a technique anthropologists refer to by the more elegant name *participant observation*), we set out to meet Americans around the country who are scraping by without medical coverage.

During 2003 and 2004, we traveled to Texas, Mississippi, Idaho, Illinois, and Massachusetts, talking with those who determine health care policies as well as those who live (or die) by those policies. We spoke to people whose stories represent the more than twenty million middle-income families and the millions of working-poor families who are uninsured. We listened to Americans who had seen loved ones die because they did not have medical coverage. And we heard the stories of Americans who were forced to declare bankruptcy or sell their homes to pay for medical care. By the end of our journey, we had conducted wide-ranging interviews with more than 120 uninsured Americans and with approximately four dozen physicians, medical administrators, and health policy officials.

We met uninsured men and women through local churches, community organizations, friends, and colleagues; at yard sales, bars, and libraries; in lines at local pharmacies and grocery stores; and via notices tacked up in public places. One contact often led to another. Our conversations covered matters directly related to illness and medical care as well as more general personal anecdotes, family stories, political opinions, observations about neighborhoods and workplaces, and a fair amount of laughter and tears.*

Not everyone we met wanted to speak to us. Some people were embarrassed that they were uninsured; some were too busy managing several part-time jobs. Other individuals, based on past experiences, had learned not to trust strangers who come asking personal questions. Still others simply were not interested in talking about private matters.

But many individuals welcomed the opportunity to speak their minds. For some of our interviewees, the $25 honorarium we offered represented their family's next few meals. Others appreciated the chance to talk to their heart's content to someone who really listened—it was important to them that we could witness the truth of their experiences. And some people made it clear that they agreed to talk to us because they wanted to help change the system by letting other Americans (often referred to as "the big shots in Washington") know how hard it is to get by without adequate health care.

*We have changed the names of our uninsured interviewees in order to protect their privacy. Physicians, administrators, and officials are identified by their real names and titles.

Reflecting the common expectation that women are responsible for the health of their families as well as for their own health issues (which often are seen as more "complicated" than men's issues), many more women than men shared their stories with us. We met with twenty Hispanic families and twenty African Americans. These numbers echo the fact that Hispanics and African Americans are more likely to be uninsured than white Americans, though white Americans constitute the absolute majority of the uninsured. Our youngest interviewee was nineteen, and the oldest sixty-four; most were in the middle of that age range. People spoke with us about the health concerns of their entire families over periods of many years.

On our journey, we gained a better understanding of the legitimate economic forces that must, in one way or another, place some limits on health care access. We learned, too, what it means to be part of the group of Americans who have been involuntarily assigned by society to carry the burden created by those forces and whose bodies bear the scars of that burden.

THE "PROBLEM" OF THE UNINSURED

The familiar phrase "the problem of the uninsured" conjures either an image of troubled, "problematic" individuals or the notion that these unfortunate persons constitute a "problem" for the rest of society. The real problem, however, begins at a far more basic level. The inability of a large portion of the U.S. population to access health care services in a systematic and medically competent manner is a consequence of social and economic developments that predate and underpin individual life histories.

Unlike the medical systems of most other Western countries, America's health care structure centers on an increasingly for-profit system of employment-based private insurance. Employer-sponsored health coverage expanded rapidly in the United States during World War II, when the shortage of civilian workers encouraged employers to look for creative ways to attract and retain employees. In order to prevent inflation, the War Labor Board put a ceiling on all wages. It ruled, however, that unions could bargain for health care benefits without violating the wage freeze. At the same time, the Internal Revenue Service ruled that health insurance premiums would be treated as a nontaxable business expense.*

During the postwar era of economic growth, employment-based health insurance became the norm in the United States, and it indeed worked reasonably well for many Americans. During this period, millions of blue-collar workers held long-term union contracts guaranteeing health care benefits, and white-collar workers expected to remain with and rise through the ranks of the companies in which they built their careers.

In recent years, however, the relationship between employment and health care has become increasingly problematic. First, as the nature of employment has changed globally, fewer people are able to stay in the same job for many years. As a result, jobs no longer serve as stable platforms for health care arrangements. Second, the fragmented nature of the American health care system, together with the political dominance of the medical, insurance, and pharmaceutical industries, has allowed health care costs to soar far above the costs for comparable products and services in Canada, Great Britain, and continental European countries. As the cost of health care rises, more employers look for ways to avoid providing insurance to their employees. The millions who find themselves uninsured are now priced out of the health care marketplace.

For growing numbers of Americans, the convergence of these two developments means that their lives have become trapped inside what we call the *death spiral.*

HOW THE DEATH SPIRAL WORKS

In insurance lingo, a death spiral occurs when a health plan starts attracting sicker patients, which causes the price of premiums to go up, which

---

*This IRS ruling was especially important because special wartime taxes on excess profits meant that marginal tax rates could reach as high as 85 percent.

causes more healthy people (who have other options) to leave the plan, which causes the remaining pool to be proportionately sicker, which causes the price of premiums to increase even more, eventually resulting in the company going bankrupt—in other words, dying.

The image of a death spiral is a useful metaphor for thinking about the role of access to health care within the larger context of American social and economic life. Because employment and health insurance are tightly linked, job disruptions such as layoffs or firings, starting one's own business, or taking time off to care for small children or elderly parents can lead to the loss of health coverage. That loss can easily lead to health concerns going untreated, a situation that can exacerbate employment problems by making the individual less able to work. Alternatively, the downward spiral can begin with health problems that lead to employment problems, making it less likely that one will have health insurance and thus reducing the chances of solving the original health issues.

Whatever the starting point, once a person enters the death spiral, it is difficult to escape. Because employment adversity is so thoroughly intertwined with medical adversity, those caught in the spiral cannot amass either the bodily or the financial resources needed to break out. Descent through the death spiral, for millions of Americans, leaves irrevocable marks of illness on their bodies and souls.

In a broader sense, the death spiral serves as a metaphor for the deep changes taking place in American society as the demarcation between rich and poor—a traditionally fluid distinction in our society—hardens into a static barrier between the caste of the healthy and the caste of those who are fated to become and remain sick.

PORTALS INTO THE DEATH SPIRAL

Individuals are pulled into the death spiral through many different portals. Corporate restructuring, outsourcing, divorce, family crises, chronic illness, serious accidents, and racial discrimination open some of the most recognizable doors. Indeed, given the number and diversity of entrances, all Americans, except for a small number of extremely rich individuals, are vulnerable to the death spiral's pull.

The majority of people we met in our travels across the country lack consistent access to health care of reasonable quality despite having been employed all or most of their adult lives. Approximately one-third of the people with whom we spoke are well educated but have had the misfortune to end up in jobs that do not offer insurance: substitute teachers, adjunct professors, part-time social workers. These Americans have not chosen to be uninsured; rather, their employers—like Loretta's—have found it cost-effective to reduce the number of permanent full-time positions while maintaining an unprotected pool of workers whose jobs by definition do not offer benefits.

Contingent workers now represent more than 25 percent of the American workforce. Some industries, such as the food industry, employ temporary, part-time, transient workers almost exclusively. Other industries retain some full-time employees but outsource certain jobs that were formerly performed in-house. In the Rust Belt, manufacturing plants employ increasing numbers of temporary workers through temp companies such as Manpower. These job slots have replaced the full-time, unionized jobs of previous years, allowing employers to cut costs by not providing benefits.* Those beginning their working lives are particularly hard-hit by the scarcity of jobs with good benefits: one in three young adults between the ages of eighteen and twenty-four in the United States lacks health care coverage.

Some people described in this book lack insurance because the industries in which they worked have all but closed down: mining, forestry,

*For example, Shelly, an administrator and home health aide at Collective Home Care (described in chapter 6), explains: "Many agencies keep the home health aides at part-time, nonbenefited, and don't provide training. They tell you to work here for six months and then [they'll] give you training, and then it doesn't pan out. Temporary hires—that's the way some agencies like it. They don't have to pay benefits."

cotton fields, steel mills, or manufacturing plants that have relocated to other countries in order to tap into a lower-wage employee pool. Barely treading water, the workers left behind now labor in temporary jobs—especially in the service sector—that do not offer health insurance. Unable to sell their homes in towns that have lost their economic foundation and then their population base, these workers are locked into futures that look grim indeed.

Some of the people we present are between jobs. Some are starting new jobs that require a six-month waiting period before insurance is available. Others work for such low salaries that they cannot afford insurance; still others work for employers who do not offer insurance at all. A small number of those we met—typically (but not always) the sickest, poorest, and oldest—have been able at one time or another to turn to the government for a program that provides access to health care. But far more simply fall through the cracks: they are not eligible for government assistance, and their employment situation does not make health insurance possible.

Some people in this book are uninsured because, like Greg, they struck out on their own and opened small businesses. With limited cash flow, especially during the first years of operation, health insurance is a fiscal impossibility. Others are uninsured because they work for a small business whose precarious financial situation precludes providing health benefits for employees.

Other portals into the death spiral originate in difficult, challenging, or shifting family situations. Many people have health coverage through their spouse—which means that divorce can lead to a break in health care coverage. Several of the women we interviewed had fled abusive or violent marriages and thus lost their health insurance. One middle-aged woman explained to us that her health insurance disappeared when her husband of twenty years "traded me in for a new model." Other women lost their insurance when they had to quit work or reduce their working hours in order to care for aging parents, sick children, or disabled spouses.

Some people whose voices are heard in this book are unable to work because of chronic illness: back pain (perhaps caused by an earlier job-related injury), high blood pressure, mental illness. In some cases, these people would be able to work at jobs that do not demand constant physical stress, but such jobs simply are not available to them. Without employment, they cannot obtain the medication they need to manage their chronic illnesses, and so they find themselves caught ever more tightly in the death spiral. Most of the people we met work despite suffering from an assortment of chronic illnesses. In addition to the strain of working with pain or other symptoms, they live with fears about how they will manage if or when their conditions deteriorate. Indeed, we have come to see chronic illness as both a portal into the death spiral and an integral component of the descent pattern.

A small number of those with whom we spoke lack insurance because they do not understand how the health care system works. They do not quite grasp that they spend more money paying out of pocket for treatments and medicines than they would spend paying for insurance. A larger number of people understand the system only too well: they are caught between squabbling companies—health insurance, workers' compensation, and automobile insurance companies, for example—with each company claiming that the other should be covering the patient's medical costs. Often, the individual caught in the middle quietly goes bankrupt, paying out of pocket while the corporate bickering goes on.

Finally, we spoke to Americans who have health insurance but have been caught in the death spiral nonetheless. We do not address the issue of underinsurance in this book (the topic deserves its own comprehensive treatment), but we do note that even for people who have health insurance, systematic gaps in coverage (such as limited or nonexistent mental health or dental care benefits) can be disastrous. Because of pre-existing condition clauses, many Americans find themselves not covered for the one condition that matters most. Moreover, many policies have high co-payments, holding the individual responsible for 20 percent or more of all bills in addition to a hefty deductible. Especially in cases of serious illness, 20 percent of a large bill can lead to the same outcome as not having insurance at all.

THE CONSEQUENCES OF SCRAPING BY

When we began mapping out this project, our initial working title was *Scraping By: How the Uninsured Cope with the Health Care System.* By the time we completed our trips to Texas, Mississippi, and Idaho, we had abandoned that title. First, we learned that, for most uninsured Americans, there is no health care "system." Rather, they deal with a blotchy and frayed patchwork of unreliable and inconsistent programs, providers, and facilities. Second, we learned that many, if not most, uninsured Americans are not scraping by very well at all.

Many of the people portrayed here either have had insurance or have been enrolled in Medicaid or another government program at one time or another. Others live in households in which some members (often the husband) are covered by employment-based insurance but others (often the wife) are not. Frequently, some family members (usually children) are eligible for Medicaid but others (usually parents) are not. All of our interviewees describe using a chaotic collage of health care services— local emergency rooms, a private doctor when they can afford an office visit, a state or county clinic when their income is so low that they are defined as "indigent," a church clinic that operates one evening a week, if they are lucky enough to get sick on the day the clinic is open. No one reported having a family doctor who knows the medical histories of family members, who knows how the patient has responded in the past to particular medicines, who knows the family's risk factors, who has any inkling about the family's ability to follow through on medical instructions, or who is poised to provide any sort of health education, nutrition counseling, or continuity of care.*

*Burstin, Lipsitz, and Brennan (1992) examined the medical records of 31,249 patients from hospitals in New York and found that the uninsured were more than twice as likely to receive substandard care and were more likely to

Such a sporadic approach to health care does not serve anyone well. Continuity of care is associated with greater use of preventive services and better control of many chronic illnesses, such as hypertension and diabetes. It also leads to fewer hospitalizations and to lower overall health care costs. Patients and physicians agree: patchwork care leads to poorer management of health problems and greater feelings of frustration all around.

Our interviewees routinely experience delays in getting care for a variety of medical problems. This means that small tumors may be left untreated until they become big and metastasize. Diabetes is not managed properly, leading to amputations, end-stage renal failure, and expensive dialysis treatments. Asthma goes untreated until the individual ends up unable to breathe, turning blue in the emergency room. Hypertension progresses until it becomes a completely disabling disease, preventing the individual from working. A small cavity in the tooth becomes a huge abscess, requiring an extraction. Sore throats become systemic infections, bladder infections become kidney infections, and earaches become the source of hearing loss. Americans without health insurance rarely go to the doctor for a checkup, rarely receive ongoing supervision of chronic problems, and rarely get treatment until pain becomes unbearable or intractable complications set in.

Without consistent access to competent medical care, uninsured Americans are left to their own devices to manage their health problems. Thus, Mexican Americans and Anglo Americans in the Rio Grande Valley cross the border into Mexico, where drugs that are prescription-only in the United States are sold over the counter. College-educated uninsured residents of Massachusetts often know someone who knows someone who knows a doctor who is willing to write a prescription or give out free drug samples without seeing or examining the patient. Across the

---

experience an injury from substandard care in the emergency room. The uninsured were also less likely to receive follow-up care after discharge from the hospital and were less likely to receive complete discharge instructions.

country, many Americans take only half of a prescribed drug dose so that their medicine will last longer. They share prescriptions with friends and relatives. When their medicine runs low, they skip doses until they can afford a refill. And they play a high-stakes guessing game when they choose which of the several prescriptions ordered by the doctor they can afford to purchase in any given month.

In lieu of consistent and adequate medical care, most of the people with whom we spoke self-medicate in ways that would appall trained health care providers. Most noticeably, they take large and frequent doses of over-the-counter pain medications such as ibuprofen and Tylenol in order to get through the day or night. Many people we met live on homemade "cocktails" combining a variety of over-the-counter medicines, sometimes with alcohol or illegal drugs, in desperate hopes of feeling better.

The consequences of this hodgepodge of erratic treatment and self-medication are demonstrably negative. A recent review by the Institute of Medicine documented that the uninsured receive less preventive care and poorer treatment for both minor and serious chronic and acute illnesses. In many cases, they live shorter lives than comparable insured populations.

The financial impact of being uninsured is also negative and often extreme. The uninsured are commonly billed at higher rates. New York Methodist Hospital in Brooklyn, for instance, charges health maintenance organizations $2,500 for a two-day stay for an appendectomy, while uninsured patients pay approximately $14,000. Emergency room visits typically cost about four times as much as treating the same problem in a regular office visit. But many doctors will not see uninsured patients who owe money for previous visits, compelling these individuals to use the emergency room for all their health problems. Moreover, many hospitals charge interest at higher than market rates on the debts patients accrue, which means that even a simple hospitalization can turn into a ten- or twenty-thousand-dollar debt. Serious or prolonged illness can lead to debts that seem almost preposterous—some of the uninsured men and women we met owe as much as $200,000 or more.

Most of our interviewees owe money that they will never be able to pay to a variety of hospitals and clinics. While some hospitals have charity care programs that provide free services for the indigent and the poor, many (including not-for-profit hospitals) simply bill the patients and then sell the accounts to a collection agency thirty or sixty days later for ten to fifteen cents on the dollar, allowing the collection agencies to work as they see fit. As a consequence, just about everyone told us about receiving threatening letters and harassing phone calls from collection agencies. Their credit ratings are ruined. Most fear going back to these medical facilities, and they are cross-examined if they do return.* Some people are able to shrug off the harassment; others cannot sleep at night. Some scrape together small monthly payments of $20 or $25, knowing (or not) that it will take them a century or more to pay off the debt; others become so discouraged that they abdicate responsibility for their own health, throwing their hands in the air, literally or figuratively.

Health care has become a leading cause of personal bankruptcy in the United States. Of the record 1.57 million personal bankruptcies filed in the United States in 2002, between one-third and one-half resulted from medical bills.

Claudia Lennhoff, executive director of Champaign County Health Care Consumers in Illinois, has seen local hospitals garnish patients' wages, put liens on their homes, and sue them in court. "What we see, the people who are in court, are overwhelmingly poor people, and the hospitals know this and the providers know this. Sometimes, some of the people in court, if you look at their records, you will see that they are

---

*A survey conducted by the Access Project (2003) found that 46 percent of America's uninsured were in debt to a medical provider. A study funded by the Kaiser Family Foundation reported that 39 percent of uninsured respondents had been contacted by a collection agency about an unpaid medical bill (*News-Hour with Jim Lehrer*/Kaiser Family Foundation 2000).

the hospital's charity care patients. They actually already have qualified for and received some charity care, so the hospitals are suing their own charity care patients!"

Some hospitals have been known to implement even more drastic measures. Hospitals in Connecticut, Indiana, Kansas, Michigan, and Oklahoma have arrested and jailed uninsured patients who failed to appear for court hearings concerning their debt, a tactic known in the legal community as "body attachment."* Yale–New Haven Hospital, for instance, took such action sixty-five times in a recent three-year period, from 2001 through 2003.

FROM CLASS TO CASTE

As more and more Americans are drawn down into the death spiral, we are witnessing a fundamental shift in the nature of American society.

In sociology courses in the 1970s and 1980s, we were taught that the vast majority of Americans identified themselves as middle class. In fact, we were told, so many Americans were middle class that the United States had essentially become a classless society. Our college professors further explained that money itself was not what led Americans to regard themselves as middle class. After all, a secretary earning $25,000 a year and a lawyer earning $250,000 clearly had very different levels of purchasing power and disposable income, yet both considered themselves—and were considered by others—to be middle class. Rather, what made most Americans middle class was a set of social and cultural understandings.

*Several interviewees told us that they had not shown up for court appearances. Their reasons included being unable to take off work (not surprising for minimum-wage and contingent workers), the belief that nothing they could say could change the balance of power (the hospitals have expensive lawyers and will win regardless), and the sense that a court judgment doesn't really matter because—as one person noted—"they can't squeeze blood from a turnip."

Middle-class Americans saw themselves as part of the American mainstream. They shared American values of family and work, they saw themselves as economically upwardly mobile, and they believed themselves the social equals of almost all other Americans. Perhaps most important, millions of middle-class Americans followed the same clothing fashions, chose the same hairstyles, spoke in similar accents, shared the same standards of "beauty," and—at least superficially—*looked* like members of the same social grouping. In other words, the outward markings of the middle class were more or less the same for the secretary and for the attorney: one would have to look at the labels hidden inside the shirt to know whether it was an expensive designer blouse or a cheap knock-off.

The concept of *caste*, we were taught, differs from the idea of *class* in significant ways. Using India as the example of a caste society, our professors explained that caste systems are characterized by the absence of mobility—you are stuck in the caste into which you are born. Caste tends to be institutionalized through recognizable external markers such as clothing or hair. Caste also is occupationally framed: the so-called untouchables in India, for instance, members of the lowest caste, were connected with the most basic human functions and performed work that put them in contact with waste, sickness, and death. Finally, the caste system is construed as a moral system: in India, lower-caste members were considered "polluted," whereas members of the highest caste—Brahmins—were associated with lofty pursuits and moral virtues. In an important sense, class is about what one *has*, while caste is about what one *is*.

The current American system in which health care is linked to employment is creating a caste of the chronically ill, infirm, and marginally employed. Because health care is so tightly linked to employment, once an individual or a family is caught in the death spiral, it is nearly impossible to find a way out. Unemployable or marginally employed because of poor health, members of this new "untouchable caste" are denied consistent access to medical care. Sick, lacking reliable health care, and locked in employment situations (especially in the service sector—the same sector to which India's untouchables were consigned) that do not offer medical benefits, they find it increasingly difficult to escape.

What about the other typical traits of caste systems? Does this new American "untouchable caste" carry outward markings on their bodies? Illness itself constitutes a physical marker: rotten teeth, chronic coughs, bad skin, a limp, sores that don't heal, obesity, uncorrected hearing or vision deficits, addiction to pain medication—all of these signal caste in basic ways.

Echoing the classical Indian caste system, membership in the American caste of the ill, infirm, and marginally employed carries a moral taint in addition to physical markings and occupational immobility. This taint is a product of the moral value that American society has traditionally placed on productive work and good health. Work has long been construed as a moral virtue; we need only think of the generations of American women who embroidered samplers proclaiming that "idle hands are the devil's playthings."

Uninsured Americans around the country noted the stigma of lacking health insurance, citing medical providers who treat them like "losers" because they are uninsured. Similarly, the providers we spoke to emphasized the problem of "noncompliance" among the uninsured, complaining about "difficult" patients who don't follow the instructions of physicians. Sickness increasingly seems to be construed as a personal failure—a failure of ethical virtue, a failure to take care of oneself "properly" by eating the "right" foods or getting "enough" exercise, a failure to get a Pap smear, a failure to control sexual promiscuity, genetic failure, a failure of will, or a failure of commitment—rather than society's failure to provide basic services to all of its citizens. The belief that illness is a marker of personal failure, together with popular images of the unemployed as unworthy 'bums' or 'welfare queens,' function as ideological glue that makes the link between health care and employment appear sufficiently rational to stand up to decades of efforts to change the health care status quo.

We hope that our use of a term as heavily laden as *caste* will stimulate meaningful public discussions regarding where our current health system is taking us as a social entity. We recognize that we are not writing about a caste system in the legislative sense that characterizes traditional Indian society. Rather, we have chosen to introduce the language of caste to describe a social arrangement that is emerging de facto from the political economy of our country at this time. As writers, we embrace the shock that readers may feel at hearing the term *caste* uttered in relation to American society. An intellectual jolt often is needed to recognize the cumulative impact of incremental cultural and economic changes such as those that have occurred in the United States over the past decades.

Devon, a recent college graduate we met in Massachusetts, offered a take on class and caste in America that was markedly different from the one we learned during our own college days. Speaking about what it means to scrape by without health insurance, Devon said: *"I just feel that the way the system is set up is like a bizarre version of natural selection, where the people who are poorest can't afford to keep themselves healthy, and so they die."*

WHERE ARE THE BODIES?

Many portals lead into the death spiral, but few lead out. The sick and dying bodies that Susan asked Rushika about are hidden inside the death spiral, in three primary locations.

Where do we hide the bodies? In emergency rooms and end-stage hospital wards across the country.

America's hospitals are legally obligated to stabilize the condition of emergency patients and to treat any life-threatening condition regardless of the patient's ability to pay. Emergency rooms are not, however, required to provide any definitive treatment or any therapy to prevent the condition from recurring. For those who are pronounced terminally ill, the Social Security disability program provides health care services through Medicare. Thus, we do not provide care to prevent emergencies or to stave off terminal illness, but we do offer a place to land at the bottom of the spiral.

We don't see corpses on the streets of Chicago or Des Moines because when people get sick enough, they are hidden in emergency rooms and end-stage treatment wards. In a bizarre economic and ethical twist, the chronically ill, if they are uninsured, are allowed to deteriorate to the point at which hospitals are legally required to take them in. They are covered if they have terminal cancer or renal failure, but not before.

Where do we hide the bodies? In homeless shelters across the country.

People we met spoke with terror about losing their homes. Medical debt can lead to liens on one's house or to bankruptcy, and illness disrupts household income and interferes with rent or mortgage payments. In what we see as a classic death spiral dance, once you are homeless, your health deteriorates further (shelters are hardly healthy places to sleep), and your outward appearance makes you unemployable (homelessness limits opportunities for personal grooming and care of clothing), thus making it less likely that you will find a job with health care benefits.

Only a small number of our interviewees had experienced periods of true homelessness, but many spoke about tough times during which they had to move in with relatives or forego necessities in order to pay their rent or mortgage. Even more, including those who looked and sounded "middle class" and whose incomes over the years had been in the range of $35,000 a year, spoke in hushed tones of the fear of losing their homes. These people understand that a middle-class income does not provide adequate protection in case of illness or job loss. Those who have more resources—financial, educational, family, and community—available to them are less vulnerable, but for most Americans (all but the very richest), enough disasters clustered together can spell an inexorable downward descent.

According to a recent study of homeless shelters in New York City, the death rate among homeless men and women was four times greater than the death rate among the general U.S. population.

Where do we hide the bodies? In prisons across the country.

Studies show that morbidity rates among America's prisoners are extremely high. This is especially true of those with mental illness. Indeed, the *Washington Post* in 1999 reported that more than 280,000 mentally ill people were locked up in our nation's jails and prisons and that the Los Angeles County Jail and New York's Riker's Island were the country's two largest "treatment facilities" for the mentally ill.

In a pattern typical of the death spiral, we fill our prisons largely with people who have committed petty (mostly drug-related) crimes. We reclassify many of these crimes as felonies, which means that, once released, the former prisoners cannot find reasonable employment. Thus, they lack access to health care, which means that they get sick(er), which means that they need to find ways—legal or not—to obtain life's necessities, including medication. And they end up back in jail, sicker than before.

The likelihood that prison will serve as a repository for sick bodies is not distributed evenly across the American population. Men more than women, African Americans more than whites, and the mentally ill more than the physically ill are in danger of finding that their death spiral slide ends behind bars.

SEVERING THE LINK BETWEEN EMPLOYMENT AND HEALTH CARE

Seeing the death spiral in action in the lives of men and women across the country has convinced us that, as a society, we must cut the link between employment and health care in order to prevent millions of Americans from being sucked into a lethal vortex of ill health, medical debt, and marginal employability. The link between employment and health care might have made sense when it was fashioned in the 1940s. But in the new millennium, new conditions make the link counterproductive at best, and deadly at worst. Employment patterns are changing, resulting in less job stability, weakened labor unions, and the movement of jobs into the low-wage service sector. Family dynamics are different: fewer people now live in conventional nuclear-family households, for example. And even the nature of illness has changed, as ever greater numbers of people suffer with chronic illness. In today's world, potential portals into the death spiral are too numerous, too diverse, and too unpredictable for patchwork safety nets to be sufficiently protective.

We learned an additional lesson on our journey—one that crystallized as we monitored our own reactions to the people we met and the stories we heard. We discovered that the death spiral intensifies as more people fall through its portals and that its growing strength reaches throughout our society, to affect both the insured and the uninsured.

If millions of American children do not have reliable, basic health care, all children who attend American schools are at risk through daily exposure to untreated disease. If millions of restaurant and food industry workers do not have health insurance, people preparing food and waiting tables are sharing their health problems with everyone they serve. If uninsured residents of Texas routinely take unregulated courses of antibiotics from Mexico, antibiotic-resistant bacteria will develop and threaten us all. If tens of millions of Americans go without basic and preventive care, we all pay the bill when their health problems turn into complex medical emergencies necessitating expensive and specialized treatment. And if we condone a health care system that contributes to the formation of an untouchable caste of the ill, infirm, and marginally employed, all of us, as a society, will lose the right to feel pride in the democratic values that we claim to cherish.

For these reasons, we have come to believe that the most efficient and effective way to break the power that the death spiral holds for so many Americans is to make the provision of basic, comprehensive health care a public rather than a private responsibility.

CHAPTER ONE

FROM WORKING CLASS
TO WORKING POOR

THE DEATH OF INDUSTRY IN AMERICA'S HEARTLAND

A sense of impermanence is blowing through the labor force, destabilizing everyone from office temps to high-tech independent contractors to restaurant and retail clerks. Factory jobs are being outsourced, garment jobs are morphing into home work, and in every industry, temporary contracts are replacing full, secure employment. In a growing number of instances, even CEOs are opting for shorter stints at one corporation after another, breezing in and out of different corner offices and purging half the employees as they come and go.

Naomi Klein, *No Logo: No Space, No Choice, No Jobs—Taking Aim at the Brand Bullies*

DAVE'S STORY: A UNION TALE

Rising out of a prairie dotted with purple wildflowers, the silos and smokestacks that mark this small manufacturing city seem to appear out of nowhere. The outskirts of Decatur, Illinois, have no real boundary— they simply trickle away into the grasslands and merge into the surrounding corn fields, soy fields, and bean fields.

Two signs representing drastically different eras and different mindsets stand on the highway at the entrance to Decatur. The first—"Welcome to Decatur, Pride of the Prairies"—is a voice from the past, a time of thriving industry, good jobs, and the booming plants that manufactured so many of the material goods that bolster American prosperity. The second sign—"Welcome to Decatur, Former Home of the Chicago Bears"—is a voice of the present, in which the city's claims to fame are long gone; Decatur has become the "former home" of an American icon.

We came to Decatur to meet people who had grown up in the secure arms of America's heavily unionized upper Midwest, commonly known as the Rust Belt. Having read about massive plant closings in the midwestern heartland, we wanted to understand how people who had been accustomed to secure jobs and reliable health benefits were coping with the uncertainties of the new postindustrial economy. Believing in our heart of hearts that we ourselves would not know what to do if we lost our health insurance (Susan pictured herself standing in a hospital lobby, clutching her sick child and sobbing), we wanted to hear whether others were more resilient than we imagined ourselves to be.

It didn't take long to see that Decatur has not responded well to the new economic era. Ever since the large Firestone tire plant closed, unemployment has been rampant in the area. Ironically, the richest farmland in the United States surrounds Decatur, but the supplies at the food banks are running low. Former blue-collar workers, victims of plant closings, swallow their pride and come to the food banks, only to see the shelves stocked with less and less food. The so-called law of supply and demand has hit the people of Decatur hard: the world no longer demands items manufactured by union workers and sold at prices reflecting hard-won union salaries, especially if comparable items can be produced for a fraction of the cost elsewhere. Of course, as residents told us, workers who are paid a few dollars a day to toil in Asian sweatshops are not likely to devote the same careful attention to their products as the former Decatur workers, who had prided themselves on their work ethic.

Loss is tangible in Decatur. The large Firestone tire complex, which in earlier times employed several thousand workers, is closed. The front gate is locked. Nothing moves inside the formerly bustling buildings.

Many of the people who used to work at Firestone and other plants have left Decatur. Boarded-up houses, sometimes several to a block, pepper the poorer neighborhoods. In the more middle-class neighborhoods, "For Sale" signs stand on many front lawns. We are told that even the smelly pollutants that formerly poured out of Decatur's factories are almost gone: the only really stinky area these days is in the vicinity of the Archer Daniels Midland (soy processing) plants.

Business owners tell us that their businesses have failed or are failing. Social service and health care providers observe that people in Decatur are depressed and that lots of folks have started taking Prozac (which would have been heavily stigmatized even a few years earlier). Young people declare that they are planning to leave, seeing no work and no future in Decatur. Working-class men tell us how "they" (the government, big business, the unions, the outside world in general) let Decatur down. Women note that Decatur has gained a reputation for being the murder capital of the United States; this reputation isn't fair, they acknowledge, but they would like to take their kids out of the public schools, and we might want to think twice about going out at night. A Catholic Charities staff member states, "There's a lot of bankruptcy going on here. I've seen a lot of people selling houses and moving into apartments and different things. And if you miss a rent payment, then you're out on the street."

Downtown Decatur has become a ghost town: few restaurants, places of entertainment, or white-collar businesses remain open. At night, the downtown streets are deserted. Large trucks continue to lumber along Decatur roads, and trains continue to crisscross the city, but the trucks' horns and the trains' whistles echo through increasingly empty neighborhoods, as Decatur's population has fallen by 20 percent over the past decade.

Dave and Judy epitomize the sense of loss that characterizes Decatur.

Broken in spirit by cruel life events, Dave and Judy broke our hearts as well. A lovely couple, physically attractive and well-spoken, they wear their stories in their eyes and on their bodies. Dave, at age fifty-five, carries himself like a once-strong man beaten down by life. Judy carries herself with an aura of sorrow so thick, so tangible, that, inured to emotion as we were after conducting dozens of interviews, we soon shared her tears and felt ourselves engulfed in her pain.

We met Dave and Judy at a chain restaurant in Decatur. The wait staff, and many of the customers, seemed to know them. Apparently, they come to the restaurant often, though they rarely eat—Dave is slim, and Judy is painfully skinny. Mostly, they just sit and stare as they drink endless cups of coffee and smoke cigarette after cigarette. But they keep coming, Dave explains, because he wants Judy to get out of the house, away from the train whistle that reminds her of her daughter's death. Besides, the restaurant provides a convenient setting for him to spread the word that he is selling his lawn mower, truck bed, roof rack, and other prized possessions in the wake of the massive layoffs at the plants around Decatur, where he has worked for more than three decades.

At age sixteen, Dave took the first of a series of low-paid, unskilled factory jobs. Quickly realizing that the key to a good future lay in acquiring professional skills, "I got an apprenticeship in construction, in '76, I guess it was. It took me almost a year to go through the whole process, and I finally got hired in '77. And, boy, that was great. It started out at six dollars and fifty cents an hour, which wasn't a lot, but I had been making five dollars. So that was a lot for me. And then every six months or a year, I got another raise. And it just kept going up, and it was wonderful. And everything was good. You could buy a new car once in a while; you could have a home."

For most of his career, he had union jobs at Caterpillar, Firestone, and other plants in the Decatur area. As a member of the Pipefitters' local, he is called when work is available. Until recently, a skilled worker like Dave was almost always employed, with a fairly steady stream of work. During the past few years, however, all that has changed as waves of plant closings have devastated the local economy.

The 2001 Firestone closing is the one that made the news, linked in the media to defective Firestone tires (which, as people in Decatur angrily pointed out, actually were manufactured while the union was on strike and nonunion replacements, known as "scabs," were working at the plant). But other plants have been laying off as well, more quietly. According to federal law, a company does not need to make a layoff public knowledge if fewer than fifty people at a time are affected. Thus, Caterpillar, another large Decatur employer, made incremental layoffs of fewer than fifty employees in each round, keeping the downsizing quiet and the labor unions from negotiating severance packages. All in all, the economic picture in Illinois is bleak: in the 1980s alone, west-central Illinois lost 64,033 jobs in manufacturing through layoffs and mergers of corporate mainstays such as Case, John Deere, and Caterpillar.

CORPORATE RESTRUCTURING AND THE AMERICAN DREAM

> [We now have] a society in which firms have been merged and acquired, downsized, deindustrialized, multinationalized, automated, streamlined, and restructured. In the process, the rich have gotten richer, the poor poorer, and . . . life for the middle class more and more precarious.
>
> Bennett Harrison and Barry Bluestone,
> *The Great U-Turn: Corporate Restructuring*
> *and the Polarizing of America*

The link between health care and employment developed in the United States as one piece of a broader cultural ethos often called the American dream.* Cultivated during the twentieth century and especially during the post–World War II era, this dream has offered hope and inspiration, and spawned endurance and sacrifice, in the American workplace. In pursuit of the dream, people like Dave and Judy worked long hours and expended all the resources they could in order to ensure that their children's lives would be better than their own. In return, they came to

---

*The American dream, just like nighttime dreams, has always incorporated layers of complexity, contradictions, and reversals of reality. Most important, to a large degree racial minorities, and in many situations women, have been systematically excluded from realizing the dream.

expect a living wage, some measure of job security, government protection in the form of workplace safety standards and unemployment insurance, opportunities for economic and social upward mobility, a reasonably healthy life, and the prospect of homeownership.

The post–World War II economy provided avenues for blue-collar and white-collar workers to pursue the American dream. During this period, American industry boomed, corporate management practices associated with expanding companies opened up avenues for white-collar employees to ascend the career ladder, and strong labor unions helped blue-collar workers receive health insurance and other benefits as part of their employment. As labor unions made gains during the twentieth century, manufacturing jobs became dependable avenues for social mobility. The labor often was grueling, but the accompanying wages provided incentives and rewards. For workers like Dave, hard work paid off because employers were compelled to treat their employees fairly and because jobs came with benefits—such as health care coverage—that helped employees make it through hard times and illness.

In recent decades, a fundamental paradox inherent in the dream has surfaced ever more clearly: although both employers and workers may share the vision of the American dream and may even share a belief that it can best be achieved when all pitch in for a common goal, the reality is that the means to attain that dream comes from one finite pot—company revenues. Gains on the part of workers come at the expense of profits for employers; labor compensation (wages, benefits, and other costs) makes up a large percentage of company expenses. Thus, as health care costs have soared over the past decades, many employers have come to see providing health insurance to employees as a burden.

During this time, conflicts intrinsic to employer-worker relationships have increasingly overshadowed the common good envisioned in the American dream. Developments in computer technology and transportation have made it easier for corporations to take advantage of looser government trade regulations, lower taxes, and cheaper labor in new geographic locations, mostly outside U.S. borders. International trade organizations such as the World Trade Organization and agreements such as the North American Free Trade Agreement (NAFTA), heavily supported by large American corporate interests, extended and enabled these developments.

Goods that used to be produced by workers like Dave in places like Decatur now are produced in manufacturing facilities in Malaysia, China, or Mexico, where occupational safety standards and environmental regulations are less rigorous than in the United States. In short, moving manufacturing from places like Decatur to South America or Asia allows higher corporate profits.

At the same time, the U.S. government has retreated from attempts to block trusts and mergers of major competitors and now rather routinely rubber-stamps the formation of megacorporations. As corporations gained more power and influence, trade unions—which once energetically protected workers and negotiated benefits on their behalf from a position of strength—declined in membership and political influence.

These changes have chipped away at the sense that workers and employers share a mutually dependent relationship serving the interests of both parties. As the structures and feelings of mutuality have evaporated, the link between health care and employment has become increasingly tenuous for growing numbers of Americans.

Dave and Judy learned this as blue-collar workers, but the same sea changes have affected white-collar workers as well. Over the past few decades, upper-level corporate management has chosen to invest dollars in carrying out acquisitions and mergers rather than in upgrading existing facilities or increasing worker benefits. Through mergers and acquisitions, corporate leaders eliminate "redundancy" (read: jobs) at all levels of management. Corporations also now turn to outsourcing and third-party specialists, a trend that further dilutes the old model of employer-worker mutuality.

Throughout the 1980s and 1990s, low- and mid-level managers and staffers were laid off at alarming rates in both Illinois and the rest of the country. More than 1.5 million mid-management jobs were slashed in the 1980s, 3.1 million were eliminated through reorganization in the first half of the 1990s, and, according to observers, these trends continue in the new millennium. For the most part, laid-off middle-management workers have not fared well in the new economy. Many end up either permanently unemployed or "underemployed" in lower-level positions, at lower wages or lower skill levels.

There is some debate about whether corporate management structures have in fact shrunk; that is, whether the millions of white-collar layoffs represent permanent elimination of those jobs or simply a turnover of personnel as companies lay off higher-paid managers and replace them with lower-paid, younger managers. However one parses the statistics, the reality is that millions of people who formerly worked in low- to mid-level management jobs found themselves unemployed and thus uninsured for short or long periods of time. If they were unlucky enough to become sick during those periods, they may well have ended up accruing enormous medical debt, declaring bankruptcy, or finding their health permanently damaged—even to the point of ruining their future employability. When they do find employment, they frequently are offered less compensation and fewer benefits in their new jobs, as average earnings and benefits for those middle-class workers have declined, in real money, over the last two decades.

We spoke with a former factory worker who is currently employed by a union as a peer counselor, charged with helping "displaced" (laid-off) workers enter job retraining programs in south-central Illinois. He clarified the impact of deindustrialization on the strong union towns of the Rust Belt: "When they build a plant in Paris, Illinois [a very small town in rural, southern Illinois], you've got people coming from all over Appalachia and the rural South to work there. They're not unionized. From what I've heard—I have a friend who works there—they're working them like twelve hours a day. People get fed up and they're quitting, and so they're hiring as fast as they fire or quit. The turnover rates are off the scale! Here in Danville, and in Decatur, there are skilled workers who want jobs, but I think in order to keep the unions out, [the companies] don't want a lot of big manufacturing jobs here, because this has been a highly union town forever.

"You know," he added, "they move the plants down to Mexico to those—what do they call them?—*maquiladoras*—like sweatshops, with no unions and no benefits. And they pay them peanuts to work like slaves. I don't blame those people for taking our jobs. They need to eat, too. I feel sorry for them."

BUYING AMERICAN

Both for people like Dave and Judy, who worked in secure blue-collar jobs, and for millions of Americans who have worked in mid-level managerial jobs, the bottom line is that the corporate culture of mergers, acquisitions, and downsizing has created a context in which the kinds of jobs that historically carried benefits, stability, and upward mobility have been dramatically destabilized, leaving millions of workers susceptible to the pull of the death spiral.

In specific terms, what do these developments mean for Dave and Judy?

Dave suffers from several chronic health problems. Five years ago, he had open-heart surgery to bypass four blockages in his coronary arteries. He suffers from high blood pressure, treated with medication, and he is supposed to take Lipitor for his high cholesterol. A few weeks before we spoke, his last bottle of pills had run out. "I had to order new medicines last week. It cost me, oh, I forget what it cost—a hundred fifty dollars for three prescriptions, one for Judy and two for me. The Lipitor I had to let go, because I didn't have enough money to buy any more."

The sorry state of employment in south-central Illinois means that the union can no longer support the comprehensive health benefits that workers like Dave and Judy had taken for granted for so many years. Dave's union now offers a plan that includes a substantial deductible—$500 per year per person. Judy says, "By the end of last year, we just met our deductible. And then the year starts over again. So we never get anything paid [for by the insurance]."

Dave adds, "We can't afford to go to the doctor. Once the deductible is covered, we'd be okay. But I'm still paying doctors from last year. And now that it's the new year, [again] we can't go to the doctor when we get sick." Their health plan recently eliminated dental and eye care completely and added a deductible for medications. "Our insurance only covers eighty percent of medical expenses now. If I go to the hospital for something, they pay eighty percent and I pay twenty percent, up to where my share is five thousand dollars maximum per person."

The biggest problem with the new insurance system is that when the number of hours worked by an enrollee falls below a certain threshold, the enrollee must pay the entire premium (including what is usually the employer's share) as well as the deductible and co-pay. Dave explains, "Well, right now, with things the way they are, they have also changed our insurance so that you have to work ten out of twelve weeks in a quarter in order to qualify for the insurance. So, now, I've been laid off a month. I no longer will qualify after this quarter. So I'd have to self-pay. Well, our self-pay is like—what are the rates, twelve or fourteen hundred dollars? It's way up there per quarter. I can't pay that."

In fact, a majority of adults who are uninsured are employed full-time (see figure 1). A majority of these workers are not even offered coverage; some, like Dave, however, are offered insurance but at rates so high that they cannot afford it (see figure 2).

At the time of our conversation, Dave's coverage for medications had become, in his words, "pretty useless." He had not been to the doctor in quite a while and thus has not had his blood tested either for cholesterol levels or for liver damage (a possible side effect of Lipitor). The last time it was checked, his blood pressure was "150 something."

To no one's surprise, given the unexpected downturn of his fortunes in recent years, he also takes two antidepressants: "Once in the morning of one kind, and I take another one at night. I ran out of that a week ago, and I haven't had any since, because that's another one I can't afford."

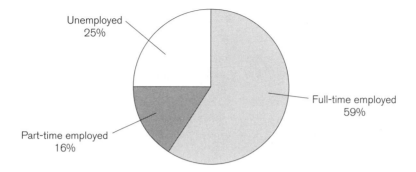

FIGURE 1. The uninsured, ages 18 to 64, by work status, 2001. *Source:* Fronstin 2001, table 2.

Dave now goes for weeks without work. When he does pick up a job, it is often located several hours away. Over the past year or two, Dave and Judy have had to sell a number of their possessions and, for the first time in their lives, have had to limit their purchase of necessities, including food.*

We ask Dave whether he might not be better off working at one of the local plants that still have union contracts.

"I'm fifty-five. I can't go to ADM and get a job. They probably wouldn't hire me, not at my age. And even if they did, I couldn't do what the young men do. I'm not physically able anymore. You spend all your life working with your back and your arms, and then pretty soon you get run down."

A job retraining administrator in Decatur explains: "Factory workers like Dave worked extremely hard. They worked terrible hours. They

---

*According to the *Decatur Impact Project Report,* a study of the 1,250 workers laid off when Firestone closed in June 2001, 13 percent had put their homes on the market, 21 percent had attempted to sell personal property or possessions in order to make ends meet, and, by January 2003, approximately 25 percent reported various symptoms of stress and tension that affected relationships with family and friends (Spannaus and Hironimus-Wendt 2003).

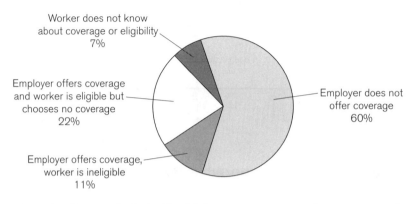

Worker does not know
about coverage or eligibility
7%

Employer offers coverage
and worker is eligible but
chooses no coverage
22%

Employer does not
offer coverage
60%

Employer offers coverage,
worker is ineligible
11%

FIGURE 2. Reasons for lack of health insurance among workers ages 19 to 64, 2001. *Source:* Collins et al. 2003, chart 3, p. 3.

worked on shifts. They would work at night. It's filthy inside the plants, dangerous, very hot and very noisy, up to a hundred twenty degrees, with no air conditioning. The work was dangerous. They would risk life and limb. They worked really hard for their money, and they felt they deserved what they earned. Having lived through all that, they now want a job with low stress and a job that's less physical. Sometimes it's necessary because they have arthritis or other kinds of degenerative problems as a result of the very hard work, the heavy lifting, and repetitive lifting they've done inside the plants."

All over Decatur, we saw signs and bumper stickers urging us to "Buy American." Many Americans, of course, need no such urging: they have always believed that American-made products were of better quality than those manufactured elsewhere. A local teacher who has been assisting displaced manufacturing workers told us, "These people have always bought American, American shoes, American belts, American shirts, and American cars. They believe in supporting each other and supporting the community. And it came as a big shock to them when all of a sudden the plants closed and they lost their jobs. And here they were, they always bought American, and now the companies are owned by international corporations, and their world has just fallen apart."

JUDY'S STORY: A WRECKED LIFE

Dave does not bear his troubles alone. He and Judy have been married for five years. This is a second marriage for both of them—Judy divorced her first husband when she found out that he was committing incest with their oldest daughter. Like many child molesters, the husband had done a good job of keeping his acts hidden. And like many victims of incest, the daughter became involved with drugs and gangs.

Thinking that hers was a solid middle-class family, Judy remembers that she couldn't understand why this child, of her four, was so wild. She began to pray that God would give her an answer. "God listened to my prayer." She discovered the incest and ended the marriage. Wishing to immediately get her daughter as far away from the husband as possible, she refused to become involved with court cases or monetary negotiations over a divorce settlement. She picked up the children, left, and let her husband take everything.

When Judy met Dave, he had also been divorced recently and had split assets with his former wife. Although both Judy and Dave were hard workers, they began their life together without any substantial savings, thanks to the divorces. Still, they were happy to have found love after all they had been through and didn't mind starting over from scratch in their late forties.

Judy has worked both inside and outside the home all her life. Starting in her mid-thirties, she found employment at the local Eagle supermarket, where she worked for sixteen years. She appreciated the job because of its stability—she liked working with the same group of co-workers year in and year out—and especially because of the good benefits, including health insurance. Three years before we met the couple, however, she lost her job—and her cherished health benefits—when Eagle closed down, forced out by a Wal-Mart that opened outside Decatur. Unlike the supermarket, Wal-Mart rarely provides comprehensive health benefits to its employees, which helps it undercut the prices of other stores. Dave says, "Wal-Mart comes in and cuts their prices until they close everybody else, and then they raise the prices."*

Within a month after losing her job, a far worse disaster struck Judy's household. One of her daughters was killed, at the age of twenty-three, when she was hit by a train.

Within a month, Judy had lost her job, her health insurance, and her daughter. Now, she adds, it's a struggle to get up and face each day. Her whole life has shut down, and she feels completely worthless. Judy tells us, "You know, they say there are different stages of grief. Well, I keep waiting for the anger, but it never comes. I just never get out of sadness."

After her daughter died, Judy did not know how to get through the days and nights. Out of desperation, she and Dave purchased a computer, which she would use for hours at a time, often entire nights, looking up information about trains. Then, to get her out of the house, Dave encouraged her to go shopping. Judy recalls that she would buy a shirt, a blouse, "anything, hoping that it would make me happy." By the time she realized that her sadness would not be helped by new clothing, they had accumulated substantial bills.

When we met Dave and Judy, their financial situation had become so dire that they had given up their cable television and their newspaper

---

*Wal-Mart has built its success on its ability to cut costs, including the cost of benefits for its 1.16 million workers. It has cut health costs per worker to $3,500 a year, fully 40 percent less than the U.S. average of $5,646, and 30 percent less than the average paid by other retailers ($4,834). New hourly workers are not eligible for benefits for six months and then are not covered for preexisting conditions for the following year. Deductibles for the low-cost plans are $1,000, with employees responsible for 20 percent of all costs above that figure. Plans do not cover all flu shots, eye exams, contraceptives, child vaccinations, and other routine services. Monthly premiums for a worker and spouse run roughly $200 per month, more than 20 percent of the take-home pay of a cashier making $8 an hour. Because of the high cost of premiums, only about 60 percent of Wal-Mart's 800,000 eligible workers sign up for coverage (Wysocki and Zimmerman 2003).

and cut their budget down to bare bones. "We went like three days without eating, in between waiting for his unemployment check. We had three weeks with no money, none," Judy said.

She tried to go back to work a number of times, but she found herself virtually unemployable. When she first started looking for a job, she was in such a state of fresh grief that no employer was interested. "I was just crying and crying and crying," she remembers. Jobs are tight in Decatur, with many laid-off workers seeking employment, and the disadvantages that any middle-aged woman faces in the job market are compounded, in Judy's case, by the wrenching grief that emanates from her eyes. "I can't take a gun and put it to their heads and say, 'Hire me.' You know? And I'm that age, not to mention I've been out of work for three years. They kind of question that."

Judy and Dave believe that it might be a good idea to move. The problem with their house, they explain, is that it is near the railroad tracks. Judy can hear the train whistling all day and all night, relentlessly reminding her of her daughter's death, bringing her back to her sorrow any time she does manage to distract herself. Dave adds, "I think that if we didn't have the money problems right now, with both of us being out of work, that would help her a lot." He notes that when she was out in Arizona for a few months, taking care of her elderly mother, "she was much better. You don't hear train whistles out there."

But Dave and Judy feel paralyzed, both emotionally and financially. Given Decatur's slumping economy, they are afraid to give up the one thing they feel sure of—their home. In any case, in the current economic climate in the area, it is unlikely that the sale price of their house would be enough to allow them to buy elsewhere in the country. Despite years of a solid middle-class lifestyle, Dave and Judy are aware of the specter of homelessness that haunts those who fall on hard times. Giving up their home for a rental apartment elsewhere—in light of Dave's untreated heart problems and Judy's untreated emotional problems—is likely to lead to the bottom of the death spiral.

IS HEALTH CARE THE ANSWER?

The devastating grief that Judy lives with, and will continue to live with, cannot be erased by money or medicine.

So why have we chosen to include the couple's story in this volume? Could consistent access to health care have eased some of their pain and prevented some of their slide?

We believe that the answer is yes. Because Judy did not have insurance at the time her daughter was killed, she was not able to receive counseling to help her over her initial anguish. Because she had inadequate insurance later on, she was not eligible to access any sort of psychotherapy or counseling to help her develop even minimal coping skills. All she received was a quick prescription for an antidepressant drug. She knows that therapy would not have made her pain go away. But a solid relationship with a therapist could have stopped some of the emotional and financial unraveling and perhaps could have helped the couple make the decision to sell the house and leave behind the incessant train whistles.

In a sad irony, the cost of accessing even minimal care for Judy has contributed to the couple's burden. During the first year or so after her daughter's death, Judy went to the doctor every few months to adjust her antidepressant medication, resulting in bills that they cannot pay. At this point, they are not sure whether their doctor would be willing to see them despite the bill. In any case, they are embarrassed to ask for what, to them and probably also the doctor, might feel like a handout or a favor. As of our last conversation, then, Dave was not taking the blood pressure medication he needs, Judy was not receiving the therapy she needs, and in order to scrape by they were selling off their various possessions.

Access to medical care would not bring Judy's daughter back, nor would it bring back the industry that has fled southern Illinois for Mexico or Southeast Asia. It would, however, keep Dave healthy enough to continue bringing some money into the household; and it might help

Judy break out of some of the worst layers of the grieving process, help temper some of her overwhelming sorrow, and enable her to once again contribute to the financial stability of her household.

Dave and Judy are not "losers." They do not have a long history of being chronically unemployed, they are not without marketable skills, and they are not mired in decades of unpaid bills. Rather, they were unfortunate enough to experience a horrifying personal tragedy at a time when the local economy faltered. This combination of events has sucked them into a quagmire of debt and depression. Under the best of circumstances, Dave and Judy probably have sufficient personal resources and social networks to hold on until the economy improves. But if Dave's chronic health conditions (heart disease, high blood pressure) continue to be untreated, it is likely that he will join the ranks of the unemployable before long. Judy, we suspect, already has joined those ranks.

SAFETY NETS AND THE WORKING POOR

Throughout south-central Illinois, the health care providers we met reported seeing more illness than in years past, and they attribute the rise in poor health to the stress caused by the economic changes that have afflicted their communities. A job retraining counselor in Decatur put it this way: "It's really hard. People get frustrated. They're struggling. They're desperate. Some have sick kids or were going through adoptions when they lost their jobs, and this has disrupted their whole lives and taken away the resources they counted on. Some of the people we see are letting their health slide; they're not doing the kind of health maintenance they had always done. Some were in the middle of some kind of [medical] procedure and they've just stopped—they're not completing it. It's ironic: the main employer around here who's doing a lot of hiring is Decatur Memorial Hospital."*

*For the most part, these hospital jobs pay low wages and are nonunion.

The safety nets that are in place—a patchwork of Medicaid and charity care—were designed for "outliers" who, temporarily, do not have "normative" employment-based health coverage. This patchwork is not equipped to provide ongoing care to the many Americans who live in the new economic reality of the twenty-first century. Dave and Judy are not eligible for Medicaid—Dave continues to work, though not steadily, and his income places them above the threshold for Medicaid eligibility.

Cheryl Rome, a long-time social worker in Danville, explains that, in Illinois, Medicaid recipients are assigned a "spend-down" based on their household income. A household's spend-down is the difference between what it earns and a precalculated figure. (No one we spoke to knew exactly how this figure was calculated.) "So let's say for a household of one person, the figure on the spend-down chart is seven hundred fifty dollars a month. Let's say you earn fifteen hundred a month. You're very likely to be eligible for Medicaid, but your spend-down is going to be seven hundred fifty. That means you have to pay that much for medical care before you can access Medicaid."

This leads to a situation, Rome continues, "in which people can't take care of their small, chronic, ongoing health problems until they become really major and catastrophic, at which point, you know, they can easily reach the spend-down, and Medicaid kicks in." In short, Medicaid does not function as a safety net for people like Dave and Judy.

Men and women in similar circumstances who live in Danville might be able to get some stopgap care at the all-volunteer Vermillion County Clinic. The "only" price they would pay is the public admission that they have become charity cases. A former mid-level manager who lost her job in a plant closing in Danville shared with us how she feels about having to turn to a charity clinic for health care: "When we find ourselves unable to provide for ourselves, and we've always been independent, it adds an emotional burden. You're trapped in a cycle you hate."

In any case, Decatur has no free clinic, so this is not an option for Dave and Judy at this time.

Rome offers sociological insight into the impact that plant closings have had on the local health care system. "People here used to work in factory jobs where they had a comfortable lifestyle with union contracts at General Motors and other plants. They had good, stable insurance." The hospitals and other health facilities, she notes, were kept "in pretty good shape because [those workers] balanced the case mix that otherwise consisted of Medicaid and uninsured patients." In other words, Rome explains, by having a large number of blue-collar workers whose medical expenses were fully paid by insurance, the hospitals could absorb or balance out the losses incurred by treating Medicaid patients, for whom the government reimbursement is low, and uninsured patients, many of whom cannot pay their bills. "But now there's hardly anyone with good benefits anymore. When the factories closed, there became a new classification of people needing health care benefits. *The 'working poor' is what was created in our community*" (our emphasis).

One of the first things we learned when we began this project was that many of our interviewees are deeply offended when they are called "the working poor." Identifying as a member of the "working class"—especially in the heavily unionized Rust Belt—carries with it a certain pride in one's ability to work hard, build things, produce goods, be the "salt of the earth," and be a part of building the American dream. Being labeled as a member of the "working poor," to our interviewees, is a stigma. The phrase is a synonym—as more than one individual told us—for "loser."

CHAPTER TWO

MEDICAID, WELFARE REFORM, AND LOW-WAGE WORK IN THE NEW ECONOMY

Susan, please turn your tape recorder back on—there's something important I want you to tell people for me. I think that the world penalizes you for being poor. Your credit rating is down because of your income, you're not allowed to make payments on things—or if you do get payments, you have to go through Rent to Own, which is higher payments and higher interest, and the poorer you are, the higher interest you pay. That's my experience, which is bull crap, because if you're rich you should have higher interest, not if you're poor. And the same goes for doctors' bills and things. It seems to me that I know people who paid less to go to the doctor, and they made more than me, and I don't understand that. Or they paid less because they have a credit company that gives you cash back if you make quantity purchases and stuff. And why can't they have programs for poor people who need it?

Misty, Idaho

GINA'S STORY: THE NEW BRAND OF LOW-WAGE WORK

When the pains in her stomach first started, Gina, a plain and tired-looking young Idaho woman with faded blonde hair, thought that they were probably caused by a mixture of stress and indigestion. Gina had been experiencing a great deal of tension lately. After working for ten years at a clerical job at Home Depot, she quit to go back to school to learn a skill that would give her better occupational opportunities.

Looking for a profession that would make her more employable and perhaps allow her to use some of her artistic talents, Gina took out a student loan of $7,000 for tuition and another $8,000 for living expenses and went to school for fourteen months to learn to cut hair. As soon as she finished her fourteen-month training program, she was hired by FabuCuts—a chain of beauty shops specializing in low-cost cuts for walk-in customers.

As is the practice at this kind of establishment, Gina does not have a steady salary. Instead, she is paid per customer: She averages approximately $3.80 per haircut—that is, 38 percent of the total price of the cut. In order to earn enough to pay rent ($400 a month for a small one-bedroom apartment), utilities (expensive in the cold Idaho winters), car insurance, gas, food, and college loans, Gina needs to work for about nine hours each day. Now in her mid-thirties, she is finding it difficult to stand on her feet for so many hours. Nonetheless, she prefers the nine-hour days to the days that she sits and waits for customers: without customers, she is paid nothing. Gina calculates that in an average month she makes about $900.

Like many haircutters, Gina is bothered by shoulder pain and expects that she will not last any longer in this job than most of her colleagues; a high turnover rate is the norm among women who work in haircutting salons. But she cannot contemplate quitting at this point because of the load she carries for her student loans.

FabuCuts does offer health insurance to its employees—for $200 per month. With a $1,000 deductible and substantial co-pays, insurance is absolutely out of Gina's financial reach. And this is where her current problems began.

At first, she had stomach pains only after she ate. And then she also began to have pains when she didn't eat. The pain became terrible, and she went to the emergency room, where she was diagnosed with a bladder infection and told to see her regular doctor if she wasn't better in a week. From the start, Gina would have preferred going to her own doctor—the one she had seen for years when she had insurance—but "they weren't seeing me because I have to pay money to go see them. I have to have the cash [up front]." And so, although she suspected that she didn't have a bladder infection, she purchased and took the antibiotics prescribed in the ER.

The pain didn't go away, and Gina decided that she really needed to see her own doctor. "This had never happened to me in the years that I had insurance, but this time the receptionist told me that the doctor couldn't fit me in and sent me to some kind of physician's assistant instead." The PA ruled out a bladder infection, diagnosed a kidney infection, and prescribed more antibiotics.

After another few weeks, the pain was worse. She made another trip to the ER, where more tests were done. This time, the bill was $5,000. Her condition still didn't improve, so she scraped together another $80 to go back to her own doctor's office. This time, the doctor saw her and told her that the problem was her gall bladder.

He sent her back to the hospital for more tests, including injecting her gall bladder with radioactive dye. This visit cost her $4,000. The tests determined that her gall bladder wasn't functioning properly and that she needed to see a surgeon. But the surgeon insisted that she pay $200 up front before he would see her. When she spoke to the surgeon's receptionist, she learned that her doctor had already told the surgeon's office that she didn't have insurance. That was several months ago, and she still hasn't seen the surgeon—she can't scrape up the money.

"I just wish we were kind of like Canada, where everybody has insurance," Gina comments.

At this point, Gina's pain comes and goes. She knows that stress makes it worse, but stress is one thing she can't seem to avoid. A friend told her that if her gall bladder isn't treated, it can rupture, and then she will need to have emergency surgery. The thought of the surgery terrifies her and exacerbates her gall bladder pain. But her friend is right.

Gall bladder rupture could cause her to lose parts of her bowel, become infertile, or even die from uncontrolled infection

Gina has become accustomed to the discomfort she lives with, but she can't get used to the fear: Her sister's ovary "exploded," and Gina is afraid that, without ongoing care, the same thing will happen to her. She has learned to handle the pain: she switches between ibuprofen and Tylenol tablets, taking eight or so each day. She has also used alcohol to dull the pain but no longer lets herself drink to excess. Between the pain and the pills, she is constantly tired and has to drag herself to work every day.

Gina and her husband would love to have children, but they can't even consider a pregnancy in their current financial situation. Gina has a long history of gynecological problems—cysts on her ovaries and endometriosis, which causes cramping and heavy bleeding. She typically has to stay in bed for the first day of each menstrual cycle. When she worked at Home Depot, she went to the gynecologist regularly, had annual Pap smears, and had several surgeries to keep the gynecological conditions under control. Now that she no longer has insurance, she has not been to the gynecologist in three or four years, nor has she had a Pap smear (particularly important because of her health issues).

Gina's husband works at a chain store as a freight manager, earning $6.25 per hour. The store keeps him at slightly below full-time hours and thus does not offer him health insurance. A year or two ago, his mother decided to pay for health insurance for him, but she will not pay for Gina's insurance. This bothers Gina because her husband is healthy and doesn't really need the insurance, whereas she is suffering and needs consistent health care. Still, Gina says, she can't expect much from her mother-in-law, who is "a very selfish woman."

Gina's mother, who works for Washington State University as a gardener, would like to help, but she lacks the financial means. Like many other large universities, WSU maintains many of its workers as temps and avoids providing health insurance. After Gina's mother works a thousand hours, she is laid off for three months and is then called back to work another thousand hours. "That way, they don't have to give benefits."

Gina wears her blonde hair in a tightly bound ponytail. Of average height and weight, with heavy glasses and sad, plain features, she has a peculiar mannerism of keeping her mouth closed even when speaking. Toward the end of our conversation, Gina explained why. She has always taken good care of her teeth and went to the dentist regularly when she had insurance. Now she has not been able to afford dental care for three years, and her front tooth has a cavity and is rotting away. She shows me. "You see, there is a hole there, or a gap, and I've never had a gap there before." Insightful about her own deteriorating situation, Gina is aware that, because of her teeth, she is beginning to look like a member of the new American caste of the ill, infirm, and marginally employed.

After we tell Gina repeatedly that we can't see the hole unless we practically stick our heads into her mouth to look, she grins with a smile that is electric enough to light up the room. For a few seconds, her pain and stress recede, she beams out a thousand watts of delight, and plain Gina turns into a beautiful young woman.

LOW-WAGE WORK AND POOR HEALTH

Today, an increasing percentage of jobs pay low wages and are located in the retail and service sectors. More than one in four Americans earns less than $8.70 an hour, a rate that produces an income below the federal poverty line for a family of four, even for full-time work.* Women and

---

*Many believe that these poverty line figures greatly underestimate the number of families who struggle financially. A report by the Economic Policy Institute, a nonprofit, nonpartisan think tank in Washington, D.C., showed that families earning between one and two times the federal poverty level were as likely as a family living below the poverty line to experience a financial hardship such as going without food, housing, or necessary health care (Boushey et al. 2001). Thus, the real number of people living in poverty is actually much higher than the numbers based on official poverty levels.

minorities are disproportionately concentrated in jobs that do not allow them to make ends meet. In *The Betrayal of Work: How Low-Wage Jobs Fail 30 Million Americans and Their Families*, Beth Shulman explains, "Women of color are four times more likely to hold a low-wage job than white men. White women are three times as likely as men to hold a low-wage job. And men of color are one and a half times as likely as white men to do so."

The employers of low-wage workers frequently do not offer health insurance. Nearly 90 percent of workers earning more than $15 an hour are employed by firms that offer health insurance. But only 65 percent of those earning less than $10 an hour work for such firms. When low-wage workers are offered health benefits, the price tag can be unaffordable. In recent years, as premiums soared, many employers raised the share that employees must pay, pushing low-wage workers even harder against the wall.

Moreover, the insurance packages now offered to low-wage employees increasingly tend to include stripped-down policies with spotty coverage or severe limits. The insurance plans provided to low-wage workers often lack coverage for prescription drugs, dental care, vision services, and care of dependents. Overall, whereas only 8 percent of workers with incomes over $75,000 a year are uninsured, nearly a quarter of those earning under $25,000 do not have health insurance (see figure 3).

Scraping by without heath insurance is a harsh burden for low-income Americans, who, overall, tend to be less healthy than more affluent individuals. Numerous studies report that poverty is related to high rates of chronic illness, self-reported poorer health status, higher levels of disability, and lower life expectancy.* A study conducted by the Philadelphia Department of Public Health, for instance, found that mortality rates for residents of high-poverty census tracts were three times higher than those in low-poverty census tracts. Similar differences

---

*These differences persist even when studies control for lifestyle issues such as smoking, diet, and exercise (Adler 2002).

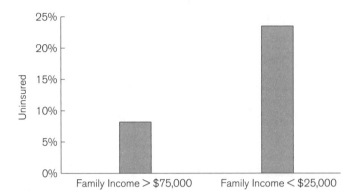

FIGURE 3.   Yearly income and lack of health insurance, 2002. *Source:* U.S. Census Bureau 2003, p. 2.

have been observed throughout the country, cutting across gender lines and reflecting the experiences of all racial and ethnic groups. Poverty is linked to less successful outcomes in almost all disease categories, including heart disease, arthritis, most cancers, psychiatric illness, and lung disease. What that means, put bluntly, is that lower-income Americans who are diagnosed with serious diseases are more likely than affluent Americans to develop disabilities and to die.

A variety of factors link poverty to poor health. Fresh, nutritious foods tend to be expensive and hard to find in poor neighborhoods. Often, the only places to buy food in low-income communities are convenience stores and gas stations, which rarely if ever stock fresh produce or whole-grain foods. An unhealthy diet is a contributing factor to obesity, which—with all its attendant health problems—is far more common among poorer Americans. Low-income Americans also tend to be exposed to more toxins—from pesticides sprayed on agricultural fields, chemicals used in manufacturing, and hazardous waste from power plants or dumps located near poor neighborhoods. The best-documented example of this differential is exposure to lead: studies find that poor children and adults show up to a sixfold increase in high blood levels of lead compared to high-income individuals.

The direct negative impacts of inferior food, working conditions (think of the hours Gina stands on her feet each day), and housing are compounded by the impact of stress. Like other aspects of poverty, stress forms part of a cyclical relationship with illness. Working poor families such as Gina's, who live their lives teetering on the edge of the death spiral, are subject to high levels of stress. The knowledge that she is one disaster, one accident or illness, away from falling over the edge is never far from Gina's thoughts. A substantial body of recent medical research demonstrates that stress in and of itself has a deleterious effect on health, weakening the functioning of the immune system and exacerbating a wide range of other pathologies. We cannot know for sure whether any of Gina's health problems are directly caused or only exacerbated by stress, but we do know that the stress she now lives with makes her more vulnerable to further illness.

MISSISSIPPI BLUES

Driving through the Mississippi Delta to meet Alisha, one of the millions of American women who move between low-wage jobs and public aid, we begin to realize that it's more about what you don't see than what you do see. The cotton fields are empty. Mississippi terrain does not lend itself to the large machinery that makes cotton profitable for the landowners. We pass by miles upon miles of pine trees. The U.S. Department of Agriculture often pays farmers *not* to farm, and so they plant pine trees in the somewhat unlikely hope that they might turn a profit by logging sometime in the future. The landscape is pleasing to the eye but provides neither cash nor food for local residents.

Mississippi's unemployment rate is higher than the national average. What little industry once operated in the state is now in retreat, since NAFTA encouraged companies to move to Mexico in search of lower wages and looser regulation. The largest growth in jobs is now occurring in the service sector, mostly in jobs that pay at or near minimum wage.

Mississippi bears the unfortunate distinction of being the poorest state in the nation, with the lowest per capita income: $19,387 for whites, $10,042 for African Americans. Everywhere we drive, we see tiny storefronts with large signs: "Cash Loans on Car Titles," "Easy Check," "Quick Pay." All you have to do is hand over the title to your car, and you'll be given a high-interest, short-term loan. If you miss a payment, well, that's your problem—your car will be repossessed.

Convenience stores dot the landscape, but we are hard put to find a supermarket with fresh fruit and vegetables. The big chains don't find rural Mississippi very profitable. The Wal-Mart out on the highway is not a feasible option for those who don't own cars.

Mississippi leads the nation in prevalence of diabetes and heart disease and ranks third in the rate of cancer deaths. It has the worst standing of all states in premature mortality (the number of preventable years of life lost before age sixty-five) as well as in overall life expectancy and infant mortality. The infant mortality rate for African Americans in Mississippi is exceptionally high: 15.1 deaths per 1,000 births, comparable to the rates in Bulgaria, Costa Rica, and Chile.

There's plenty of illness in Mississippi, but few health care options for the working poor, especially in rural areas. In most "clinics" (actually, private offices), you need to pay before you see the doctor. Once you owe money at a clinic, you can't come back. For those who can't pay, the only option is the crowded urgent care clinics in the hospitals, where sick people sit for hours and hours and still might not be seen.

Pharmacy shelves display almost no over-the-counter medicine—not many people can afford to buy it, anyway. In the pharmacies, we notice more aisles of processed snack foods and cola than of medicine.

Everywhere we go, we see substandard housing at exorbitant rents. A two-bedroom duplex in a shoddily built subdevelopment with dirt roads and poor drainage rents for more than $500 a month. Monthly rent for a room in a boarding house with bars on the doors and windows and a shared kitchen and bathroom is more than $200. It is more profitable for landowners to rent out poorly constructed housing than to sell the land to the African American residents who have worked it since the days of slavery.

ALISHA'S STORY:
AFTERMATH OF A "MISSISSIPPI APPENDECTOMY"

Alisha moved into her house in Philadelphia, Mississippi, just a few weeks before we met her, but she already feels at home in this community, where the kids play outside and the mothers take turns watching them. Alisha's house is immaculate despite a flock of small children (hers and her neighbors') and a stack of unpacked boxes in the corner of the living room. Alisha herself is a personable woman with a pleasant and hospitable smile.

Offering us seats on the sofa, Alisha sits down gingerly on a straight-back chair. Though careful to put us at ease in her home, she can't help holding herself stiffly, at an awkward angle, while we talk. Her vivacious face and voice make her seem younger than her thirty-eight years; her posture and rigid movements belong to a much older woman.

Having lived in Ohio part of her life (she moved to Mississippi recently in order to help care for her aging grandparents), she welcomes us as fellow northerners and is eager to share her reflections on health care in both parts of the country.

"I just think it's terrible here in Mississippi, because I'm from up north. In Ohio, they will give you health care—even when you work—you know, they don't just cut you off Medicaid. They try to give you six months to get established on your job and get health insurance. Here in Mississippi, if I call my caseworker today and said I was working for so and so, I make six dollars an hour, and I work forty hours a week, they punch it in the computer right then. Within three days, I'll have a letter saying as of next month, because of your income, you will be cut from Medicaid."

Like other residents of her neighborhood, Alisha has worked at a variety of low-paying jobs. Most recently, she was employed as a home health care attendant taking care of a paralyzed, elderly woman eight hours a day. She liked the job even though it was rough work and did not provide health insurance or other benefits. "She is a nice lady. She keeps her spirits up." Alisha was sorry to leave the woman who had become dependent on her and who offered her so much inspiration. However, "I had to leave that job because my back hurt, and I couldn't afford to buy the medicine for me to be able to do my job." Alisha understands that this is a lose-lose situation for all concerned: the elderly woman lost an excellent home health aide, Alisha lost a job in which she felt needed and competent, and society as a whole lost a productive worker.

Diagnosed with scoliosis at the age of fourteen, Alisha knows that in order to function she needs Naproxen (an anti-inflammatory), pain pills, and muscle relaxers. With the appropriate medication, she is able to work. Yet if she works, she is ineligible for Medicaid. Even her $6 hourly wage as a home health aide meant that she was not eligible for Medicaid; the clerk at the Medicaid office stated that if Alisha's income exceeded $236 per month, even with three children, she would not be entitled to free health care.

As soon as she left her job, Alisha applied for Medicaid. She recalls the day she received the letter informing her that she had been accepted. "The mail came at nine o'clock, and by nine-thirty I was sitting at the doctor." Still, Alisha is worried. She currently receives child support only from the father of her middle child. The father of her baby will begin paying child support soon, which will push her income above the cut-off line, once again knocking her off Medicaid.

Over the years, Alisha has found some creative ways to handle her medical problems. She suffers from asthma, but she uses her sister's inhaler sometimes, since she can't afford one of her own. Her children, who suffer from more severe asthma, receive from Medicaid "a breathing machine, and they get three hundred packs of medicine for the machine in the box." Alisha uses their medicine when she needs it. She doesn't feel bad about using her children's medicine because "if they start needing three hundred doses, they have a medical problem, and they need to be in a hospital."

Far more disturbing is the heavy bleeding she has been experiencing for the past three years, since her last child was born. After her last pregnancy, Alisha's tubes were tied. Following a common chronology in Mississippi, the tubal ligation was performed shortly after the birth, while Alisha was still entitled to Medicaid by virtue of her pregnancy.* A few months later, when she began menstruating again (typically, women do not menstruate for a few months postpartum), the profuse bleeding began. But her Medicaid eligibility was over, and she was not able to afford a medical assessment or treatment.

As Alisha explains, her periods were brief, regular, and painless before her tubes were tied. But about four months after the baby was born (a month after Medicaid ran out), her period "started with the heavy, heavy bleeding, and the days lasted longer. And then it started going longer and longer into periods being heavier and harder for me. Sometimes I just lie on the floor and push real hard until it's time and then get up and get on the toilet and then the blood clot comes. So I have periods like that now."

We ask Alisha, "When you began bleeding so heavily, what did you think it was?"

"I thought [the doctor] had messed up tying my tubes."

"Weren't you scared to be bleeding so much?"

"Of course. I mean, of course. But I didn't have insurance."

"But you didn't go back there. Did you try to call?"

---

*As we talked with women during our time in Mississippi, it became apparent that many had been offered tubal ligations immediately after they had given birth, while they were still covered by Medicaid. When we asked these women why they had their tubes tied, very few of their answers led us to believe that it had been a truly informed choice. In fact, tubal sterilizations are so frequent in Mississippi that they have become known in the medical community as "Mississippi appendectomies."

"No. There wasn't any use. They would make an appointment, and I couldn't keep it. Because I couldn't afford to."

Now that she is no longer able to work and thus is eligible for Medicaid once again, she has seen a doctor to have the problem evaluated. The doctor has given her medication in an attempt to regulate her hormones and reduce the bleeding, but the pills are not working so far. The plan is to do a D and C (a dilation and curettage, where the doctor scrapes out the lining of the uterus in an attempt to remove any abnormal tissue) if the pills don't work.

Alisha considers the doctor's proposal sensible, but it does have some drawbacks. In another month or so, when the child support check arrives, Alisha will be cut from Medicaid. The additional $100 a month she will receive from the baby's father will make it impossible for her to follow through with the doctor's plan.

Again, Alisha will fall victim to a lose-lose situation. The taxpayers who funded her diagnostic visits to the doctor will have wasted their money because the doctor's treatment plan cannot be pursued. The doctor will face the frustration of trying to offer quality health care to a patient whose access is, at best, erratic. Alisha will go on bleeding until she becomes too debilitated to work at all. And when the bleeding becomes too unbearable or too frightening (for her or her children), she will make another expensive trip to the emergency room for another stopgap solution.

WELFARE REFORM AND OTHER HOLES IN THE SAFETY NET

Like many low-wage workers, Alisha turned to the welfare system at various times in her life when poor health and poor employment options became too much to handle. Unfortunately, as she learned the hard way, the safety nets that supposedly are in place to safeguard all of us fail all too often.

In 1996, the U.S. Congress enacted a system of welfare reform dubbed the Personal Responsibility Act. This legislation, which replaced Aid to

Families with Dependent Children (AFDC), supplied a new name for public aid: Temporary Assistance to Needy Families (TANF). Touting a moral ideology that promotes the virtues of paid employment, TANF sets a five-year lifetime limit for aid, regardless of need; a two-year limit for finding full-time employment; and a requirement to be involved in a work experience program for twenty to thirty-five hours per week within two months of initial receipt of aid. The new policy also requires mothers of infants as young as three months to work outside the home, prohibits aid to most immigrants, and allows states to set up residency requirements for public aid.

Reflecting the word *temporary* in the name of the program, the number of welfare recipients declined from 12.2 million to 5.3 million by 2001. According to Sharon Hays, author of *Flat Broke with Children: Women in the Age of Welfare Reform*, "although nearly two-thirds of former welfare clients had found some kind of work, half of those were not making wages sufficient to raise them out of poverty. [And] the fate of those who were without jobs or welfare—over one-third of former recipients—remained largely unknown."

Those who crafted the new law promised that families who moved from welfare to work would not be made worse off by losing health insurance or food assistance. However, as researchers Robert Greenstein and Jocelyn Guyer found, "the proportions of poor families that are served in Medicaid and food stamps have declined since 1995. Although eligibility for neither program is dependent upon welfare receipt, the dramatic declines in cash assistance rolls appear to have resulted in large numbers of eligible working families failing to receive Medicaid or food stamp assistance."

Greenstein and Guyer cite an Urban Institute study of single-mother families who left welfare between 1997 and 1999. "Close to half of the children in these families—and nearly two-thirds of the parents—lost Medicaid after ceasing to receive welfare." The vast majority of these families are living on incomes that stay close to the poverty line, and few of the parents work in jobs that provide health insurance.

Hays suggests that cutting the welfare rolls contributes in very significant ways to the creation of what we call the caste of the ill, infirm, and marginally employed. "Work requirements and time limits [of TANF] throw millions of desperate women into the labor market and put them in a position where they must accept low wages, the most menial work, the poorest hours, with no benefits, and little flexibility."*

Who are these former welfare recipients, and are they positioned to hold down jobs or to use an entry-level job as a stepping-stone to better future employment? First, exceptionally high numbers of women who receive or have received welfare are victims of domestic violence, bearing the emotional and physical scars of abuse. Unfortunately, however, as Hays argues, TANF actually gets in the way of women leaving abusive husbands. The Personal Responsibility Act of 1996 begins with this sentence: "Marriage is the foundation of a successful society." It then describes the problems of teenage pregnancy, out-of-wedlock births, children raised in single-parent homes, and fathers who fail to pay child support, linking these social conditions to high rates of violent crime, children with low cognitive skills, and other highly negative imputed outcomes. As Hays observes:

> Indeed, a reading of this statement of the law's intent would lead one to believe that the problem of poverty itself is the direct result of failures to live up to the family ideal. . . . Single mothers on welfare are effectively punished for having children out of wedlock or for getting divorced. The punishment they face is being forced to manage on their own with low-wage work. . . . Removing the safety net and forcing welfare mothers to work is actually a way to reinforce all women's proper commitment to marriage and family.

Second, many welfare mothers and other women care for disabled family members, a point to which we return in chapter 4.

*Hays (2003) further points out that low-wage employers not only benefit from this large pool of eager new workers but also gain greater control over their existing workers—who are now under pressure to accept their current working conditions or face being replaced by former welfare recipients.

Third, many welfare recipients are not healthy, as Hays explains:

A recent study by the U.S. General Accounting Office, following the same methods used to track disabilities nationwide, found that a full *44 percent of welfare mothers report some form of physical or mental health disability*—a rate that is over three times as high as the national disability rate (16 percent). . . . For more than one-third of TANF recipients, the General Accounting Office notes, these disabilities are "severe enough that the individual was unable or needed help to perform one or more [simple, everyday] activities, such as walking up a flight of stairs or keeping track of money or bills." (emphasis added)

One would have hoped that our society would not have removed the old safety net of AFDC without providing a new safety net that could catch the most disadvantaged (physically or otherwise) of those who formerly would have qualified for public aid. And in fact, the federal Supplemental Security Income (SSI) program is designed to provide for adults with disabilities serious enough to prevent work at any job. "However," note Sheila Zedlewski and Pamela Loprest, "SSI provides eligibility only for those unable to perform any substantial work because of a medical condition expected to last at least one year or result in death. A large proportion of those [who had received AFDC] experienced health and personal difficulties that did not meet SSI's strict disability definition but still made it difficult to hold a job."

What happens, then, to this population of women, all of whom are raising children and almost half of whom suffer from substantial physical or mental health challenges, when they are pushed into the low-wage employment market? Their own health challenges, combined with the rise in temporary and contingent labor in the United States as a whole, make it unlikely that they will remain in one workplace for very long. Thus, even if they are fortunate enough to land a job that offers benefits, they may well have left that job before the waiting period for health insurance (anywhere from three months to one year) has ended. Summarizing the findings of a number of local and national studies, Karen Seccombe writes: "Studies report that one-quarter to one-third of adults and at least 15 percent of children are completely uninsured after leaving welfare."

Then, given the high rate of health challenges facing these women and the low likelihood of receiving insurance, their health may well deteriorate, making steady employment even less likely. At some point, their health problems may become sufficiently severe for them to qualify for SSI (a solution that is hardly fiscally efficient for the country's tax coffers). What is more likely, however, is that they will become entrenched members of the caste of the ill, infirm, and marginally employed.

CHAPTER THREE

FAMILY MATTERS

DIVORCE AND DOMESTIC VIOLENCE

DIVORCE, HEALTH, AND HEALTH INSURANCE

Laura is a happily divorced woman. Since separating from her husband, she has fulfilled a lifelong dream by going back to school, where she is about to complete her PhD. Her only regret is that she has lost her health insurance in the wake of the divorce.

Laura explains to us, "Sometimes women are forced to stay married because of insurance. That happened to a friend of mine, who's married to a man who is a bum."

"What do you mean he's a bum?" we ask.

"He's just a bum. He's a drinking bum, he's a gambling bum, he's just a no-good bum. He's someone that everyone will call 'just a bum.' And she can't get divorced from him because she needs his insurance—which he gets through his employer. And she would be uninsurable if she left him, because she has neurological problems. So she's locked into a marriage with a guy who is a real bum because she is dependent on his insurance."

Laura's perceptions are on target. With some variation by state and socioeconomic group, divorced women overall are about twice as likely to lack health insurance as married women. A recent study in Ohio found that only 8.1 percent of married women were uninsured, com-

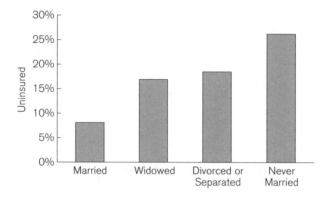

FIGURE 4.   Women's marital status and lack of health insurance, Ohio, 1998. *Source:* Ohio Department of Health 2001.

pared to 18.5 percent of divorced or separated women. Widowhood had only slightly less impact than divorce on women's insurance status: 16.9 percent of widows were uninsured. Equally disturbing, 26.2 percent of never-married women were uninsured (see figure 4).

The declining likelihood that women will have health insurance if they are outside a standard marriage relationship is part of an overall picture of loss of economic protection for women at the end of marriage. In a study of women who were divorced, separated, or widowed, Leslie Morgan, author of *After Marriage Ends: Economic Consequences for Midlife Women*, reports that all three groups experienced a significant decline in family income, a decline that was sustained over time, indicating that there was no substantial recovery of income "as long as the women remained outside the boundaries of marriage." Morgan explains: "Poverty was a fairly common outcome among those who became widowed, separated, or divorced. . . . Not only do rates of poverty, per se, rise after marriage ends for women, but there are also substantial numbers of women whose households balance on the brink of poverty."

The negative experience of divorced women vis-à-vis health insurance reflects a component of the health care–employment link that is rarely noted in policy discussions: because employment-based insurance often covers dependents (a spouse and minor children), the current system of linking health care to employment favors married people. Each member of a married couple has twice as great a chance of being insured as each individual would on his or her own. As for same-sex couples, although increasingly the largest employers are offering benefits to domestic partners, this is purely at the discretion of the employer. As a result, gay men and women are also at a disadvantage in terms of coverage.

Lenore Weitzman, author of *The Divorce Revolution*, writes: "During a marriage in which only one spouse is employed outside the home, the members of the employee's family are covered as his or her dependents and share in [health insurance] benefits. Upon divorce, the nonemployee (typically the wife) and minor children generally lose this coverage because of the traditional assumption that the rights to insurance belong only to the worker." Weitzman cites a number of examples, noting in particular the case of military wives (see Annette's story, later in this chapter), who spend years aiding their husbands' careers, only to lose their insurance benefits when now-successful husbands trade in their wives for younger models.

The family model that is institutionalized in the current link between employment and health care also favors people who live in nuclear family households—husband, wife, and children. Members of extended families are rarely covered as dependents in employment-based health insurance policies. This structure is particularly problematic in the many immigrant communities in which younger people are expected to help care for older parents and grandparents, ill siblings, and other members of the extended family who may or may not live with them at any given time.

This bias toward the nuclear family has a number of highly damaging consequences, especially for women. As chapter 4 discusses, women are far more likely than men to serve as primary caregivers for dependent family members—including those outside the nuclear family. Living with and caring for a disabled relative does not earn one the right to health insurance. And, as this chapter points out later, the link between employment and health care and its bias toward the nuclear family can force women to remain in nasty or even violent marriages, and it can prevent women who leave abusive marriages from continuing to access the medical care they need.

ROBERTA'S STORY: TAKEN BY SURPRISE

Roberta was born into a prosperous, well-educated family in Boston. In the late 1940s, the family moved to Vermont, where her father established his own business. A bright and studious young woman, Roberta completed a master's degree in education at a prestigious midwestern university. After teaching for two years, she became a doctoral candidate in federal education policy at a large state university, and in time she took a position on the research faculty at that university.

Deeply committed to social justice, Roberta became involved in national antiwar politics and presidential campaigns in the 1960s. Her professional and personal aspirations seemed achievable in the 1970s, when she met her future husband, a psychology professor who shared many of her goals and interests.

Roberta remembers that the second time they met, he told her that he had been invited for a job interview at the University of Illinois. Her immediate reaction was to laugh and tell him that she'd never consider living in downstate Illinois. Yet, as Roberta points out, "life happens while you're making other plans," and in 1971 she and her husband moved to the University of Illinois at Urbana-Champaign.

"Given my professional background and interests, at that time I considered this a disaster because the University of Illinois was not very far along with affirmative action. I began to apply for jobs, and I was told that I didn't need a job because I was a faculty spouse," she recalls.

Over the next few years, as her husband built up a solid academic career, with a good salary and a respected professional reputation, Roberta held short-term academic positions at the university, pursued her political interests, and undertook myriad volunteer and charitable activities in the community.

Shortly after their son was born, they took a three-year leave and moved to Washington, D.C. In the third year, Roberta took a position in the Carter administration. As things unfolded, it became clear that the future would entail making a permanent move to Washington, where the opportunities for a dual-career family were more plentiful. Roberta also was intent on finishing her dissertation and working professionally in her field, in addition to performing her roles as a wife and mother. "I was enthusiastic about the move to D.C., and I did not want to be back in Illinois at all."

As they prepared to make the permanent move from Illinois to Washington, in the late 1980s, Roberta's husband announced that he wanted a divorce. "I didn't go for a divorce. No, no, no. I was committed to the marriage and did what I could to see that we moved through the difficulties of the relationship. I'm a fairly independent and strong-minded person about things that I believe in.

"When this all happened, I was back in Illinois to prepare for the move to the D.C. area. I was devastated . . . and could not believe that my marriage was crumbling. I was probably naïve in this respect, as many women often are. In retrospect, I can only say that my husband turned fifty that summer, and I later felt that this was his midlife crisis. I felt very betrayed at the time, and it certainly took an emotional toll on me.

"When it became clear that the divorce was . . . a fait accompli, our son was in elementary school and was doing very well in school. I quickly shelved my own ambitions and made a firm decision that we were going to stay in the house in Illinois. We had friends here, a lot of social support, and, given my values, it was very important to keep my son's life stable and weather the marital storm."

Ironically, Roberta's husband soon left the University of Illinois. Roberta dug in her heels and remained in the community in which she had become active. She served on the boards of a campus religious foundation and numerous other community organizations. Over the years, she has had a number of research and teaching jobs at the university, but as an adjunct faculty member, she has never had health insurance. In her current job, working for a church, she receives a medical stipend but no insurance.

"When I first was divorced, I continued to be covered by my husband's health insurance. As part of the divorce settlement, I had been given two years to become reestablished professionally, including completing my doctoral dissertation at the state university where I had started my PhD. Given the age of my son and the distance involved, this became a difficult task. When I began to experience problems with the child support provisions of the divorce settlement, I went back to court. It took over a year to get a hearing, but I was able to see us through this period, as I have always been good at managing money and squeezing blood out of a turnip if necessary!

"When the court hearing finally took place, I did receive an additional award of child support. However, I did not receive a continuance of health insurance, which I thought was totally unconscionable. After that hearing, to be very honest with you, it's a question of, do you feed your child and keep your house going, or do you insure yourself for the one time a year that you might go to the doctor because you have the flu?

"During this time, I managed to complete the payment of the mortgage on our home out of my own funds. However, I also became increasingly depressed, as the divorce had been terribly upsetting to me. I did seek out counseling and in the process received effective antidepressant medication to put my life back into perspective.

"And then it was in 1999 that I discovered that I had this lump in my breast. It was shortly after another very good friend of ours had died from breast cancer."

Roberta had spent most of her life as part of the privileged caste—she always had access to health care when she needed it (which was not often, since her health always had been excellent). Thus, her shock at discovering that she had breast cancer was compounded by the shock of finding out what it is like to be sick and uninsured in America. As is true for all cancer patients, Roberta's days became filled with a parade of office visits—to the radiologist, the oncologist, the surgeon, and other physicians. At each step of the way, she was asked, "What insurance do you have?" and at each step her mind flashed through a series of responses that included embarrassment, anger, and anxiety.

"In the beginning, it was really hard to tell people that I [didn't] have insurance. I mean, how could this happen to me? They'd be thinking, 'Roberta was out there on every social cause, every political campaign.'"

She adds, "When I first detected the lump in my breast, I was totally proactive with every medical person who became involved in my treatment. Before we even began exams or treatment, I was explicit about lacking medical insurance. It was very humiliating for me to have to admit this, as I had always had high-option medical insurance prior to my divorce by dint of my own employment and/or marriage.

"Before my surgery, I went to all the various health care groups. I've worked as a reporter so, you know, I'll do anything. I thought about where the Illinois Department of Public Aid was. And I just went in and said, 'I would like to see someone to find out what, if anything, I am eligible for.' What you discover is that if you are totally indigent, everything is covered by the state. If you're a person who pays your bills and you basically manage within the parameters that you have, you're not eligible for a cent. And so then I just let everybody know that I had left no stone unturned, and everybody said not to worry.

"After the surgery, I went back to the hospital and said, 'Here's my situation. I would like to appeal any charges.' And I filed this incredible documentation with them. And they turned me down. So now I pay them a certain amount every month; and then I pay my primary oncologist a certain amount every month; and I applied to another hospital for coverage for the radiation oncology under their charitable giving program, and that was granted. At this point, I owe something like fifteen thousand dollars. I just pile up the bills and don't pay too much attention to them."

Roberta's annual expenses for medication (tamoxifen and other prescriptions) come to $1,427. She has no source of assistance for drug costs.

Roberta's education, community contacts, and homeownership have slowed her descent into the death spiral. Still, she lives in a county that has a particularly bad record for suing patients over medical debt and a low rate of free and charity care offered at the local hospitals.*

Although Roberta probably will not lose her house any time soon, the house will eventually need major repairs. If she is forced to declare bankruptcy because of medical debt, she will not be able to get the credit necessary to pay for the repairs. With luck (and a good economy), she'll be able to sell the house for enough money to buy a smaller place. Without luck, she will have to downgrade to a rental apartment. With a history of cancer and an uncertain income, rental payments could become an iffy proposition. Her articulate manner and expansive networking will keep her employed at least for a time. But without medical insurance at the age of fifty-five, the odds are high that her health will deteriorate, and the hustling and bustling that she does to maintain that networking will become less possible.

Despite Roberta's lifelong awareness of economic and social injustice, she is surprisingly unaware of the precariousness of her own situation. Just as she never dreamed that she would end up a single mother on a limited income or that she would be battling breast cancer without health insurance, she still cannot imagine herself falling any further down the death spiral. And, with a strong community backing her up, she might be right. But, as the experiences of Dave and Judy illustrated in chapter 1, once she starts to slip (pushed, perhaps, by being forced to sell her house, by enduring another bout with cancer, or by encountering other health problems of middle age), she will find surprisingly few handholds to grab as she goes down.

*This assessment was offered by Claudia Lennhoff, executive director of the Champaign County Health Care Consumers.

ANNETTE'S STORY:
THE REPERCUSSIONS OF DOMESTIC VIOLENCE

All in all, given her solid middle-class background and her homeowner-ship, Roberta is far luckier than many other women whose access to health care is contingent on staying in a miserable marriage. And, while her former husband certainly was not supportive of either her career or her self-esteem, at least he was not violent.

Annette wasn't so lucky.

We had arranged to meet Annette at her house at 6:00 P.M. When we rang the doorbell, we found her three children home alone; Annette had not yet returned from work. Happy to spend time with attentive adults, the two younger children climbed on our laps, drew pictures, read aloud from their books, proudly showed us the new shower curtain and toilet seat cover in the bathroom, and demonstrated their ability to climb on a chair and take ice cream from the freezer. They also told us about their own health problems: the eight-year-old, who has severe asthma, showed us his nebulizer; the fourteen-year-old, who has a congenital heart problem, wears a monitor that signals when she is experiencing cardiac stress.

Arriving home an hour late, Annette, an attractive thirty-eight-year-old African American woman, explains that she had to pay a complicated bill on the way home from work. With a household income of $15,000 a year, Annette frequently deals with complicated bills, utility shutoffs, calls from collection agencies, and kids who need clothes or school sup-plies that she simply cannot afford. All this she takes in stride. What she finds truly daunting are health problems.

Annette has suffered from excruciating headaches and serious visual distortions for a decade, ever since her ex-husband beat her, causing severe head injuries. Immediately after the beating, Annette was taken to the hospital. She received a CT scan, presumably to detect brain or skull injuries, and an operation was performed on her eye. At the time, her husband was in the military, and Annette had access to free medical care through the Department of Defense hospital system.

After the surgery, the doctor told her that the problem was not cured entirely and that she would continue to have some difficulties. Annette believes that the initial surgery did help somewhat, but visual problems and painful headaches continue to plague her.

Until her divorce was final (a process that took three years), Annette continued to receive health benefits through the military. She made good use of those benefits and received regular follow-up care. But once the divorce was official, she no longer had health insurance. She has never had a repeat CT scan, primarily because she no longer is eligible for benefits through the military.

We ask whether she thought about remaining married in order to keep the benefits. But Annette wisely answered, "It was not worth it." If a man beats you once, she cautions, "he would do it twice. I drove all the way from Utah to Mississippi by myself just to be free of him."

A few years ago, Annette became pregnant, which made her temporarily eligible for Medicaid. Speaking of an experience that many of us find familiar (how often do screaming children calm down as soon as they enter the doctor's waiting room?), Annette recalls: "After I got my Medicaid, my headaches stopped, eased up, and then when my Medicaid stopped, they started going bad again." We ask whether she has been back to the doctor, since the problems seem to be worsening. "I can't afford it. I had Medicaid, but they cut me off last year."

Annette continues to live with visual disturbances, which she believes have become more extreme of late. "When I look through my right eye, I see fine. But when I look at you through my left eye, you have a big old black spot on your head. All I see is everything else around you."

She also suffers from agonizing migraines, as often as twice each week.* Despite the pain she experiences when a migraine strikes, Annette

*National data suggest that migraines are more prevalent among poorer Americans. In a study of fifteen thousand households conducted by Johns Hopkins researchers (Stewart et al. 1992), prevalence of migraines was 60 percent higher among the poorest patients (those with incomes less than $10,000) than among patients who were even slightly better off (those with incomes over

must report to her job as an office manager—a job that does not provide health benefits—because if she does not show up, she will be fired. The one thing that helps the migraines is a shot she sometimes gets in the emergency room. From Annette's perspective, the most important benefit of the shot is that it allows her to "see straight."

Typically, she goes to the emergency room every month or so. The costs of the visits vary. The least she has ever paid is $250, an astronomical sum for someone living on her very limited income. The cost of the emergency room sometimes deters her from going, even when she is in terrible pain. "It was a problem last year, probably back in October. I had no job, and that was the only reason I didn't go. So I would just sit in the bed, and I would just cry and cry and cry myself to sleep. It was awful."

Annette realizes that it would be helpful for her to establish a relationship with a physician who can get to know her history and condition. Because she can't pay for office visits, however, she must rely on the emergency room, where she is seen by any of several physicians who happen to be on duty. Over the past year or so, doctors have prescribed a number of medications for her—Fioricet, Imitrex, and others. Each time she receives a new prescription, she must pay out of pocket. Unfortunately, nothing has worked so far: Fioricet seems ineffective, and she vomited after taking Imitrex.

Annette wonders whether some other sort of treatment is available: "You know, that's what I'm going to talk to the doctor [about] when I go back." She'd like something "if not as strong as Demerol, close enough to it so that when I take it, it'll put me to sleep."

In fact, a number of medications—some of them, such as beta blockers, relatively inexpensive—have been proven to reduce the frequency

---

$30,000). In the majority of the two dozen families we interviewed in Mississippi, at least one member suffers from chronic or migraine headaches. In many cases, the headaches are so severe that they require trips to the emergency room and lead to missed days of work. The financial consequences of both these situations— the minimum cost of an ER visit typically exceeds $200, and lost work days mean lost income—certainly add to the already stressful lives of women like Annette.

and severity of migraine attacks. But they must be managed and prescribed by a doctor who sees the patient regularly, thus putting them out of Annette's reach.

Like many women who have suffered from domestic violence, Annette seems to be prone to frequent illnesses. During the past year, she has gone to doctors at least half a dozen times for colds, earaches, the flu, headaches, and bronchitis. Each doctor visit costs $61, plus whatever medication is prescribed. Relying on urgent care and walk-in clinics, she rarely sees the same doctor more than once. Last year, she was diagnosed with an ulcer and took medication for it for a short while. (She no longer remembers the name of the medication and couldn't afford to purchase it even if she could.)

Annette is a bright woman. She is a high school graduate, and her dearest dream is that her fourteen-year-old daughter will go to college, get a degree, and "do better than what I'm doing." According to Annette, she "has potential. She's gifted, she's very intellectual." In many ways, Annette has done a good job at making a life for herself and her family. Her children are sweet and friendly, and she herself works at a reasonably good job.

Yet, as we spend more time with Annette and her family, it becomes increasingly clear that she is at the end of her tether. She is coping not only with her own health problems but also with those of her children and with their collective trauma in the wake of brutal domestic violence. The eight-year-old has a noticeable speech impediment and reads far below his grade level. Since the divorce, Annette has been involved in relationships with two other men, one who also became violent and another who ran up large bills in her name. The house is in disarray—when Annette comes home from work, she often collapses on her bed with a migraine.

HEALTH CARE AND THE ECONOMICS
OF DOMESTIC VIOLENCE

Unfortunately, Annette's experiences are not unusual. American women face the greatest risk of assault from those with whom they are intimate, particularly male partners. Estimates indicate that a minimum of two million women and possibly as many as four million are severely assaulted by male partners each year in the United States and that between 21 percent and 34 percent of all U.S. women will be physically attacked by a male partner during adulthood.

Injuries sustained by women in these attacks range from bruises, cuts, black eyes, concussions, broken bones, and miscarriages to permanent injuries such as damage to joints, loss of hearing or vision, scars from burns or knife wounds, and even death. Survivors of domestic and sexual violence frequently experience long-term reactions of fearfulness, anxiety, and confusion; chronic fatigue, sleep disturbances, phobias, depression, substance abuse, feelings of powerlessness, and a variety of somatic symptoms are also common. Overall, women with a history of suffering rape and other abuse perceive their health less favorably than other women and report more symptoms of illness across virtually all body systems.

Because of the ongoing and injurious nature of violence by male partners, abused women often visit physicians repeatedly, with increasingly severe physical traumas. Even with repeated trips to physicians, however, inquiries are rarely made into the cause of the injuries, and the history of victimization underlying the physical trauma may never be identified. This is clearly the case in Annette's experience. Despite frequent trips to the emergency room with severe head pain, she has received no counseling, no offers of support groups for victims of domestic violence. No one has expressed interest in trying to figure out why she has these excruciating headaches or in coming up with a plan to reduce their frequency or severity.

Abused women like Annette make substantially greater use of medical and mental health services than women who have not faced abuse. Women with a history of suffering sexual assault are likely to make twice as many visits to physicians each year as women who have not been assaulted. The outpatient medical expenses incurred by the most severely victimized women can be more than twice as high as expenses incurred by nonvictimized women. One watershed study reports that "victimization severity was the single most powerful predictor of total yearly physician visits and outpatient costs, exceeding the predictive power of age, ethnicity, self-reported symptoms, and morbidity-related injurious health behaviors." Although it is crucial for women who have experienced domestic or sexual violence to be assured of ongoing access to health care, as Annette's experience shows, the opposite may be the case: as a result of domestic violence, women can lose access to health insurance.

For all these reasons, the welfare policies of the TANF program, discussed in chapter 2, have particularly negative consequences for women who are at risk for, or who have been victims of, domestic violence. Because the long-term physical and emotional effects of abuse often create a greater need for welfare, cutbacks in public aid hit victims of domestic violence especially hard. Across the nation, research shows that women on welfare report shockingly high rates of past domestic violence. For example, a 1997 study commissioned by the Massachusetts Governor's Commission on Domestic Violence found that one-fifth of the participants in the state's Transitional Aid to Families with Dependent Children program had been abused by a current or former husband or boyfriend during the preceding year; and nearly two-thirds had been abused at some point in their lives. That survey also revealed that, compared to other women, abused women had lower self-esteem, greater emotional distress, and more physical disabilities.

Most women deal with abuse by trying to leave, but these efforts can be hampered by economic deprivation. Abused women typically flee with very little money because abusive partners tend to control bank accounts. Financial support, such as welfare payments, enables women to leave their abusers—but without such economic support, victimized women may stay in, or return to, abusive relationships.

Since abusers often demand that their victims remain socially isolated, abused women may lack the occupational and social resources necessary to begin working and keep a job. Moreover, the kinds of emotional and physical injuries abused women may have suffered can make them less employable. Battered women tend to miss days of work because of their injuries and may lose their jobs because of the abusers' disruptive behavior. Thus, whether women are on welfare or not, domestic violence can jeopardize employability and, consequently, accessible health care.

In the Massachusetts study, abused women were much more likely than nonabused women to report that a current or former husband or boyfriend opposed their attempts to attend school or hold down a job. The study concludes: "Welfare reform may unintentionally serve to keep some women from leaving an abusive situation or may cause some to return to it. The requirement for finding work or a workfare placement within two months of receipt of assistance (for women whose youngest child is school age) may not be safe for current or recent victims of domestic violence and may not be achievable for severely traumatized victims of domestic violence."

Unfortunately, many battered women who have left their abusers are compelled to return because of economic distress. They are more likely to be ill and to be only marginally employable, in jobs that are less likely to offer health care benefits. Thus, they are less able to access the medical services that could help them become more employable. In this way, the death spiral forces women back into violent marriages, where their health and employability may deteriorate further, trapping them ever more firmly in its pull.

CHAPTER FOUR

WHO CARES FOR THE CAREGIVERS?

LOVE AS A PORTAL INTO THE DEATH SPIRAL

JAMIE'S STORY:
"LIKE WE'RE PLAYING RUSSIAN ROULETTE"

Jamie lives with her husband and two-and-a-half-year-old son in a farming town set in the middle of corn fields in central Illinois. With a population of 2,700, her town is dominated by the railroad tracks and the highways that carry the crops and manufactured goods of the Rust Belt east to New York and west to California. Jamie's house has a charming middle-American feel, down to the colorful jungle gym set in the yard.

Jamie, an attractive young woman with a blonde ponytail, sparkling blue eyes, and a trim figure, has an associate's degree in early childhood education. Before her son was born, she worked at a local Head Start learning program for young children, a job that provided health insurance.

Together with her husband, she looked forward to being a first-time parent. Not even the gestational diabetes that she developed late in the pregnancy detracted from her excitement at starting a family.

But then, "Max was born over a month early, on Halloween in 2000," Jamie recalls. "He was low birth weight. He was only five pounds and two ounces. He had some bruising on his chest that the doctor was worried about, so they did blood tests to see what this was about, and they

72

found that he had low platelets. They told me that a normal baby's platelets are higher than forty thousand, and his were only four thousand. So they had to give him donor platelets immediately because he was getting so low. Then he started making platelets on his own. So then he was all right.

"But they ran tests to see why, what may have caused the thrombocytopenia [low platelet count]. And it was because he had CMV, which is cytomegalovirus. Basically what it is, is a virus that everyone gets in their lifetime. But if you get it while you're pregnant, then it can cause harm to your baby. Your baby could die or have hearing problems, vision problems, or problems with learning when they get into school. But, basically, they tested his eyes and his hearing, and they tested him for water in his brain, and everything was fine. And so he stayed in neonatal intensive care for nine days. And he ended up better, so he got to go home.

"When we brought him home, my husband stayed with him during the day, and I stayed with him at night. My husband worked nights, and I worked during the day. He is a mechanic and didn't have insurance from his job. But I still had insurance—for Max, too—through my work.

"Then my husband got a better job, a real step up. His new job is a day job, and so I stayed home with Max, which is what I always wanted to do even before I had him. The problem is that the new job is with a small company, and the insurance is more than four hundred dollars a month, and we can't afford it.

"I looked for other insurance that we could afford, and I sent away for a Blue Cross/Blue Shield plan, but they wouldn't cover Max's preexisting condition.

"So then we tried getting KidCare [the Illinois State Children's Health Insurance Program, or SCHIP]. It takes two or three months for KidCare to give you a response. They told me that we didn't qualify because my husband made too much money. But then a year and a half later, someone told me that the limit for KidCare had gone up, so we applied again, and this time we got it. So now Max has KidCare. Anyway, now my husband is going to get a raise, and so we'll lose the Kid-Care. We've actually talked about him deferring the raise.

"The problem is that during the time without insurance or KidCare, Max was starting to show signs that he has a speech problem, and I wanted to take him to be checked. As soon as we got KidCare, I took him in for a hearing test. A week later, we got the results.

"It turns out that he's got some hearing loss. He was supposed to be getting hearing tests every six months. But we didn't have insurance, so we didn't take him in for the tests. And eye screening every six months. Because of the CMV, it was important to have him checked, but we couldn't afford it.

"My husband and I have talked about my going back to work so that we can have insurance. But most day care centers don't have enough employees for the insurance rates to be cheap enough. And so I would basically be working to cover the cost of insurance and the cost of putting Max in day care so that I could go to work. I think I'd actually be losing money traveling back and forth into work every day."

Jamie prefers talking about Max, but, at our prodding, she reluctantly turns to her own health concerns. "I haven't had a checkup since the baby was born, and I'd like to have insurance for myself, especially because of the gestational diabetes. But right now, it wouldn't be worthwhile for me to go to work and get insurance because we'd lose KidCare. It's like we're playing Russian roulette.

"I want to stay home and take care of Max." With her college training and her ten years of experience in early childhood education, Jamie believes that she can do a better job of giving Max the specialized care he needs than day care workers could. "In Illinois, you only have to have six hours of training to work in a day care center, and that's what most of the staff has. . . . I know I'm more qualified to be with Max because I'm his mom and because I have my associate's degree.

"And I know if I go back to work and he goes to day care, then he'll be exposed to all kinds of illnesses and viruses. And, basically, then I'll have to [take] time off from work because of that. It just makes more sense for me to stay home with him altogether."

Jamie's house is filled with educational toys, music (to stimulate Max's hearing), textured wall hangings (for sensory stimulation), and healthy foods. Jamie is determined to make sure that her son has the proper developmental supervision and stimulation that his complex medical conditions require. She and her husband gave careful thought to the pros and cons of her staying at home with Max, and they concluded that Max's overall health and development would benefit from the one-on-one caregiving that his mother can provide.

But as long as Jamie stays home with Max, she will not have health insurance for herself. At this time, she feels well and worries only occasionally about her own health. Her gestational diabetes was severe enough to require insulin injections twice each day, and she has been told that gestational diabetes puts her at higher risk for developing type 2 diabetes. She knows that it is especially important to take care of herself because Max will likely need more help from his parents than other children would require.

Jamie and her husband have chosen to put Max's welfare ahead of their own, a choice that most Americans would respect. They are happy to live on one income, if it means that Max can receive the best possible parenting and early childhood education. Unfortunately, neglecting Jamie's own health has turned out to be part of the bargain.

THE VIRTUES OF FAMILY CAREGIVING

Jamie is one of millions of American women who spend a great deal of time taking care of an ill, injured, aged, or very young family member. All told, Jamie is relatively lucky. Because her husband earns enough for the family to scrape by without her income, she is able to avoid most of the burnout that is so common among family caregivers. For many other Americans, caregiving responsibilities are piled on top of paid employment. Although juggling two "jobs" is exhausting and stressful, the caregiver has no choice—without the income she brings in, the family will quickly hit bottom.

Caring for young, old, sick, disabled, or dependent family members constitutes a surprisingly wide opening into the death spiral. Moreover, the often overwhelming demands of caregiving can catch people unawares. A study of two-parent families raising a child with disabilities reports that, although all the mothers had been active in the workforce before the child's birth and 75 percent had originally planned to return to work, only 8 percent eventually returned to their jobs.

Nancy Hooyman and Judith Gonyea, authors of *Feminist Perspectives on Family Care: Policies for Gender Justice,* explain that a variety of factors contribute to an increase in the number of Americans who spend substantial hours at unpaid family caregiving. Deinstitutionalization of the mentally ill; the overall shorter length of hospital stays, which then necessitates longer periods of home care; reductions in funding for social services; and increasing life expectancy, including for people with disabilities—all create a growing demand for family caregiving. An estimated 11.3 million adults with chronic disabilities depend on others for some degree of care, yet only a fraction receive that care in an institutional framework. This is in addition to the many millions of young children who benefit from parental care and for whom there is no space in good-quality day care centers.

Family caregivers save our health care and social service system uncounted dollars and provide a level of personal and loving care that no institution could possibly match. Some experts speculate that without family assistance the number of elders in nursing homes would triple.

The National Family Caregivers Association (NFCA) states that more than one-quarter of the American adult population provided care for a chronically ill, disabled, or aged family member or friend during 2000. The value of the services provided by family caregivers is an estimated $257 billion a year. Yet the health care and social service systems do not take care of these individuals in return. A full-time family caregiver who becomes sick or injured is likely to be out of luck unless another member of the household works in a job that provides dependent insurance coverage. In a typical death spiral pattern, when the caregiver becomes too ill to function, the fortunes of the rest of the family plummet as well: the individual who was being cared for will need institutional care, which is far more expensive and less effective than family care.

A WOMAN'S DOOR: VALUING THE CARING BUT NOT THE CAREGIVERS

Though many American men have also been pulled into the death spiral through the portal of family commitments, a great many, if not most, women have felt its draw at some point in their lives. This portal is open to women of all ages, economic backgrounds, races, and religions. All one needs to gain entry is the vulnerability that comes from close relationships that make demands on one's time, emotions, or body.

According to Hooyman and Gonyea, "in most instances, *family caregivers* is a euphemism for *one* primary caregiver, typically female. . . . In fact, with the exception of the marital bond, men tend to assume primary responsibility for relatives with disabilities—and for household tasks—only when a female family member is unavailable." Studies cited by these authors show that about 9 percent of Americans, almost all of them women, leave the labor force in order to care for an elderly relative with a disability, and many more leave the labor force to care for disabled spouses and children. The average woman now spends nearly one-third of her life fulfilling the caregiving role, leaving the paid labor force for approximately eleven years, as compared to only one year for her male counterpart.

Full-time caregiving is both physically and emotionally arduous. For family caregivers, full-time is really full-time. Despite the overwhelming demands on their time, day in and day out, family caregivers are not considered "employed" and thus are not able to access employment-based health care. As a result, although caregivers embody socially cherished principles of loyalty, responsibility, and family values, they may find their own health endangered because they have taken on a task that we as a society claim to respect.

Caring for disabled relatives takes a heavy toll on the caregiver's health. One study of 462 older mothers caring for an adult with mental retardation indicates that caregiving is associated with poor physical and emotional well-being for the mother. Hooyman and Gonyea cite "growing evidence that family members, especially the women who have taken on the role of caregiver, experience increased personal health problems, including physical exhaustion and deterioration of their own health status." Physical ailments reported include headaches, stomachaches, insomnia, hypertension, heart attacks, and ulcers. The decline in caregivers' health is attributed both to stress and to the caring activities themselves (such as lifting for bathing or toileting). According to an NFCA members survey, 61 percent of "intense" family caregivers (those providing at least twenty-one hours of care a week) have suffered from depression, and 41 percent of caregivers have experienced back problems.

On top of the physical and emotional stress of caregiving, women all over the country find that family caregiving has a negative impact on employability and thus on access to health care. Many good jobs do not allow the flexible schedules needed by a family caregiver; and jobs that do offer more flexibility in terms of hours may not provide insurance benefits.*

All in all, Jamie is pretty fortunate. Not only does her husband have reasonably good employment prospects, but her own health seems to be holding steady, and her child will—in a few years—go to school, freeing Jamie to go back to work. Whether she can find a job that allows her to

*Studies report that young women without children earn 90 percent of men's wages, whereas mothers earn only 60 percent (see Shulman 2003a, pp. 3, 75). This phenomenon, known as the "family gap," constructs motherhood as a potential portal into the death spiral, especially for lower-income women.

care for her son after school and also provides health insurance, we don't know. But at least she has some hope.

Edna, however, sees no end in sight to the challenges she faces as a family caregiver.

EDNA'S STORY: SQUEEZING THE "SANDWICH GENERATION"

> I know I'm dying, but, luckily, I don't think it's right away.
>
> Edna

The road from Jamie's house to Rantoul, Illinois, where we met Edna, is lined with strings of pro-gun billboards. Erected among the wildflowers that dot the quiet prairie, each series tells a story or makes a rhyme:

Shooting sports

are safe and fun.

There's no need

to fear a gun.

gunssavelives.com

Edna saves lives in a way that is neither safe nor fun. As the primary caregiver for three generations of kin—"sandwiched" between an aging parent, an adult child with problems, and a grandchild—she receives no pay for her round-the-clock work, is rarely able to leave the house, and lately has seen her own health deteriorate without access to basic health care.

We first met Edna in her kitchen, a crowded room infused with the smell of down-home cooking and decorated with dozens of creatively framed photographs of family members. Cramped but comfortable, the kitchen is Edna's retreat where she talks to friends, snatches time from her family responsibilities, and sits at the table while she makes numerous phone calls to social service agencies on behalf of her increasingly confused elderly mother, her rebellious unmarried daughter, and her developmentally challenged young granddaughter.

Edna worked outside the home until her granddaughter was born, a full two months premature. "I had to stop because her mama had her young—she wasn't mama material—and I didn't want my granddaughter to be in the street with strangers."

Until the baby was born, Edna worked at the Bell Helmet plant. Although the work was hard, Edna took pride in it, sometimes even writing encouraging messages inside the bicycle helmets to the children who would eventually wear them. She was a prized employee at the plant and was allowed to take substantial time off work to care for her baby granddaughter. "They allowed me to do things they wouldn't normally allow anybody else 'cause I'd been there so long. They didn't pay me, [but] they let me not work."

By the time the baby was released from the hospital and seemed sturdy enough to be left with a babysitter, Edna's own health had deteriorated because of arthritis (common among people whose work involves repetitive motion, such as assembly-line work). She tried going back to the factory, but her productivity declined from her usual twenty-five helmets an hour to only twelve. Lower productivity meant lower take-home pay, making it difficult to justify paying a babysitter while she was at work. In any case, as a result of being born early, the child had substantial developmental delays—in Edna's words, "She's not dumb or anything, but she's just a little slow catching on"—and Edna was reluctant to leave her with just anyone. From that point on, she explains, "I'm the mama, I'm the grandmother, and I'm the babysitter. I'm everything."

Edna had saved money over the years and had accumulated a fair amount of funds in a 401K. She used that money to support herself, her daughter, and her granddaughter over the next five years. When her granddaughter entered kindergarten, Edna began to look for a new job. It was at this time, however, that her mother became sick.

"She can't do anything. She can walk to that door and walk back to her room, that's the most she can do. She can't stand up long. She can't even make a cup of coffee. Her back aches. She's eighty-four years old, and everything is coming out of whack. Just had a hysterectomy, which she is very lucky, at eighty-four years old, to live through it. Of course, she went through hell for the next eight months after it was over with, but she came through that fine.

"I can't work because I can't leave my mother alone. I remember a time when I went to the store one day, and she took it in her head to go to the kitchen and cook. I said, 'Ma, wait till I come back.' She said, 'No, I want this now.' You know, eighty-four years old, they're stubborn, like a two-year-old. When I came back from the store, she was in the room eating, and the gas was still on. She had totally forgot to turn it off."

Since Edna left her job, she and her household scrape by on about $800 per month. Fortunately, her mother is covered by Medicare, and her granddaughter is covered by KidCare. But Edna herself—the glue that keeps this family from sliding into a nursing home (for her mother), foster care (for her granddaughter), and perhaps even prison (for her daughter)—has no health coverage at all.

Edna suffers from a number of health problems. Most troubling for her day-to-day functioning is her narcolepsy. She takes a variety of over-the-counter drugs (mostly caffeine based) to keep herself awake. The narcolepsy was an even bigger problem when she worked in factories, where falling asleep on the assembly line can be dangerous.

Edna remembers that some years back, she went to a doctor at a sleep clinic and spent two days sleeping there to prove that she had narcolepsy. "He wrote it out, down, and everything, and then I had to get back to work. I'd had too much time off trying to get help for something I already knew I had, but I have to have proof of it, right? But now I've took too much time off work, and I'm back at work, and he sent me a let-ter saying that 'Yes, you have narcolepsy. We have to get together' and stuff. But I couldn't take more time off. And it's like a rock and a hard place."

She would like to go back to the doctor to see if anything can help the narcolepsy, but she can't afford the visit. Edna lives in Rantoul, and the sleep specialist is located in Champaign. Since she does not drive, and there is no public transportation that would take her to Champaign, she would have to pay for a taxi—about $20 each way, which is beyond her budget.

There are doctors in Rantoul, but she still owes them money from numerous visits during her daughter's teenage years, when, as Edna says, the girl was a "total bozo" and "went through so much trauma from age fourteen to eighteen. Boys, running away—and it made the medical bills add up." Because of those unpaid bills, Edna cannot use the local Rantoul physicians.

For someone in Edna's situation—no health insurance, no Medicaid, and no independent resources—accessing ongoing health care often proves impossible. Three years ago, Edna learned that she has diabetes. When she was first diagnosed, she had money to pay for medical care. At that time, she saw a nutritionist, who put her on a food plan and gave her various food samples. She was also given pills to reduce the swelling in her feet. (She has since run out of the pills and cannot afford to buy more.) This regimen worked well, and Edna felt that the diabetes was under control. Then, however, she ran out of money. For a while, her doctor continued to see her, letting her run up a bill. "But she wanted to get paid, and I understand that. [But] I can't afford to pay on that."

The absence of good medical care forces Edna to overuse the one option that America's poor and uninsured can count on—an expensive visit to the emergency room. Edna knows that she needs continuing care for her diabetes. "I know diabetes, and especially among black folks, it is a very, very bad thing to have." She finds it unreasonable that she can get care only when she has an emergency—"when I'm two steps from death."

She tells us about a typical recent encounter with the medical system.

"When I talked to you last night, my feet were so bad. I don't know if it was that diabetes, right? And I can't put my feet on the ground. And I called the hospital, and she was very nice, and I told her my problem was that I had diabetes, that I can't come to your hospital because I owe you. And I said was there anything I could take or something I could do. And she was telling me what I could do is put the feet up, which I was doing anyway. And I had told her that aspirin usually takes the swelling down, so that helped me a whole lot, and she said, 'Well, you need to come in here.' I said, 'I know it, but I owe you people so much money.'"

Edna recalls what happened the last time she went to a doctor in Champaign for a diabetes-related matter. "I go in there, the doctor, oh, yeah, she did not even touch me. Here's my fifty dollars, right? I get in there, and waited forever, and she said, 'Oh, you don't have health insurance.'

"'Actually, no.'

"'But you know it's going to be very expensive?'

"Now this doctor is supposed to be asking, 'What's the matter with you?' But she ain't said nothing about me, only about the insurance. I'm sitting there. My feet are all swollen. She said, 'Well, oh, I see you don't have insurance.'

"Then she says, 'Well, have you tried Francis Nelson Clinic [a county clinic with a sliding-scale fee]?' And I said, 'No, I didn't.' And I'm waiting for the doctor to ask me where does it hurt.

"Finally, after about five minutes of talking about the insurance thing, where I could get help and everything, she said, 'Well, what's the problem?'

"I said, 'Well, I know I'm a diabetic. I just want you to look at my feet or something and tell me what I could do, and maybe you could give me the pills that I was taking before that had helped my feet.'

"And she looked at me like I'm looking at you right now [from across the table]. She never touched me. We never got closer than you and I are right now. And she said, 'Well, it's Francis Nelson. They do free treatment and stuff like that, because this is going to be very expensive.' And she looked at my feet from a distance, and then she went back to talking about Francis Nelson.

"I said, 'Is that it?' She said, 'Yeah, that's it. The lady at the front desk will help you to book for Francis Nelson.'

"I just looked at her, and I said, 'Why did you take my fifty dollars then?' We never talked about my health or nothing. She never came closer to me than you are right now, sitting there with that pencil in her hand, asking me about how I'm going to pay the bill. That's exactly what she did. It was right then and there the tears came out of my eyes."

To add insult to injury, when Edna approached the receptionist at the front desk for help in setting up the appointment at Francis Nelson (which has a substantial wait for non-emergency appointments), she was told, "Oh, we don't do that. But I could write down the number where you can call them to make an appointment."

"Then she said, 'See you next time.' I thought to myself, 'No, you won't either,' and I walked out the door. I was sitting in the hallway waiting for my son to come and get me, and there I was crying like a fool, because I saw right then if you don't have health insurance, you can forget it. They did it nicely, but they got rid of me. One, two, three. Nobody asked how I was feeling, what hurt, if I could refer you to so-and-so. They didn't do none of that."

Now, Edna tries to manage her diabetes herself. She borrows test strips from her mother, who also has the illness, and if her blood sugar tests high, she stops eating and drinks only water in order to "rinse all of that out of me." After about three days, she usually finds that her blood sugar goes back to normal, although the fasting makes her tired. "I don't know if anybody notices, because I'm the one taking care of this family." Edna knows that these swings in her blood sugar are not healthy and can accelerate the onset of diabetic complications, but she sees no other option.

A few months ago, Edna spoke to a caseworker about trying to get Medicaid. She filled out numerous forms, but she became stuck on the requirement that she send in a letter from her doctor documenting her medical problems. "They wanted medical papers, which I did not have. Remember, I don't have a doctor. But they're not listening to me. Anyway, so I called the office that I used to go to, and the lady said that the doctor I had seen before is no longer there. I mean, how could I get an okay from a doctor? The doctor is no longer there!"

Edna suspects that she might be eligible for other forms of public aid, but she dreads the application process. "See, that's the thing. I don't know how to do that. I guess I really don't want to do it, but I've got to do it now because I've used up all my savings. And every time I go to ask for assistance, I say the wrong things. I'm not smart enough that way, I guess."

As we see it, Edna is quite smart—smart enough to have saved sufficient money to support her family through years of crisis, smart enough to manage the complicated physical and emotional needs of three generations of female kin. What Edna lacks is the kind of job that our society rewards with a salary and health care benefits. As a result, she has entered the death spiral, taking her mother, daughter, and granddaughter with her.

There is something else Edna lacks—experience with the system of public aid. Having worked at steady jobs that provided benefits for the first three decades of her adult life, Edna was ill prepared for the kinds of welfare-savvy strategies she would need when, within the space of a few years, her unmarried daughter gave birth to a premature baby and her mother experienced the onset of Alzheimer's.

But then again, who would have been prepared for that?

CHAPTER FIVE

THE FOX GUARDING THE HENHOUSE

WORK-RELATED INJURIES AND THE VAGARIES
OF WORKERS' COMPENSATION

> When I came aboard a little over a year ago, . . . it was understood that it was my own responsibility [if I got hurt]. And we had a joke that whenever you go on the roof, remember, if you fall off the roof, you're fired before you hit the ground.
>
> Ethan, construction worker, Massachusetts

STEVE AND MARY ANN'S STORY:
TALES FROM AN IDAHO BAR

The sharp contrasts of northern Idaho overwhelmed our Boston eyes. The clichés are true—we'd never seen such blue skies, clear rivers, green trees, and spectacular mountains. Nor had we ever seen so many steep, winding, frighteningly unmaintained roads; such large distances between towns; so many men with arms, back, or legs marred by injury; such a high proportion of pharmacy shelves devoted to orthopedic equipment; or so many bars in such tiny communities.

Three bars punctuate the short main street of the town of Troy, Idaho, population one thousand. Each bar, we are told by our friends in Troy, has its own flavor: two sponsor karaoke (one for country music and one for rock), and one is the place to play pool. One attracts the older set, another focuses on younger people, and the third draws the serious drinking crowd. On a Friday night, the bars are hopping; we couldn't find a parking spot near the town center.

We met Mary Ann and Steve one mid-afternoon at the serious drinkers' bar, where they had been self-medicating their various injuries and aggravations for a good while. In their mid-fifties, they both dress and talk like actors trying out for the role of "tough Idahoans" in a Western film. Mary Ann has tattoos on her upper arms; Steve walks with a swagger and peppers his speech with ultra-macho cowboy slang. Both hold their drinks like old friends. If we were the casting directors, Mary Ann definitely would get the part. Steve's performance, unfortunately, is undermined by the large truss he wears around his torso.

Steve was injured in 1994 while working at a seed plant. Bags of seed weighing 110 pounds each fell on top of him, pinning him to a forklift. When other workers moved the forklift to try to pull him out, the whole pile of seed bags came tumbling down on him.

Steve continued to work for several years following the injury, receiving sporadic treatment that, with constant arguing and negotiating, was mostly paid for by workers' compensation insurance. Mary Ann remembers that "the first doctors that he was seeing kind of tended to want to rush him off and tell him that it was all in his head." The problem, she explains, is that workers' comp has developed a reputation for being hard to deal with, and consequently physicians don't want to work with workers' comp patients.

From the start, Steve received shabby care. For example, he was not given physical therapy to help him recover from the skeletal and muscular injuries, nor was he given an initial MRI to determine whether his internal organs had been damaged. He was not sent to an orthopedist; a general practitioner was the only physician who saw him after the injury. Steve estimates that more than a thousand pounds of seed bags fell on top of him. One might assume—even expect—that a thorough clinical examination and substantial rehabilitation services would have followed, but that was not the case.

Throughout the past seven years, Steve has engaged in constant negotiations and bickering with workers' comp over medical bills. Right now, for example, he is fighting over a $2,900 bill. "They tried to say they didn't okay the brain scan and MRI that they gave me last year, but we have the written letter documenting that they okayed the tests."

Steve and Mary Ann have been resolute in their demands that Steve receive what he is due from workers' comp. Thanks to their persistence, until recently most of his medical care was eventually covered.

That state of affairs changed about a year ago, when he was diagnosed with both degenerative arthritis* and a pre-cancerous condition.

Mary Ann believes that if Steve had had better care, his arthritis might not have progressed to this point. "It's been kind of a struggle all along to get them to listen to him, and I finally started going with him to doctors' appointments. And I just told them flat out, I said, 'Look. The man's been active all of his life. He's done things that three men couldn't do, just because he's that stubborn. And now he can't even mow the lawn with a power lawn mower in one try. He has to stop and rest.'"

Because of the pain medication that he takes for his back and neck, Steve goes for blood tests to check his liver functions every six months. A test one year ago discovered M protein in his blood. This often is a precursor to developing a serious blood cancer called multiple myeloma.

"Once that came up, workers' comp wanted to stay out of it all." Workers' comp claims that this condition is not related to his injury. But

---

*Degenerative arthritis, or osteoarthritis, is a chronic joint disease characterized by the breakdown of joint cartilage and adjacent bone in the neck, lower back, knees, hips, and/or fingers. As the cartilage wears down, the bone ends may thicken, forming bony growths, or spurs, that interfere with joint movement. Bits of bone and cartilage may float in the joint space, and fluid-filled cysts may form in the bone, limiting joint movement. Steve's type of osteoarthritis typically is caused by an earlier infection, injury, or deformity. Arthritis can dramatically affect a person's ability to become or stay employed. In a study from Ontario (Badley and Wang 2001), men with arthritis were 2.7 times as likely (and women with arthritis 1.9 times as likely) not to be working as similar people without arthritis.

Steve and Mary Ann feel otherwise: "His job was handling chemicals and treated seeds, and, you know, this multiple myeloma is linked to pesticides, herbicides, Agent Orange. Other guys around here have this, too, and none of them are getting workers' comp, though they've tried."

Reflecting the experiences of many workers who find that workers' compensation is more likely to cover one-time injuries than the diseases caused by cumulative hazards such as toxins, Steve adds, "They're saying that this is not work related, which is a bunch of BS."

To make matters worse, because of the multiple myeloma precursor, workers' comp has now refused to continue paying for his back and neck medicine. "Their own doctors that they sent me to the first time for an evaluation said that I needed to see a doctor every six months, and I needed to stay on the medication. That was their doctors. And now they ain't paying nothing."

Seriously disabled at this point both by his immune disease and by the neck and back injuries, Steve has applied twice for Social Security disability benefits. He has been turned down, but now has a lawyer to help him apply a third time. (Actually, his former employer is paying for the lawyer, in the hope of getting Steve off workers' comp and onto Social Security.) Social Security has told Steve that he should be able to find "meaningful employment." Since he can neither stand nor sit for more than a few minutes at a time, it is unclear exactly what sort of employment the agency has in mind.

Between the injuries and the bureaucratic hassles, Steve's state of mind is far from positive. Mary Ann tells us, "It frustrates him that he can't do what he used to do, and he gets fidgety, and he gets depressed. I can usually tell when he's depressed because of the big sighs, and then he'll kind of pace around."

In addition to her constant battle to reassure Steve that he is "still a man," Mary Ann has her own problems with workers' comp. She is a school bus driver for the local rural township. Her route takes her through unpaved, bumpy, winding mountain roads. Like many others employed by the school system, Mary Ann finds her work time restricted to eighteen and a half hours each week; because she works fewer than twenty hours, the school system does not provide her with health insurance.

After twelve years on the job, she says, "my joints and my thumbs are degenerating, from the repetitious movements and the vibration of the steering wheel."*

Shouldn't workers' comp cover her treatment, since her thumb problem is work related? we ask.

Mary Ann answers, "Well, by rights they should, but two years ago, I had to threaten workers' comp with a lawsuit to get them to finally pay for the surgery I needed for my thumb."

She takes a great deal of over-the-counter pain medication: Tylenol and Aleve every morning and evening, and alcohol throughout the day. She watches her joints deteriorate and is not receiving any treatment to slow the process. She would like to find a job that would be gentler on her joints, but she has no skills or experience in anything other than physical labor. Mary Ann laughs, "I did waitress work for a long time, but I can't hold the plates anymore without dropping them on customers."

Steve and Mary Ann clearly get a kick out of watching our "wuss" reactions to their horror stories. As we offer to buy him another drink, Steve shows us his grotesque-looking left hand—what looks like a bone

*Repetitive stress injuries are an increasingly significant source of work-related disability. Caused by recurring or constant use of the same muscles or tendons or periods of repetitive vibrations, they can cause pain, weakness, and more serious disabilities. The American Academy of Orthopedic Surgeons estimates that such injuries cost $27 billion yearly in medical bills and lost work days (cited in Sunley 1994). The National Education Association reports that 88 percent of school bus drivers who responded to an online survey described physical pain related to work, including back, shoulder, elbow, hand, and knee problems as well as headaches (Weiss and Leonard 1999). The study notes that those with repetitive stress injuries are often not believed by employers, who want to avoid the costs of improving work conditions and paying workers' compensation claims.

sticks out the side. When he was younger, he broke his hand. "The doctor wanted to operate on it. And because I didn't have insurance, well, I was like, 'I ain't gonna have it operated on.' The doctor said, 'Well, I can wrap it for you with an ace bandage.' I said, 'Ahh, let's do that then.'"

Steve is not the only rugged guy we met in northern Idaho, nor is he the only man we interviewed who enjoys boasting about his many injuries and his ability to "suck up" the pain without medical intervention. As we finish our drinks, we ask our final question to Steve and Mary Ann: "Just wrapping an ace bandage around broken bones—we hear a lot of stories like that around here. Do you think that this is a macho thing, or is it really a money thing?"

Mary Ann needs no time to think before answering: "It's a money thing."

Tough they may be—we could not tolerate the levels of pain that both Mary Ann and Steve live with daily—but stupid they are not. If medical care was affordable; if the cobbled-together patchwork of insurance, disability benefits, and workers' comp didn't have so many holes; if doctors were compensated fairly and equitably for all their work so that they wouldn't be reluctant to treat uninsured patients; if large industries were forced to take responsibility for the cumulative negative effects of working with toxic chemicals; and if employers couldn't get away with manipulating workers' hours to deny health care benefits—if any of this came to pass, Mary Ann and Steve would be healthy enough to work. Then they could save their socializing at the saloon for the weekend and wouldn't need self-medication, either through an ace bandage or a rum and coke.

WORKERS' COMPENSATION: WHAT WENT WRONG?

Steve and Mary Ann understand that injuries at work cannot always be avoided. What frustrates them is that the programs that are in place to help and safeguard workers—employment-based health insurance, workers' compensation, and disability benefits—have failed to protect them.

Workers' compensation is the primary mechanism for providing medical and living expenses to people who have been injured on the job. This program is crucial to all working Americans because typical health insurance policies do not cover work-related injuries or illnesses.

The way workers' compensation operates is that employers pay a certain amount into an insurance pool. Workers injured on the job can then apply to that pool for medical expenses and for financial compensation for work days lost. In exchange for that benefit, however, workers cannot sue their employers for damages, even if the help they receive from workers' comp seems insufficient or unjust. The system is an institutionalized trade-off in which the injured worker receives certain benefits and the employer is protected from a lawsuit. Thus, while workers' compensation safeguards workers to some extent, it also takes away their right to avail themselves of the judicial system.

Making matters worse, not all employers acquire workers' compensation insurance, even in states where it is legally required. Recall, for instance, Ethan's remarks, quoted in the epigraph that began this chapter. During our interview, Ethan explained that in the construction trade it is common for employers to fictitiously label their employees as subcontractors, thus absolving themselves of the responsibility to pay into workers' comp.

Alan Conilogue, bureau chief of the Department of Benefits and Administration of the Idaho Industrial Commission, agrees that this indeed is the case in his home state. Under Idaho law, it is mandatory for all employers to provide workers' compensation insurance. Conilogue knows, however, that a substantial number of employers do not pay for such insurance—but no government agency is mandated to go after delinquent employers.

Conilogue shares his observation that many people in Idaho who are injured on the job never make it into the workers' comp system, even if their employer does carry workers' comp insurance. "When I mediate cases, again and again and again they would say, 'Well, I got hurt, but I didn't want to turn in a claim. I just wanted to come back to work, and I know it costs [the company] money. And I just sort of sucked it up.' I don't know what the number is, but it is a significant number, for several reasons.

"One, there are a number of employers who will say, 'If you turn in the company [that is, file a workers' comp claim], you're fired.' Another thing they'll do is—and this is very common, *very* common—they will have incentives. 'If we go a quarter with no work comp claims, you get this little bonus.' And they assume if there is a person who does get hurt, one, they want the bonus, and two, they don't want to be the person who ruins everyone else's bonus. So those injuries don't get recorded.

"Then there are people who get hurt and just don't report it for whatever reasons. They want to be a trooper. And then there's a fourth group, I think, that just aren't aware of workers' comp, or it doesn't occur to them that it ought to be a work comp injury. They just wake up and their back hurts one day, and they go to the doctor. And they turn it on the health insurance,* and they don't want to give it a thought. I don't know [for sure]. But that's significant. I bet it's in the double digits—twenty percent or more."

FIREWALLS AND OTHER HASSLES

Even when an employer provides workers' compensation insurance, the actual coverage that employees receive often does not reflect the true costs of their injuries. In a thorough study of the workers' comp system, J. Paul Leigh and colleagues conclude that this insurance actually covers only 27 percent of all occupational illness and injury costs and that injured and ill workers and families absorb about 44 percent of the costs.

*This scenario assumes that the individual has health insurance. But it is unlikely that employers who avoid carrying workers' compensation insurance (which is legally required) would be generous enough to provide health insurance (which is voluntary).

The typical scenario that we heard described across the country is one in which the workers' comp insurance company delays accepting and paying the worker's claim. In the meantime, the injured employee racks up medical and other bills and then, in desperation, accepts a lump sum monetary settlement that does not come close to covering medical expenses or replacing lost wages and, even worse, precludes the possibility of seeking further compensation if the injury leads to further physical deterioration.

Lisa Cullen, industrial hygienist and author of *A Job to Die For*, confirms that this scenario often occurs:

> Denying payment is a common ploy by insurance companies because it is so difficult for sick people to fight. Many patients give up seeking payment for all or at least some of their bills and pay them directly—to argue over each one is too difficult. Called "starving them out," this tactic often brings workers and their families—already suffering from an injury or illness—the added burdens of depression; stress, financial loss, or devastation; divorce; drinking and even suicide. One injured worker was actually told by an insurer "not to take it personally. It's just part of the game."

As Conilogue explains, "Instead of paying the benefits out over time, the insurance companies say, 'We're going to give this to you all at once. But in exchange for that, we're declaring that the claim is done.' If anything flares up again, you're toast."

We ask whether people tend to accept the lump sum settlements. "Well, they do, and that's another problem of the system, because they often are starved out by that time. And they often don't have a choice. They're so desperate for money that they do it just to get the money, because the insurance company has been resisting paying. [The company is] saying, 'Oh, no. You're not disabled. You can go get a job right today if you go and get off your duff. So you're not entitled to this money. But if you take our settlement, we'll give you something.' This is a classic starve-out that we see all the time. People get desperate.

"We have an off-the-cuff saying: *'If you're off work and you've got no benefits coming in, after three months you lose your truck. After six months you lose your house, and after a year you lose your spouse.'*"

Echoing Steve and Mary Ann's perception that the system is exceedingly complicated to navigate, Conilogue notes that physicians may not want to work with workers' comp patients because doctors are not paid for the time they spend dealing with the paperwork. What especially bothers physicians is the time it takes to give a legal deposition certifying the injury or illness.

"So some doctors are charging outrageous sums of money for these depositions, to the point where it's hurting their patients' case. The patients cannot get the testimony they need, because they can't afford to pay the doctor. Some of them are charging like twenty-five hundred dollars an hour or more. It is crazy. And so the patient cannot afford that. Frankly, that seems kind of unethical to me. [The doctor] should treat the whole patient. That's part of the patient's problems. But it's not pleasant for the doctors. Some of the lawyers just really rake them over the coals."

Looking at the situation from a wider perspective, it seems that attorneys are making money because various segments of the health care system are trying to push patients off onto someone else's turf. If an injured worker does not receive adequate workers' comp (which costs both the employer and the insurance company), he or she will turn to government disability programs or Medicaid for help.

It is crucial to understand that the workers' compensation system is part of the large network of private insurance companies. One way the insurance industry protects itself (that is, protects its profits) is by constructing a firewall between health insurance and workers' compensation. Cullen clarifies: "Regardless of how good the policy, private health insurance is not responsible for workplace injuries or illnesses. That's why dental and medical claim forms have a little check box next to the standard question, 'Is this claim related to a workplace accident?' If the yes box is checked, they can and will deny the claim."

This firewall is beneficial to the insurance industry, but it is detrimental to the health of Americans for the simple reason that the body's limbs, organs, immune system, bones, muscles, and mind are an integrated whole. When one part of the system is damaged, the effects spread to other parts of the system. As Cullen explains: "It is difficult to identify all occupational diseases and link them to specific workplaces. Among the confounding factors: diseases can have long latency periods; people switch jobs and relocate; and exposures occur off the job that may influence disease or progression." As a result, it is easy for insurance companies first to deny workers' comp claims by arguing that the injury or illness is a preexisting or chronic problem and then to deny health insurance claims by arguing that the problem is work related. This is what happened to Steve. Despite his obvious injuries, workers' comp refused to continue paying for his back and neck medication after doctors diagnosed his pre-cancerous condition.

Steve's impaired health at this stage of his life is the result of several injuries, some sustained on the job, some at home, some on the road. He has several medical problems that clearly are work related (back and neck injuries); others (his pre-cancerous condition) may or may not be connected to employment. Unlike the insurance industry, our bodies—complex physical, psychological, and social organisms—do not have firewalls separating work-related pain and disability from non-work-related problems. The discrepancy between the holistic reality of the human body and the bureaucratic demands of the for-profit insurance industry serves to pull millions of Americans into the death spiral.

"OLD MAN BOB": BUILDING AMERICA
AND DESTROYING BODIES

Steve's injury was sudden and dramatic. Other men we spoke to shared stories of the cumulative smaller injuries that wreak havoc with their health. Joe, a soft-spoken man in his early forties, injured his knee working on construction sites and now has painful calcium deposits. His shoulders and wrists are hurt from the repetitive motion of pounding and hammering, and especially from using jackhammers. He injured his wrist several times and had surgery to fuse the bones back together. Although the doctor declared it fixed, Joe recalls that it broke "in about five minutes" when he went back to work. His wrists indeed look deformed, swollen, out of alignment. Joe estimates that he has had thirteen surgeries, several on his shoulder because of injuries related to using the jackhammer. The jackhammer, used to break up concrete, weighs about a hundred pounds. "It stresses your body because it shakes and pounds. Most guys who use them a lot have wrist and arm problems."*

Over the years, he has received some help from workers' comp, but, Joe tells us, he had to fight for everything—and still did not get all the medical care he believes he needed.

Throughout his adult life, Joe has had employment-based health insurance only sporadically. As a result, he has received bits and pieces of medical treatment, stopping treatment when his benefits stopped.

We ask how he manages without health care, when he so clearly is in pain. Joe explains that he delays surgery and instead "does things like steroid shots to get me through." He's had shots in his wrists and knees, "just when you can't stand the pain. The shots cost two hundred fifty dollars a pop, and they like to do a series of four over a few weeks." That is a lot of money, but the surgery for his knees would cost $47,000.

Joe understands the overall toll that construction labor takes on the body. He would like to work in another occupation, but he has no other skills, a predicament shared by many of his co-workers, especially the older men. The partner with whom Joe has worked for the past five years is sixty-two years old. He and Joe split tasks so that Joe does the harder labor, digging ditches and holding the weight of pipes. His part-

*A number of construction workers complained to us that they were forced to use jackhammers that were heavier than the accepted worker safety standards allow and that they were told to work with the jackhammer for hours at a time, although the industry standard calls for frequent breaks.

ner has two prosthetic hips, and his knees and shoulders were replaced. He would like to quit working, but two years ago, at age sixty, he went bankrupt because of medical debt. Joe, understandably, is worried that he will end up in the same situation.

Joe's partner is a well-recognized type in the world of construction. Donny, thirty-four years old, owns his own small and floundering contracting business. (He made about $10,000 last year.) "At the rate I'm going now," he tells us, "I was kind of thinking in my head [that] in five or ten years I'll have to either stop or destroy my body altogether and wind up like Bob. Old Man Bob, we call him. We use him part-time sometimes when we're kind of behind . . . but he's had one hip replaced already and can barely walk around. He's talked this summer about getting the other hip done this year or next year."

We ask him just how old Old Man Bob is.

"Not sixty yet; about fifty-four or something. But he has to work so that he'll have income."

Old Man Bob lives in Idaho, but during our travels in Mississippi, we met a sixty-one-year-old man who fit the description of Old Man Bob to a T. Daniel has worked in construction his whole life, although it became hard for him to continue during the past two years. Unlike Joe's partner, who filed bankruptcy because of medical debt, Daniel owes no doctor or hospital bills; he just doesn't go for treatment if he doesn't have the money. Daniel explains that he has always been healthy, but he has sustained a number of injuries over the years, and now they are catching up with him.

Although he is a skilled carpenter, he has often been forced to take unskilled jobs because labor is considered so replaceable in Mississippi. "Well, you have to work if you're going to get paid. So they gonna try to keep you down." Over the years, he occasionally has had health insurance for six or eight months at a time but never has found a long-term construction job that offers insurance benefits. Typically, construction work is short term, much of it in the form of subcontracting, which allows the employer to dodge responsibility for workers' compensation or health insurance.

Daniel's vision has deteriorated, and he no longer feels comfortable climbing ladders, a necessary part of his work. He has arthritis in his back and still suffers the effects of a bad fall in 1979 in which he fractured his neck. His back has bothered him since he was injured on the job lifting a heavy pipe while working on a Navy base back in 1966.

Believing that continuing to work would be hazardous both to himself and to his co-workers, Daniel recently decided to file for disability benefits, but the process has not been going smoothly. He already has been turned down.

Daniel is so obviously disabled (he is missing one eye, walks crookedly, has grossly deformed hands, and cannot move several of his fingers—and those are only the obvious external injuries) that we were interested in hearing about the medical exam that determined his ineligibility for disability benefits.

An MRI was performed on Daniel's back, but the doctor did not test his finger, hand, or arm strength. We ask how much time the doctor spent with him. "Well, the doctor didn't spend any time. All they did— really did—was take the x-rays and send me through that [MRI] machine. And that was it."

As part of the application process, the disability office asked Daniel for the name of his doctor. Like many uninsured Americans, Daniel does not have a doctor who knows him or his problems. In fact, shortly before he applied for disability benefits, he tried to see a doctor who had treated him a number of years earlier. When he arrived at the office, he was told that the doctor wouldn't see him unless he paid fifty dollars up front. He did not have the money, so he left. When the disability office asked which physician had been treating him, this was the only doctor Daniel could name.

At this point, Daniel knows that his application for disability benefits has been turned down, but he does not know why. The way the process works is that Daniel must ask for a hearing in order to find out why his request was rejected. On the advice of friends, he has hired a lawyer to represent him at the hearing.

"SUCKING IT UP": MASCULINITY, WORK, AND MALE BODIES

We wrote this chapter during the weeks leading up to the 2003 World Series. One of us an avid Red Sox fan (Susan) and one a devoted Yankee fan (John), we paid close attention to the language of masculinity that filled the newspapers and radio sports shows across the country. With Red Sox star shortstop Nomar Garicaparra experiencing a prolonged batting slump, members of the media repeatedly asked Red Sox manager Grady Little whether he would replace the slumping Nomar with another player. Little's response, reiterated over the course of a week, offers insight into culturally accepted images of working male bodies. Little told the press that he would "ride the horses that got us here [into the play-offs]." While a casual listener might think that Little was managing a polo team rather than a baseball team, the reality is that men's bodies often are described using the language of animals, especially strong, heavy animals.

Hooked on sports radio, we found ourselves catching the football news as well. On Wednesdays, football coaches announce the weekly injury lists, which sometimes include half a dozen or more players per team. The injury reports follow Sunday's public spectacles at stadiums around the country in which concussions are glibly spoken of as "cleaning his clock" or "getting his bell rung," neck injuries are euphemistically called "stingers," and players are praised for staying on the field with broken limbs and playing through the pain. Of course, the coach has a full quota of substitute players waiting on the sidelines to take the place of those who are too badly injured to go on.

What we are describing is a cultural ethos that portrays the ultimate man (the star athlete) as animal-like in strength, insensitive to injury, able to "suck up" pain, and, when all else fails, expendable.

Most men, of course, are not professional athletes. Nevertheless, men we interviewed (and not only in Idaho) described a masculine work ethos that combines wider social expectations of muscular manhood with expectations by employers that blue-collar workers should be able to "suck it up." In work environments ranging from the armed services to warehouses and factories, from farms to construction sites, men are often pressured to push the physical limits of their bodies while they also stretch their luck.

Especially in sectors of irregular employment, such as the construction and logging industries, the primary means of securing a string of jobs is through personal contacts and reputation. Having a reputation for "whining" (that is, reporting injuries or occupational hazards), being scared (read: safety conscious), or being lazy (unwilling to push your body) limits the chances of being hired at the next work site, especially in a competitive market, whereas a reputation for bravado and bravery as well as competence (measured in production) will lead to the next job and the next. Reporting workers' compensation claims and missing work because of injury or illness can damage a worker's reputation, both among employers and among co-workers.

The culture of masculinity extends beyond the workplace when injury or long-term ailments debilitate body functioning and affect day-to-day lives. Not being able to live up to images of masculinity can lead to depression, frustration, and insecurity in private lives as well. The men we interviewed were reluctant to talk about this issue, but their wives were keen to share their perspectives with us. Mary Ann, as we saw earlier, spoke movingly about Steve's fidgeting, pacing, and sighing.

Misty is married to a man who suffers from crippling degenerative arthritis after half a lifetime of inadequately treated construction job injuries. She speaks poignantly about Nathaniel's low self-esteem, feelings of humiliation at not being able to support his family, and fears that his sexual inadequacy will cause Misty to seek other romantic partners.

"My husband just thinks that he should be bringing in the income, and he thinks that the world is judging him because he's not. So he almost just doesn't want to tell people that he's disabled, because they're like, 'Oh, another one of you,' you know? And, yes, he does get sexually frustrated, because he can't—he just can't anymore. I think depression has a lot to do with your sexual activity, too. You have to overcome that mental barrier, that I'm just a cripple, just to have sex with your wife.

"He thought I would—Oh, my God. I was playing bingo with older people than him. I mean, everybody in the hall was old, and he thought I was going to leave him for some of these people playing bingo. And I was like, 'What?!' And I just kept playing bingo because I didn't want him to think that, you know, that in any way. . . . It's so hard to convince him that I think he's my hero, and no matter. So it's really hard to keep him in that frame of mind."

VALUING THE WORKER OR THE WORK?

Joe, Daniel, Steve, and Nathaniel are four very different men. One is young, two are middle-aged, and one is approaching old age; three are white and one is black; one is college educated and three are not. But all are injured, all live with constant severe pain, and none are able to access appropriate medical treatment. All have entered the death spiral because of the "sin" of having worked too hard.

America values building: building up, building out, building taller and bigger, building roads, monuments, malls, and houses. What America does not seem to value are the workers who do all that building. For men like Joe, Daniel, Steve, and Nathaniel, the sexist expectation that men's bodies are infinitely durable and able to withstand pain has crashed headlong into the economic ethos that values profits more than the workers who produce those profits. For the four of them, as for so many American men and women, the workplace has proven to be the site of illness and injury rather than the source of health care benefits.

For women on the job, hospitals and nursing homes, ironically, are among the most dangerous workplaces. Nurses and nursing aides routinely lift heavy patients, handle toxic substances, are exposed to infections, and work erratic shifts. Almost all of the nearly two dozen nurses and nurses' aides we interviewed described the problem of working "short." When a nursing home employee does not come to work, the other workers on that shift are expected to pick up the absent worker's patient load; supplementary workers are not called in. Hospital nurses describe chronic understaffing, which forces them to lift or move patients single-handedly when no one is available to help and results in a work load that makes it impossible for them to follow mandated safety precautions.

Injuries on the job open portals into the death spiral for far too many working Americans. According to Leigh and colleagues, 165 Americans die each day from occupational disease, while 18 more die from work-related injuries. Annually, a shocking 7.1 percent of workers are injured or made ill on the job.

The particular injuries and illnesses vary by occupational niche. White-collar workers face job-related health issues ranging from carpal tunnel syndrome to ailments linked to toxins that reside in the ventilation systems of office buildings. Blue-collar workers can be harmed by sharp blades, heavy machinery, repetitive motion, and exposure to hazardous chemicals. Retail workers are vulnerable to injuries resulting from standing on their feet all day (often in shoes required for dress codes but not designed for extensive standing or walking), repetitive motion, and violence during hold-ups or at the hands of irate customers. Health care workers stress their bodies by lifting heavy patients and are exposed to illness-causing germs, which pervade their workplace.

As a society, we claim to value hard work and those individuals who perform it. It is difficult, then, to understand why we tolerate high rates of work-related injuries and illnesses and an ineffective system of workplace safety enforcement. Equally difficult to understand is why we lack a comprehensive system of providing medical and other help to those who are sickened or injured on the job. It seems the ultimate irony that in a society that links health care to employment and claims to place such a high moral value on work, employment itself can turn into a portal into the death spiral.

In workplaces across America, management far too often views attention to safety standards as a hindrance to productivity or as unwanted government interference. The guarantee that workers who are injured or sickened on the job will receive the care they need (whether that means treatment enabling them to return to work or services that allow them to retire in dignity) has become a matter for lawyers and insurance companies to bargain over—on the backs of the workers themselves.

In fact, in the contemporary marketplace, we would argue that putting health care in the hands of employers (whether in the form of health insurance or in the form of workers' compensation) leads to substantial conflicts of interest when employers are charged both with increasing profits and productivity and with providing a safe working environment and health insurance to their employees. In today's world, expecting employers to fairly and fully take responsibility for the health and safety of their workers—when doing so means a substantial financial outlay on behalf of employees, who are assumed to be short-term and replaceable—is like asking the fox to guard the henhouse.

JOHN'S STORY: SELF-MEDICATING AT THE LOCAL SALOON

Wearing a cowboy hat, boots, jeans with a large belt buckle, a silver tie clip sporting two dangling stars, and a full mustache, the fifty-one-year-old John could be an extra in a film set in a saloon of the Old West. Down to his slightly bow-legged walk, John evokes the stereotype of a western frontiersman. The day that Steve and Mary Ann introduced us to him, he was playing the role of gregarious bartender/local psychologist, wholeheartedly empathizing with the hard-luck lives of the bar's regulars.

In common Old West imagery, cowboys expected regular encounters with injury—thrown from horses, bitten by snakes, caught far from shelter in a sudden storm, or hit with a bottle in a barroom brawl. This imagery is not all that far from the experiences of those who work today in the rugged employ of the western extractive industry or in other rural environments.

John was never thrown from a horse, but he was pinned under a rig for four and a half hours when he was a young man. When the jack slipped and the rig fell on him, his front teeth were knocked out. He was never hit with a bottle in a barroom brawl, but he was hit in the head by a combine when he was working in the fields one summer, and his jaw was broken. John says that he and ladders don't get along well—he has fallen from ladders several times, including one accident in which "I tore my foot up." He also broke his ribs when he was whacked by a two-by-four while building a roof for his house. And he broke a few more ribs when he fell on an icy Idaho road.

These injuries—most left untreated both at the time and later on—have taken their toll on John's body. He can no longer hunt or fish, a serious problem in a community where hunting and fishing provide much of the high-quality food available to the local residents. No longer able to work as a skilled mechanic, John is now the manager of the bar, responsible for everything from sweeping the floor and paying the bills to hiring and firing the employees. John's work days often stretch to fourteen hours or more. For this, he is paid $1,050 a month and offered no benefits.

Except immediately following a few injuries sustained on jobs that offered short-term workers' compensation, John has never been to the doctor. When he broke his ribs the second time, his neighbor who works at a hospital brought him some bandaging and wrapped his ribs for him.

Now, in his early fifties, John lives with severe chronic pain in his back, ribs, and legs. On a regular basis, John needs medication—painkillers and muscle relaxers—simply to be able to get out of bed and come to work. "You just go around to the people and negotiate a little bit." By "people," he means friends, pharmacists, and, above all, his current girlfriend, who is a nurse. John purchases some of his pain relief over the counter. For example, on a typical day, he takes eight ibuprofen (which he calls "Ironman"), waits two hours, and takes another eight. (The maximum recommended dosage is six pills in a twenty-four-hour period.) When he needs something stronger, he turns to friends who were injured during military service and have access to pain medication through the Veterans Administration system.

John could pose for the cover of a self-help magazine. He is—literally—an expert at scraping by. John has what he calls "bad feet." On both feet, the bone in the little toe has "fallen down," and a spur grows on it. "The only way they can fix that, get that pressure off, is surgery. They have to lift the bone back up. The foot doctor gave me a price just for his part: it would be right at a thousand or twelve hundred dollars, not counting anything else, not the hospital or anesthesia. That is just to bring the bone up and to get pressure off that foot to get rid of the spur."

We ask him, "And you can't afford that?"

John replies, "Are you kidding me? I just take a tool, and I shave it. I have to do that like twice a week, get it down to where I can walk on it. I just take that spur and put the sander to it. Squint your eyes and grit your teeth. It really hurts, especially when it hits the real skin. I can shave it down, and three days later it's right back to where it started."

With true western bravado, John tells us repeatedly that he doesn't trust doctors, that the foot doctor was a young "fuck" and he didn't want him working on his feet, and that he has never had his blood pressure checked and never plans to.

Still, at the end of our conversation, as John painfully stood up and tried to straighten his back, he dropped his bluster for a moment and confided: "It's hard to live without health insurance, I'm here to tell you. I mean, there are times when I should've gone to the doctor, but I couldn't afford to go because I don't have insurance. Like when my back messed up, I should've gone. If I had insurance, I would've went, because I know I could get treatment, but when you can't afford it, you don't go. Because the harder the hole you get into in terms of bills, then you'll never get out. So you just say, 'I can deal with the pain.'"

Invoking the fear of a final descent into homelessness, which haunts all those who enter the death spiral, John turned his head and whispered, "But I can't deal with not paying the bills, because I am not going to sleep in the street."

CHAPTER SIX

RISKY BUSINESS

THE SELF-EMPLOYED, SMALL BUSINESS OWNERS, AND OTHER AMERICAN ENTREPRENEURS

JUSTIN'S STORY: THE RUGGED INDIVIDUALIST

Americans born in the 1950s grew up venerating the rugged individualist, the Lone Ranger who refused to conform to society's norms and who chose an independent path with no clock to punch, no boss, and no mind-numbing routine. Justin, born in Idaho in 1970, embraces those same old-time, frontier values: physical strength, independence, the open air, and freedom.

An avid outdoorsman who likes working with his hands and relishes the frigid Idaho winters, Justin followed his father into logging, a job with enough independence to suit his self-sufficient personality. But a year or so after he married Jessica, when they began building their family, Justin quite sensibly left logging—a dangerous job that did not provide health insurance—and took a job at a nearby lumber mill in order to have health benefits for himself and his family.

Jessica recalls, "He hated [the lumber mill]. He had rotating shift work, and he had no self-esteem; he would just babysit a machine. What kept him there were the health benefits. Then finally he decided he couldn't do it anymore. He didn't want to grow old there. It was a dead-end job. He still has friends that work there. His friends just wish that they could quit, but they can't because of the insurance."

Eight years ago, with Jessica's support, Justin left the mill and began his own construction business. Jessica worried about giving up their insurance, and for the first few years that Justin worked on his own, they paid for a major medical policy that would cover disasters but not regular office visits or medicine.

"We paid and we paid and we paid. Then we would go to the doctor, and we would still have to pay the doctor bill. Then we decided we don't want to do this anymore. We just wanted to pay our medical bills and save the money that we had been paying on the premiums."

We spoke to Jessica in the cozy kitchen of their house, built on the edge of a precipitous bank overlooking the Clearwater River. Justin and Jessica built the house themselves—literally—with their own muscle power. The house is beautiful, constructed with the attention to quality and aesthetic detail that reflects their values.

A strong woman despite her petite size and gentle demeanor, Jessica speaks in a matter-of-fact tone as she tells us about her husband's injury the previous winter. "Justin was riding a horse, and he fell off and broke his neck." Just hearing about this terrifying accident, in the dead of winter, high up in the mountains on their isolated forest property, causes our knees to go weak. Jessica, however, kept her cool at the time. She carried him to the car and drove him four miles down the steep and icy deserted road to the Clearwater Valley Hospital.

Because of the severity of the injuries—his neck was broken in three places, and he had dislocated a disk—he was transported to a larger hospital in Lewiston, where he spent four days in intensive care before undergoing surgery. Worried about his injuries but equally worried about the mounting hospital bills, he left the hospital the day after the surgery.

"He should have stayed in longer. When he came home, he was in so much pain that he had to go back and get a halo [a traction device bolted to the head]. He just got that off about three weeks ago. He is doing a lot better. Now he just wears a brace."

Justin is a handy guy, good at what he does and hard-working, and he charges relatively low prices for his work. But it had taken some time to build up the construction business—the most he had earned was $30,000 in the year before his accident. Justin and Jessica had no savings on which they could draw after the injury.

For several months, they had no income at all. Medical bills, however, they had in abundance. "We are dealing with forty-five thousand dollars' worth of bills right now. The Lewiston hospital turned it over to the Clearwater County Social Services Department, [which] is the county's indigents' assistance program. And they voted whether to help us with the bills, and they rejected the request. They felt that he could pay the bills in—I think they figured in three to five years, he could pay the bills off."

Justin's accident has brought home to Jessica the importance of having health insurance, and she desperately wants to purchase insurance right away. But this may not be simple. "Now we have so many medical bills every month that it is going to be hard. Insurance is about five hundred dollars a month or more." The various hospitals, doctors, and dentists to whom Justin and Jessica owe money are willing to accept monthly payments that are smaller than the insurance premium. "Sometimes I can pay a hundred dollars, sometimes I can just pay fifty."

Jessica took Justin's broken neck in stride, but she is visibly apprehensive about their enormous medical bills. We ask her whether medical finances have created any tension in her relationship with Justin.

"Yeah, a lot, and I am really mad at him because we didn't have any insurance. He is basically in charge of the finances on the bigger scale. Because his income is varied all the time—you don't know how much you are going to have each month—so whatever we have, he gives that to me, and I write out all the bills and make it work. Yeah, we have a lot of tension because of money and finances. . . . I think deep down he feels a little guilty, and now we know we need health insurance. I think things should get better as long as nobody gets sick again. You know that it is really a gamble, especially with three children in your family."

Despite the massive medical bills and the incapacitating injury, Justin refuses to ask for help.

"He would not let me talk about our finances to anyone. He is the kind of guy who—he is going to pay for it himself. He is not going to take any charity. Now, if there is a program through the hospital or something like that, and he can fill out the paperwork and he qualifies, he will do that. But he will never take charity. It makes him look weak. I think in his eyes that would be, 'I am weak.'"

Weak is the last word we would use to describe Justin. A few months after breaking his neck in three places, he is back at the construction site, though not working at full capacity and still in a great deal of pain. It is still unclear whether his impaired working capacity will interfere with his ability to keep the business afloat.

In many ways, Justin is a throwback to another era. Building his house with his own hands, chafing at working indoors under the supervision of the shift manager, and going back to work so soon after a life-threatening injury, despite the pain—these are traits all of us admired in the superheroes of the Old West. But those superheroes, at least in the movies and television serials, never grew old, never had families to support, and never carried over their injuries from one episode to the next.

BELLE'S STORY: ANOTHER SORT OF PIONEER

Belle, now fifty-six years old, is a different sort of pioneer. A highly educated acupuncturist in Boston, she trained in French literature, worked in publishing, and founded a feminist newspaper. Because of her dedication to innovative projects, she has been self-employed almost her entire working life.

In the early 1970s, Belle signed up for a yoga class in Cambridge, Massachusetts. At the time, yoga was considered unconventional and avant-garde, but it resonated with her interest in empowering herself as a woman and an activist. At the end of each yoga class, the participants would exchange massages. "I felt that I had the gift of touch," she recalls.

"Back then, I was a pioneer in holistic health. What attracted me to yoga was 'being in the body' and working with the emotions that are held in the body."

Belle worked for thirteen years as a massage therapist and then trained in acupuncture. The training cost about $10,000, less than it would cost now that acupuncture has become more mainstream in the United States. She received her master's-level training in 1988 and since then has supported herself through her acupuncture practice.

For a number of years, Belle worked in a group practice, but she now works at home in order to cut costs and control her own space. "The downside of being self-employed is that it is erratic in terms of cash flow. You have to accept that. You have control over your life and schedule, but no security or benefits. The only benefit is the sense of freedom."

When her income has allowed, she has paid for health insurance, but more often than not she cannot afford it. "The last time was about five years ago. It was about three hundred twenty dollars a month." Until three years ago, all her health care expenditures were for alternative medicine, primarily acupuncture and chiropractic. "It didn't seem worth it to pay for insurance which didn't cover the health care I actually used."

As she grew older, however, she decided to make a change. "Turning fifty, I knew I needed tests, mammograms. So I signed up for free care at a Boston hospital. To be eligible for free care, profit from my business has to be under eighteen thousand dollars a year, so I was eligible.

"Seven months after the first mammogram, I found a huge tumor in my breast. It was breast cancer."

Belle learned that the free care at the hospital covered hospital expenses but not physicians' fees. Her surgeon kindly waived his fee, but she has continued to make payments to the oncologist and other physicians.

During the cancer treatments, "I was a real trooper and kept working for four months. But then I had to cut back, and word got around that I wasn't working. So when I was ready to work again, I had fewer clients." Fewer clients, of course, meant less income. But there's an irony: "If I make more money, I'll lose the [free care]. Even though I'm not earning much now, my financial bracket works. So there's not much incentive to make more money." An odd commentary indeed on the American entrepreneurial enterprise.

SMALL BUSINESSES: BETWEEN A ROCK AND A HARD PLACE

Given the financial risks—and health risks—involved, why do so many Americans choose to start their own businesses or opt for other forms of self-employment? Some people, like Justin, chafe at working at a repetitive indoor job under the constant supervision of a manager. Others, especially women and members of minority groups, believe that opportunities for advancement are limited when someone else is in charge and that working for themselves can ensure that they receive the respect and financial rewards they deserve. In fact, during the 1970s and 1980s, women formed new businesses at a rate twice that of men.

We spoke to several people who left jobs at national chains because they considered the service the chain provided, or the product it manufactured, to be of poor quality. Jack, whom we interviewed in Mississippi, opened his own transmission repair shop after a national chain relocated him to three different states and then placed him in a shop where the work was consistently shoddy.

For artists and musicians such as Jonathan, whose situation is described in chapter 7, work is inherently a solo act. Many small business owners are medical or other professionals. Although most are not enamored with the details of running a business, they understand that in the current system they must manage their own practices. This is the case for Martin, the Boston area dentist described later in this chapter.

We also have spoken with people who had a great idea for a new product and, inspired by earlier generations of American entrepreneurs, struck out on their own with small capital reserves. In other instances, one person or a few dedicated people are determined to provide a service to the elderly or disadvantaged; in the case of the Collective Home

Care Agency, discussed at the end of the chapter, the founders took the risk of leaving secure government jobs in order to fulfill their sense of moral mission.

Mansel Blackford, who has studied the history of small businesses in America, notes that community involvement, local recruitment and purchasing, and an organizational structure that allows junior employees to learn the ropes are some of the ways small businesses contribute socially. Small businesses also affect America's economic vitality through their role as sources of innovation. Enterprises like Belle's excel in developing products and services that require low amounts of capital and high degrees of specialized knowledge.

In fact, in recent years, small businesses have employed more than half of all private-sector employees and generated 60 to 80 percent of new jobs. Small firms produced thirteen to fourteen times more patents per employee than large firms and generated more than half of the annual gross domestic product.

Despite these benefits to the economy, Blackford argues, "governmental policies nonetheless have often directly or indirectly furthered the development of big business in the United States." The current system does not make it easy for small businesses. Providing health insurance, which can be key to recruiting and retaining employees, is a particular challenge for many small firms. In a ten-state survey prepared for the Office of Advocacy of the Small Business Administration, Saundra Glover and colleagues note: "Small businesses [are] finding it more and more difficult to obtain affordable health insurance for their workers. This is especially so for those small businesses that have less than 25 employees and have a disproportionate share of low-wage-earning employees. This is occurring in spite of ongoing state and federal efforts to address this problem through legislation."

More than half of uninsured workers are either self-employed or work for firms with fewer than twenty-five employees. While large firms generally offer health insurance, the percentage drops dramatically for smaller employers (see figure 5).

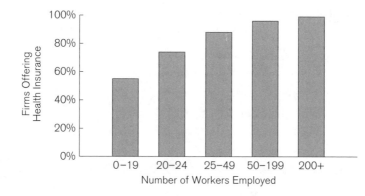

FIGURE 5.   Firms offering health insurance, by size, 2002. *Source:* Kaiser Family Foundation and Health Research and Educational Trust 2003.

According to the Small Business Administration's Office of Advocacy, 83 percent of small businesses cite the high cost of premiums as the reason they do not provide coverage to their employees. Because they lack the negotiating clout of larger businesses, small employers often pay more than large employers for similar coverage and have experienced greater annual increases in premiums. Small businesses also face higher administrative costs: the Small Business Administration estimates that the administrative costs for small firms averaged 33 to 37 percent of total claims, versus only 5 to 11 percent for large companies. In addition, whereas small businesses are subject to many state mandates for coverage (for instance, they are required to cover infertility treatment in Massachusetts), large companies are often exempted from such mandates by the Employee Retirement Income Security Act (ERISA), federal legislation passed in 1974 that, among other things, exempts self-insured large employers from state insurance benefit regulations.

Insurance companies require many small employers to "experience rate" each of their employees, which means that their premiums are based on the health risks of specific workers. Thus, even one sick worker (or child of a worker) can make insurance unaffordable for the whole group. This requirement, typically waived for larger firms, forces difficult decisions on small business owners who are trying to do the right thing for their workers as well as for their businesses.*

THE EMPLOYER'S PERSPECTIVE

The sentiments expressed by the small business owners we encountered were surprisingly consistent, given that our interviewees lived in diverse states and operated a wide variety of businesses. This sentiment can be summed up easily: they want to dedicate themselves to building up their construction/high-tech/graphic design/medical/public relations/consulting business; they do not want to be in the health insurance business.

Unlike multinational conglomerates, small business owners typically know their employees intimately and feel shame and guilt at their inability to provide health insurance. Often, the bitter decision comes down to either not offering health insurance or running the business below the threshold of profitability, which risks layoffs or even closure. The total annual cost of health benefits per covered employee (which includes both employer and employee contributions for health, dental, and vision insurance and takes into account dependent coverage) rose from an average of approximately $4,400 in 2000 to $6,200 in 2003. For many small business owners, the cost is simply too high, no matter how committed they are to treating employees well.

Liz, the owner of a small high-tech start-up in Massachusetts, manages to provide health insurance for her three employees; but she is able to do so only because she worked in human resources in a previous job and thus is unusually knowledgeable about health insurance options.

---

*A few states, generally those that are richer and more liberal, such as Massachusetts, Maine, and New York, regulate the small business insurance market and do not allow plans to increase rates when an employee of a small business generates high costs.

This knowledge has allowed her to find somewhat reasonable terms. Liz tells us, however, that "the solutions I have come up with need a lot of savvy, and most small business owners wouldn't know how to go about doing it." Even with that advantage, at the time we interviewed her, Liz had recently been forced to cut the plan in half (in terms of benefits) because the rates had increased significantly.

Like other small business owners with whom we spoke, Liz is uncomfortable with taking responsibility for her employees' health care and making decisions that have medical implications for other people. Her expertise is in the field of language recognition software, not medicine. She observes that small business owners not only are forced to shoulder the financial and bureaucratic burdens of their businesses but also are forced to deal with issues that more properly fall within the realm of medical ethics.

Will her decision to go with a plan that has substantial co-payments wind up causing an employee stricken with heart disease to lose his home or declare bankruptcy? Will adopting a plan that does not cover birth control force an employee into an unwanted pregnancy? Will her selection of a plan that severely limits mental health visits cause an employee to commit suicide? If she chooses a plan with a limited number of doctors, will an employee be unable to see the appropriate expert when a rare or complex medical problem arises? These are not decisions that Liz wants to make, nor does she believe that small business owners like herself are particularly competent at making them.

Equally distressing, Liz explains, is that owners of small businesses take a particularly hard financial hit to cover employees who have serious health problems. In a larger company, the higher cost of providing health insurance to one or two very sick people is distributed over a wider field. For small business owners, one very sick employee can cause rates to rise to a point where the employer is forced to cancel the insurance, close the company, or release the employee (which is not legal).

With sadness and rage in her voice, Liz tells us, "I know for a fact that employers are reluctant to hire people with chronic illnesses. Absolutely.

They can't out and out discriminate—for example, they can't ask if someone is sick—but if someone comes in for an interview and has a visible illness such as MS, who would hire that person?"

MARTIN'S STORY: A DENTIST'S DILEMMA

Martin, a Boston dentist, has had his own practice since 1990. A gifted (and amazingly painless) dentist whose reasonable prices attract both low-income and affluent patients, Martin enjoys and takes pride in his dentistry but hates running the business side of things. "I'm not a business man. I like the dental stuff. I'm not trained to run a business, and I hate it. I like going in and doing my work. I don't like managing the finances, ordering supplies, paying the staff, making sure insurance forms are filled out properly."

A few years ago, Martin was diagnosed with severe coronary disease. As a small business owner, he had no larger company to help carry him through the months that he couldn't work. Moreover, he had to keep the office running at least minimally, even when he was too sick to see patients. During the months in which he was struggling to stay alive and keep his business intact for his return, he was terrified that he wouldn't be able to keep up his insurance payments. "Friends actually gave us money. It's a scary thing."

A dental assistant and an office manager have worked for Martin since shortly after he opened his practice. The two women are more like friends than employees. As is the case in many small businesses, Martin participates in their family events and they participate in his. Both women are from the Dominican Republic, and Martin has developed a passion for their Dominican salsa and merengue radio station, with which he sings along while he works on patients.

During the time Martin was ill, he relied on his office staff to keep the business running. When he returned to work, weakened from surgery and other treatments, he relied on them to help him make it through the days of working on his patients' teeth.

Martin believes that everyone should have health insurance and that it is his responsibility as an employer to make sure that his employees are covered. He has offered insurance to both employees through the plan that he has for his own family from the Small Business Association.

"I told them that I would pick up half the cost. I was honest with them. I told them they could choose between a raise and health insurance. They know that I'm not rich and out to exploit them. One said she has her husband's insurance. The other said that she prefers the raise. She gets free medical care through the hospital. She makes a bit more than twenty-five thousand dollars a year, but she is a single parent, so she is eligible for free care. She thinks of the hospital as her doctor, so the hospital free care satisfies her.

"Anyway, I am glad they turned the insurance down, because it's expensive. To be honest, I didn't press them.

"Most dentists are small businesses with tremendous overheads. My insurance is a thousand dollars a month for my family. That is what I offered to split fifty-fifty with the employees. My half would have been five hundred dollars a month for each of them. So I am relieved that they preferred the raise.

"I think that most dentists are not running to offer insurance to their employees. It's a hard thing to be generous with. Many dentists only hire part-time help. Instead of one full-time person, they'll have two workers at twenty hours a week each, so as not to have to do insurance."

Other dentists handle the dilemma of insurance for their office staff in a variety of ways. Two dental assistants we interviewed, one in Texas and one in Idaho, told us that their employers do not provide insurance for the staff (though they do have insurance for themselves and their families) but do try to help out as best they can (at least, in the eyes of their rather devoted assistants). Both of these women mentioned that the dentists they work for will write prescriptions for them when they are sick. One assistant suffers from chronic urinary tract infections, and her boss prescribes antibiotics when the infections flare up. The other assistant turns to her boss for prescriptions when she has an occasional sore throat or flu.

Clearly, this is not a medically appropriate way to manage the health care problems of the staff working for a dentist. Dentists are not trained to treat urinary tract infections or other nondental infections. Nevertheless, like the assistants, we are hesitant to judge too harshly. The dentists, we assume, are trying to do what they can to be helpful in a situation in which the link between employment and health care has pushed them into a financial corner.

COLLECTIVE HOME CARE

> The chief executive officer, who is often also the owner, runs the business personally. He or she knows the other managers and most of the workers. . . . In small companies the elaborate hierarchies of top, middle, and lower management that normally exist in big businesses are not present. Moreover, most small businesses are single-unit enterprises. . . . As locally oriented companies, small businesses commonly recruit their work forces from their communities and are deeply involved in community affairs. They are also more apt than larger firms to purchase their raw materials locally and to produce for local rather than national or international markets.
>
> Mansel Blackford, *A History of Small Business in America*

Collective Home Care (the company's real name) is a very special home health care agency. It was founded several years ago by former county employees who were frustrated by cuts in services for elders who had been covered by the state of Massachusetts. The owner, administrators, and nurses of Collective Home Care are dedicated to a dual mission of providing compassionate and high-quality care to the homebound and providing reasonable and equitable wages, benefits, and working condition to home health aides. Unlike many agencies around the country (for example, those at which Alisha, whom we met in chapter 2, works),

Collective Home Care is committed to providing health insurance to its employees.

That commitment faced a harsh test in May 2003, when further statewide budget cuts in the Department of Health and Human Services forced the owner of Collective Home Care to decide between closing the agency and halting its health insurance program.

Shelly, one of the agency's administrators and a former home health aide, explains: "The state Executive Office of Elder Affairs took a pretty big budget cut and therefore followed with massive cuts to their clients. They cut the number of hours [of care] that each client would receive. They really brought them down to such a bare minimum. We lost just tons and tons of hours, which obviously meant tons and tons of revenue. Couple that with rising costs of health care for our own employees, and we were in a position where we couldn't afford insurance. We weren't going to make payroll.

"The hardest part of it all, what we found with the state cuts, was that our clients were no longer [allocated enough hours of care by the state] and they had to choose: Do you want to have a bath during the week, or do you want home-delivered meals? . . . Or do you want Life Watch [a pendant worn around the neck that will allow the client to call for emergency help]? . . . Massachusetts is in a pretty sad state of affairs. But then again, the people that are governing these cuts have enough money to pay privately to have twenty-four-hour care for their mother and father who can't bathe themselves and feed themselves. So it's kind of hard to get them to understand."

Few other home care agencies are interested in picking up clients paid for by the state (these clients constitute about half of Collective's usual client base), because the state's payment rate for home care work is lower than the private pay rate. Thus, if Collective shut its doors, the hardest hit victims would be the poorest among the elderly. "Those are the clients that are the most needy in the community and have to have the services. If we don't do it, nobody is going to."

When the agency first opened, Collective was paying 50 percent of insurance premiums, and the employees paid the other half. The following year, Collective absorbed a rate hike, which pushed its share to 65 percent, with the employees paying 35 percent. After yet another hike, the split became 70 percent and 30 percent, and Collective added a chiropractic rider, picking up that cost also. (Home health aides and nursing assistants often strain their backs lifting patients.) That year, Shelly recalls, they were hit with a 21 percent hike in insurance costs. "I believe our payment came to just over seven thousand dollars per month for the employer contribution. That covered about thirty employees."

Devastated by the rate hikes and the state budget cuts for elder services, Sue, the agency's owner, told her associates, "I can't ask the aides to work here without having the one benefit, that one and only benefit that we've been able to offer all this time. I can't do this. We'll have to close." In line with the agency's name, however, its organizational mode is consensual and collective, and other staff members overrode Sue's recommendation. The agency remained open, but it stopped providing health benefits.

Shelly asserts, "Looking from the eyes of our home care aides, they would rather tough it out and have a job than not have a job and not have health insurance both at the same time."

As of November 2003, Collective's financial basis had begun to stabilize, and the agency was planning to resume providing health insurance. But the new plan is a lesser one. Previously, in order to be covered, an employee needed to work thirty-two hours per week. Now, the threshold for coverage will be forty hours per week. The problem with that, Shelly observes, is that home health care agencies tend to have many part-time employees, both because of the nature of the work (heavy lifting, for instance) and because clients tend to be somewhat transient, making it difficult for an agency to guarantee employees a full week's work. Although Collective has resisted the industry's inclination to hire "temps" in order to avoid paying benefits, it cannot afford to make health insurance available to all employees.

CHAPTER SEVEN

YOUNG, SICK, AND PART-TIME

THE VULNERABILITY OF YOUTH
AND THE NEW AMERICAN JOB MARKET

RACHEL'S STORY: "A KIND OF MAGICAL THINKING"

Rachel's long blonde hair is just one of the attractions she holds for the children at the Boston area day care center, who love to braid it, stroke it, and mess it up. The kids also enjoy her easy laugh, the songs she sings to them, and her willingness to get down on the floor and crawl around with them.

In the three years since she graduated from her top-notch liberal arts college, Rachel has been unable to find a job that offers health insurance. Though she works five days a week at the day care center, the work is not considered full-time (she supplements her income with tutoring and babysitting), and she is not entitled to the insurance that the center provides for some of the more veteran employees.

Rachel hopes to apply to medical school later on, but for now she would like to earn money, gain some independence from her parents, and experience working in the "real world."

Ironically, both of Rachel's parents are physicians, and she feels that it distresses them that she does not have insurance. Rachel suspects that their frustration is directed toward her as much as it is directed toward the health care system.

As a child of physicians, Rachel has access to a level of medical care that is unavailable to most other young adults. Nevertheless, her parents' expertise is within certain subfields, and they cannot help her with all her medical issues.

A few years ago, Rachel underwent a gynecological procedure because of an abnormal Pap smear. She was told to follow up with frequent Pap smears (several times each year) because this abnormality could be an early sign of cervical cancer, but she has not done so because each test costs $150. Rachel also is worried that a Pap smear might find dysplasia, which, as a preexisting condition, might prevent her from getting health insurance later on. In addition, Rachel suffers from severe menstrual cramps—she takes about twenty ibuprofen each month for the cramps—and she is concerned that this may be connected to her other gynecological problem.

Although Rachel enjoys her work with children, her real love is dancing. Over the past several years, she has been bothered by what she calls a "chronic hip thing," a terrible problem for a dancer. She would like to see an orthopedist—but without health insurance, she can't afford to go.

Though young and from a privileged background, Rachel faces two rather worrisome health problems, one possibly life threatening and the other a threat to her quality of life. Standard medical practice would seem to demand ongoing care for the gynecological problem and at least an initial work-up for her hip. Without health insurance, however, she is excluded from the world of standard medical practice.

Rachel already understands, at least in part, how the death spiral works. "It's kind of unfair that medical bills can hurt your credit, you know. If you need medical help, you need help. It's not like ruining yourself with your credit card debt. I think that it's completely unfair, and even immoral, that people who work certain kinds of jobs don't have access to health care. . . . I think that is one of our fundamental rights. If you visit any European countries, it's completely unfathomable to them, the idea that in the United States people have to fight to get proper care."

Rachel's parents provide an additional perspective on her situation. During an interview, we ask how they feel about her years without health insurance.

Rachel's mother admits, "I go back and forth about it. My physician friends are amazed that I didn't take out a policy. I guess I say to myself that she is basically a healthy kid and that if something catastrophic happens, she could get free care at the hospital. But I'm not comfortable with this. I think it is a kind of magical thinking, that nothing will happen. Also, I assume that she'll go to medical school and get insurance that way. That's magical thinking. I'm anxious, and I nudge her to find a job with insurance.

"We think about this a lot. My friend, who also is a physician, did take out insurance for his daughter, and she then had appendicitis. And we thought, 'What would we do if Rachel had something like appendicitis?'

"But we feel it is Rachel's responsibility to deal with the insurance. We also feel that if she should have a serious problem, we could probably finesse something, since we are physicians. For example, we could get her medication from our samples.

"Many of Rachel's friends are in similar situations, where they are working but don't have insurance." Rachel's mother sums things up: "It's an uncertain world."

A year after our initial conversation, we called Rachel to ask whether her health, job, and insurance status had changed. She told us that she was now working in an accountant's office as a typist. She took this job, which she dislikes, rather than continue working with children, which she loves, because it gives her health insurance. It is a dead-end job, it does not utilize any of her talents, and it does not train her so that she can be promoted within the office or within the accounting industry. While this job has, for now, allowed her to escape one death spiral, she certainly feels that she has entered another.

RAE AND MARTIN'S STORY: A PARENT'S WORK IS NEVER DONE

Young adults like Rachel shared with us their frustration at having to continue to rely on their parents to help them out financially. Whether or not to pay for insurance, and who should bear the cost, has become a bone of contention between numerous young adults and their parents.

Rae and Martin are middle-class parents living in a suburb of Boston. Like Rachel's parents, they own a home, both are professionals (he is the dentist who was introduced in the previous chapter, and she is an art teacher), and they invest a great deal of money and care in the education of their three children.

When their children were small, the family lived in Sweden, where they grew accustomed to a national health service. When they returned to the United States in the mid-1980s, they enrolled in Blue Cross/Blue Shield. They quickly found, however, that they were expected to pay a substantial deductible for each child in addition to large premiums. Given the shock they felt the first time all three children were sick simultaneously, they decided to switch to a less expensive policy that would cover only hospital costs.

When their eldest son turned twelve, the tantrums he had experienced throughout his childhood began to develop into seriously violent and psychotic behavior. Rae recalls the first time they had to make the painful decision to hospitalize their son. "The first page of the insurance said that the policy doesn't cover neurological or mental treatments. So I thought I'd have to sell the house. It turns out that, in Massachusetts, this policy did cover mental health, but there was a three-thousand-dollar deductible. The first time, he spent five weeks in the hospital.

"It kept getting more expensive for the same bad coverage. Each year, we had the three-thousand-dollar deductible. And we were paying out of pocket about three hundred fifty dollars a month for his medication, plus his therapy.

"So we [joined] an HMO through the Small Business Association. That way, his preexisting condition was covered. At this point, we pay about twelve thousand five hundred dollars a year for insurance.

"Our son has been hospitalized many times over the years, sometimes for longer periods and sometimes just briefly. We were lucky that the

Boston school system had an appropriate school for him, so he was able to live with us most of the time.

"Then, when he turned nineteen, he was taken off our policy. Shortly afterward, he enrolled in college, but he quit after a few weeks. So he was on and off our coverage and his own coverage. Both were with the same insurance company—Tufts."

Their son has had various crises, during which he breaks furniture and threatens to hurt himself or family members. "About a year ago," Rae continues, "I had to take him to the ER in the middle of the night. He had been hurting himself, making cuts. I took him to St. Elizabeth's. And they wouldn't admit him, because when they called Tufts, they were told he's not covered. Actually, Tufts screwed up and gave him the wrong number. So he was covered, but the clerk who answered the phone in the middle of the night didn't have that information. So we had to wait until 4 A.M. for a city-funded ER psych team to come to evaluate him and admit him somewhere else—Franciscan Children's.

"That night was awful. This entire wait was because Tufts screwed up the paperwork. In the morning, when the office was opened, they said he is covered."

Many of the young adults we interviewed shared similar stories of bureaucratic snafus. Because they tend to be more geographically and occupationally mobile than older adults, and because it has become common to punctuate university studies with periods of employment (both to finance the studies and to experience the real world), many young adults find themselves on and off a variety of insurance plans. Because of the fragmented nature of the system, each time they go on or off a plan, opportunities develop for administrative errors, which can lead to substantial medical debt or even denial of treatment.

In addition to the bureaucratic hassles, the cost deters many young adults from obtaining insurance. Although Martin and Rae's son was holding down a steady job at the same retail store where he had worked during high school, his employer did not provide insurance.

His parents, despite financial struggles of their own, felt they had to pick up the slack. As a single adult enrolled in Tufts through his father's Small Business Association group plan, his fee started at $315 a month. Over the course of a year or so, it went up to $340 a month.

Rae tells us: "He refused to pay. He didn't care if he had coverage. He stopped taking his medication and said he doesn't need insurance. But we weren't going to risk that; if he had an episode and we needed to get him into the hospital, we wouldn't be able to take him. He refused to pay; he didn't want to go to the doctor, anyway. We were more nervous than him.

"To be honest, I don't see how he could have paid for insurance, though he was working close to full-time and living at home. He just wasn't paid enough, and his employer wouldn't guarantee him a steady number of hours each week.

"Now he's back in Sweden, and I am relieved that he has coverage."

Given this young man's long history of mental health struggles, it is reasonable to ask why he was not enrolled in the Supplemental Security Income (SSI) program, which would have given him Medicare coverage. But, like many people who live with chronic health problems—and especially those with chronic mental health problems—he is not fully disabled. He is capable of working for months at a time, and, what's more, he *wants* to work. And, given how difficult it is for even those with clear-cut physical disabilities to receive SSI benefits (see appendix 1), it is not at all certain that he would have been accepted into SSI. In any case, his parents do not want to encourage him to see himself as too disabled to work simply in order to access medical services.

Martin and Rae's second son is having a rocky time of it as well. He is a junior at a prominent college. Last spring, he applied to a prestigious program for a semester of study abroad. By the time the program notified him that he was not accepted, it was too late for his parents to apply for financial aid at his regular college. Needing to take a break in tuition payments, and hoping that their financial aid application would be accepted for the second semester, they asked their son to postpone returning to college for one semester. When we last spoke with Martin and Rae, this son was living at home and working at a computer lab. Because he is not a full-time student, he is not covered by his parents' insurance.

Although the second son is a relatively healthy young adult, he has a long history of serious depression. His depression is not being treated at this time.

"Martin wanted to pay for [our second son's] insurance, but I said we're going to risk going without it because we're so short of money right now," Rae recalls.

We asked Martin and Rae how they feel about paying for insurance for their eldest son, but not for their second son.

They paused and looked at one another. "It's like Russian roulette."

YOUNG ADULTS AND HEALTH INSURANCE

Today's young adults are the first generation of Americans who are unlikely to become as prosperous as their parents. The economic challenges faced by young men and women looking to find their bearings in the current job market are part of a larger landscape of cultural changes that include a rise in age at first marriage and in the number of years it takes to complete college and graduate school. In today's economy, most jobs that pay enough to support middle-class life require years of advanced education. For young adults, that means years of semiautonomy in which they piece together loans, part-time jobs, and whatever money their families can provide. Many spend their twenties and early thirties shuttling between college and work, professional school and travel, community service and internships, never earning enough to settle down, marry, and raise children.

In our travels around the country, we met young people from solidly middle-class families, whose parents provided good college educations for them; who are motivated, energetic, and trying to do "the right thing" (in whatever sense they understand it); who are eager to be self-sufficient; and who are uncomfortable when they need to ask their parents for financial help. Yet, despite these advantages, many young adults are unable to find jobs that allow them to begin their own pursuit of the American dream or even to take care of their health in a reasonably adequate manner.

Typically, young adults scrape by without health insurance because the jobs they hold are defined by their employers (accurately or not) as temporary, contingent, part-time, or substitute. In the United States today, almost half of young adults ages nineteen to twenty-three lack health care coverage during some or all of the current year (see figure 6). Fully two-thirds of them are likely to lack coverage at some point over the next four years. Most policies drop young adults from their parents' policies either when they turn nineteen or when they cease being full-time students.

These uninsured young adults rarely can afford to pay the full premium under the COBRA program (named for the 1986 Consolidated Omnibus Budget Reconciliation Act's health benefit provisions), which would allow them to continue coverage under their parents' policies, or to buy individual policies for themselves on the private market. COBRA premiums usually run between $200 and $300 a month, out of reach for many recent graduates. A growing number of insurers are offering special plans for young adults (such as HumanaOne College Graduate, offered by Humana), in which premiums can start as low as $25 a month but usually jump after six months of coverage. In addition, these plans often come with large deductibles (up to $5,000 for the cheaper plans) and do not cover preexisting conditions. Because of these financial constraints, many young people forego coverage.

Financial considerations often are coupled with youthful (and unrealistic) feelings of invincibility. For many young adults, the possibility of serious illness is far from their minds. But the chance that they will need major medical care is not as low as many of the young adults we interviewed seem to think. Three and a half million young women between the ages of nineteen and twenty-nine become pregnant each year, facing

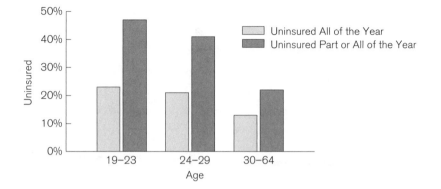

FIGURE 6. The uninsured, by age, 2001. *Source:* Collins et al. 2004.

delivery costs (even without complications or C-sections) of as much as $5,000 to $10,000 or even more. Many young people also are diagnosed for the first time with diabetes, depression, and other serious chronic diseases. Injuries are especially common in this age group; indeed, for every one hundred adults between the ages of eighteen and twenty-four, thirty-two injuries are reported each year.

Lack of insurance forces many young people to delay or skip medical care. In one study, about half of young adults ages nineteen to twenty-nine reported that they had gone without needed medical care because of cost—failing to see a doctor when sick, not filling a prescription, or skipping recommended screening tests. The result is that both minor and major conditions are likely to become more serious because they are not caught or treated in a timely manner.

JONATHAN'S STORY: ARTISTS, MUSICIANS, AND THE IDEALISM OF YOUTH

We smile at the irony of the first words Jonathan, a twenty-eight-year-old musician, speaks after we tell him about our project: "I don't have any health problems," he declares. "I don't think I'm a good candidate for your study."

We do not know whether Jonathan is giving voice to a young person's naïve belief in invincibility, to the public bravado typical of men, or to an artistic nonchalance toward matters of the body rather than the spirit. But given his frayed Salvation Army store clothing (most definitely *not* shabby chic) and his worn-out shoes, we decide to trot out a few sample questions on the fly.

"Have you been to the hospital in the last few years? Do you have any aches and pains that you try to ignore?"

"Oh, that, yes," Jonathan answers.

"Come on in and sit down. We want to hear more."

Jonathan is a singer and guitarist who has experienced some success on a number of concert tours around the country. He spends about half the year on the road, playing mostly at small venues, driving from city to city. In between gigs, he picks up odd jobs or waits tables to round out his income. His concerts bring him close to $50,000 a year, but after he pays his booking agent and travel expenses, he lives on $15,000 a year or less.

Jonathan grew up one of seven siblings in Atlanta, where his father worked for a pharmaceutical company. He doesn't know the details of his parents' insurance history, but he does know that going to the doctor was never an issue when he was growing up—his mother took her children to the family doctor when they were sick.

When Jonathan was eighteen, and still covered by his family's insurance, he developed kidney stones for the first time. His parents took him to the emergency room, where he was given Demerol for the pain and told to wait until the stones passed. A year later, he developed stones again, this time large enough to keep him in the hospital for three or four days. The third time he had kidney stones, he was no longer covered by his parents' insurance. Frightened by the pain, he went to a clinic in downtown Atlanta that had sliding-scale fees.

"The third time, I was scared of [the stones] coming. . . . Like I would feel it, and I'd get scared. And I finally just developed this thing to where as soon as I felt like I need to pee but I can't, I would just start pounding water. I would just drink probably a gallon of water in like two hours. The stone would get into the bladder, and once it was into the bladder, I wasn't worried about it. And then finally I would see it pass later on."

Over the past ten years, he has had kidney stones approximately once each year. Generally, he takes care of them by himself, drinking large quantities of water and hoping they will pass quickly. Jonathan even has developed his own folk explanation for why he can tolerate passing the stones without medical assistance: "I think maybe this kidney, like the urethra, might be just callused over, because I barely hurt anymore. Just every now and then stones come out."

Jonathan experiences other pains in his hip and lower back and isn't sure which are related to his kidney and which to the hip pointers (inflamed hip sockets) that were diagnosed when he was younger. He points to the entire right side of his body when we ask him where he feels the discomfort. Jonathan has always enjoyed sports, especially basketball, but over the past few years his pain has intensified, and he finds that he can "maybe squeak out two days in a row [of playing], but I couldn't squeak out three."

From the days when he had insurance, Jonathan remembers that the doctor gave him anti-inflammatory medications for the hip pain, but he read "somewhere" that such drugs have a bad effect on the kidneys. At this point, he does not take any medication or consult any health care provider. He has not had a checkup in five years, though "I'd like to be able to just at least know what's going on [with my hip and kidney]. I always say someday I'm going to be rich and find out."

John F. Kennedy once said, "The arts incarnate the creativity of a free people." Like many dedicated artists and musicians, Jonathan is more than willing to make financial sacrifices in order to dedicate his life to his art. He doesn't care that his clothes are shabby, that he doesn't own a car, or that he doesn't have any money in the bank. But he clearly knows and cares that not having health insurance can be disastrous both in the short term and over the long haul.

In a surprisingly resigned tone for a young man, Jonathan tells us: "I'm pretty sure someday this kidney will have to go."

TEMPORARY IN MASSACHUSETTS—
MIDDLE CLASS BUT UNINSURED

We linked up with Heather and Samantha because both were employed as temporary office workers and had been hired to transcribe tapes of interviews for this project. Young women with bundles of initiative, each (separately) sent us emails telling us how fascinated they were by the interviews and letting us know that although they were white, middle class, and educated, they also did not have health insurance.

Heather is in her mid-twenties. After graduating from college, she was accepted into graduate school but decided that she was too young for that sort of financial commitment and should work for a few years first. Over the past few years, she has worked as a substitute teacher and, like many of her peers, as an office temp. A talented stand-up comic, Heather was so popular among the students at her school that the administration asked her to stay on full-time but did not offer health insurance. She decided not to take the job.

An active young woman, Heather does not have any major health problems. She has made a few visits to the doctor for chronic rashes and other skin problems, but each time she found that after paying the doctor she didn't have enough money to fill the prescription. For now, she has decided that doctor visits are a waste of money. She also suffers from some chronic gynecological problems for which she should be getting consistent care. These problems are not life threatening, but they are uncomfortable if left untreated. And, like many of the young women we interviewed, Heather worries that even minor gynecological problems could lead to future infertility.

What troubles Heather most is the possibility that she could be in a major accident or contract a serious illness. Her mother and grandparents are her "safety net," but they are not particularly well off; helping her with big medical bills could wipe out their entire retirement savings. As a result, Heather no longer plays sports (she used to play ultimate Frisbee) because she is afraid she'll break a leg and be unable to handle the financial consequences.

Heather has been experiencing some depression, which seemed common among our young interviewees. One job she had did offer health benefits, but the plan paid for only thirteen visits to a therapist, which Heather knows is insufficient. Mirroring the experiences of many of her peers, she ended up receiving Prozac from her primary care physician with no psychotherapy and no follow-up with a psychiatrist. More to the point, Heather and her friends feel that the Prozac doesn't really seem to help. Their depression is situational, not organic: they have graduated from college into a terrible economy, and few of them are finding "real" jobs with benefits.

Samantha is the daughter of a retired California physician. She graduated from college three years ago and then signed on to Americorps Vista Volunteers. Since finishing her stint with Americorps, she has held a series of temporary clerical jobs, some of which offered health insurance but not prescription coverage, most of which offered nothing. Samantha estimates that her total take-home pay is about $700 a month. Although she has two roommates, most of her salary goes for rent and utilities.

Last year, Samantha made an extended trip to Brazil, where she volunteered among poor children. While in Brazil, she had access to health care, but when she came back and experienced what she euphemistically calls "stomach problems," she could afford only one doctor visit. Predictably, the doctor wanted to run tests for parasites, but she didn't have the money and never did the tests. Shortly afterward, she began working at a high-end catering company (which did not request lab tests, even though she told her boss that she had been in Brazil). Samantha tells us that many of her friends traveled to Third World countries after college and that many of them work for catering companies or as waitresses, potentially spreading the germs and parasites picked up in their travels.

Like Heather, Samantha sees herself as healthy and strong, but she is plagued by a few health problems made more worrisome by the prospect that they will worsen without treatment. Since graduating from college, she has been grappling with depression, though she has not seen a therapist or taken any medication. Most troublesome is that the depression is manifested in fatigue, lack of motivation, a sense of being overwhelmed, and poor concentration, all of which interfere with her ability to look for a better job that would provide benefits.

CLASS MATTERS

Rachel, Heather, and Samantha are white, upper-middle-class young women; all entered adulthood with a solid base of education, social capital, and good health; and all live in Massachusetts, which offers some of the best health care options of any state in the country. Massachusetts is tied with Minnesota, Rhode Island, and Wisconsin for the lowest percentage of uninsured individuals (8 percent). Massachusetts has the highest supply of medical doctors (434 per 100,000 population) and registered nurses (118 per 100,000) of any state in the union. It also has the highest per capita health spending, at $4,810 annually. And Massachusetts is one of the very few states to have an uncompensated care pool to reimburse hospitals for care provided to the uninsured.

The final section of this chapter introduces Kim, a young working-class woman who lives in Illinois. In many ways, Kim struggles with the same challenges faced by the more affluent young women described earlier: they work in jobs that define their status as part-time, temporary, or contingent, which means that they do not have health insurance. But the problems that Rachel, Heather, and Samantha have experienced are substantially more difficult for young people who come from less privileged backgrounds and live in states with fewer medical resources.

Whereas upper-middle-class young adults typically enter the uninsured phase of their lives with a store of good health that has been cultivated throughout their childhoods by their financially well-off parents, less affluent young adults like Guadalupe, whom we meet in chapter 8, may already have accumulated health problems that have not been adequately diagnosed or treated. And, whereas upper-middle-class young adults believe that they can rely on their parents or grandparents to bail them out if they become very sick (though they certainly are uncomfortable with the prospect of wiping out parents' retirement savings), working-class and poor young adults know that once they enter the death spiral, there is no one to pull them back up.

University of Pennsylvania sociologist Frank Furstenberg confirms our anecdotal observations regarding the contrasting experiences of young adults of different socioeconomic backgrounds. He places this difference, in part, in the context of the decline in well-paid manufacturing jobs since the 1960s, a development that affects the less educated most harshly. "The decline of union jobs also reduced the possibility of men earning a family wage, eroding the marital prospects of males with less than a high school education and, more recently, even those who completed high school. The hardest hit economically have been minority males."

Furstenberg also cites the impact of the criminal justice system and drug laws on the employment prospects of young minority adults: "Over the past two decades, harsh and punitive responses to juvenile offenses have become widespread at the federal, state, and local levels. This is especially true for drug offenses, which are treated severely and often lead to incarceration. Low-income, minority males in particular have extraordinarily high rates of involvement in the criminal justice system. . . . Upward of 25 percent of black and 15 percent of Latino males will spend some time in a correctional facility, with many having their first encounter with the criminal justice system before the age of eighteen. . . . This means that many of these young men will not complete high school and will suffer in the labor market."

KIM'S STORY: "A CHILD?! ARE YOU SERIOUS?!"

Kim, a young African American woman who lives in the college town of Champaign, Illinois, isn't quite sure whether she wants to tell us her story. That's why she has brought along a friend to the interview and asked to meet us in the middle of a bustling mall—both the friend and the mall provide a potential escape in case our questions don't sit well with her.

Born in Chicago and raised in the city's housing projects, Kim had few advantages in life other than having a father in the U.S. military. Though he did not live with the family, he did list her on his health insurance policy until she turned eighteen. At that point, his plan would no longer cover her.

After high school, Kim went to community college to study early childhood education. Like many college students, she assumed that her degree would lead to a permanent job and benefits. Since graduating from college, however, she has been working part-time at a day care center. She would like to work full-time, but the center isn't hiring full-time employees. She also works part-time at a Walgreens drugstore. Though she isn't thrilled with the work (which doesn't utilize her college training), she would agree to work full-time, except that Walgreens isn't hiring full-time employees either. Kim explained that she tried working more hours there after her boss told her that she would need to work full-time for twelve weeks in order to be eligible for insurance. But when she approached the twelve-week mark, her hours were cut, making her ineligible for insurance.

Unlike Rachel, Heather, and Samantha, Kim knows that she has serious health problems and that it is dangerous for her to go without medical care and medication. Since late childhood, she has had diabetes. She needs to take insulin and Glucophage, and she must test her blood sugar several times each day. The medicines and testing equipment cost far more than she can afford on her minimum-wage salary (she earns about $1,000 a month), and she has not been to the doctor for longer than she can remember.

We ask Kim how she can afford all her medicine and testing paraphernalia. At first, she evades our question. Suspecting that she is embarrassed and fearful that we might judge her behavior as immature or irresponsible, we reassure her that this is not the goal of our project.

Finally, she takes a breath and reveals, "Okay. I haven't been taking my medicine like I was supposed to, because I couldn't afford it. I've been having a lot of financial problems because I live on my own, I was going to school, and then plus I got car payments and stuff like that.

"I got to the point where I couldn't get help, and I was starting to feel like, 'Oh, well.' I was starting to get a little attitude. I know I shouldn't have. But it was frustrating, and I couldn't come up with the money. So I was like, 'I don't know what to do.'"

Untreated diabetes not only makes her feel worse day to day but also hastens the onset of the serious complications the disease can cause. Because she is unable to monitor and manage her blood sugars and get recommended preventive care, she is at high risk for premature blindness, heart disease, limb amputations, and kidney failure. Standard medical treatment aims to prevent or at least significantly forestall such outcomes, but Kim does not see a way to access standard treatment.

A week before we met, she had called the nurse educator at a hospital diabetes clinic where she had been treated before being cut from her father's insurance when she finished college, hoping that the nurse could arrange a reduced fee that would allow her to return to the clinic. The nurse was pleasant but not overly optimistic.

"I also tried to apply to public aid for a medical card [Medicaid], but they were telling me I have to have a child. They said that's what I need in order to get help through the system. And I'm not about to have babies right now."

We ask what her reaction was to being told that she should have a baby.

"They make me think that they're stupid, because, I mean, you have people out here like me with no kids and trying to go to school and trying to do the right thing, and I think we should also be helped, instead of [helping only] people who already have kids. I mean, I was like, 'A child?! Are you serious?!'"

CHAPTER EIGHT

MENTAL HEALTH MATTERS

A MEXICAN IMMIGRANT HITS THE BUREAUCRATIC WALL

TEXAS TOURING

Texas leads all states in the percentage of its population who lack health insurance. Within the state, the highest concentration of uninsured individuals lies in the heavily Hispanic region south of Interstate 10, tracking the Rio Grande Valley along the Mexican border. That is where we traveled to meet Guadalupe and Elena, a daughter and mother struggling with a serious mental health disability. As we quickly learned from them, the combination of a psychiatric condition and a Hispanic identity opens double-wide portals into the death spiral.

The Rio Grande Valley, to the outsider's eye, seems to offer endless health care choices. Giant billboards on the highways declare: "Foot Pain? Call New Texas Podiatry!" and "Mark Rodrigo, MD, Specializing in Maternity Care." Our favorite billboard proclaims: "Pain Specialist, Sayyid Ali, MD, call 1-877-555-HURT." On each billboard, the face of a physician who seems to be trying a bit too hard to radiate concern and competence, professionalism and affability, beams down at the speeding Texas drivers. The advertisements might entice, but the fees do not: uninsured patients generally must pay up front before the doctor will see them.

Driving across the Rio Grande Valley, we see a number of "H" signs on the highway and follow them to a brand-new, fine-looking hospital.

Strolling through the clean and well-decorated corridors, we hear almost no Spanish, although the population of the Rio Grande Valley is close to 90 percent Hispanic. This is a private hospital, providing excellent services to the more affluent northern "snowbirds" who come down to Texas for the mild winters and cheaper health care.

The local Mexican American population—the majority of which is uninsured—rarely can afford its services. In Texas, 31 percent of Hispanics live in families with an income below the federal poverty line (compared to 10 percent of whites). In addition, 61.8 percent of the state's Hispanics are uninsured, compared to 26.8 percent of non-Hispanic whites.*

We follow another set of "H" signs on the road for forty-five minutes to locate the hospital used by the local Mexican American community. Opening the door, we find ourselves in an overcrowded emergency room staffed by overworked physicians and nurses, trying to give adequate care and counseling to uninsured patients who cannot afford a primary care physician and whose only safety net is the emergency room.

Everyone we speak to in the Rio Grande Valley tells us that they go to Mexico to buy medicine. (Many drugs that are available only by prescription in the United States are sold over the counter in Mexico.) Following the directions provided by some of our interviewees, we drive across the border at Progresso and again at Renosa. Blocks before we reach the tourist souvenir shops, we see signs for dozens, maybe hundreds, of pharmacies and clinics: "Dr. Ortega Dental Associates—'First Dentist in Town,'" "Thelma Aguirre, MD—Weight Control, Dermatology, Diabetes, Hypertension, Breast Reduction, Eyelid Surgery," "Pharmacy—The Best Prices in Town, Compare and Save with Us, Amoxicillin 500 mg 96 Capsules, Augmentin, Ceclor, Lincocin, Viagra, Special Prices."

*Nationally, more than 58 percent of Hispanic noncitizens are uninsured; among Hispanics who are U.S. citizens, 27 percent lack health insurance (see Doty 2003a and 2003b).

Modern medicine is not the only healing option in the Rio Grande Valley. Both in cities and in towns, we see *botanicas* in every neighborhood, sometimes on every block. These shops sell Mexican herbs, Cuban charms, Catholic saints, New Age crystals, and votive candles customized for every possible physical or spiritual ailment.

Pentecostal churches hold healing services. At the Wings of Healing Apostolic Church, the pastor tells how he prayed for a child with leukemia and the boy recovered, how he himself had a heart attack and the doctor said he wouldn't make it through the night, but he prayed and here he is, many years later. "People ask, 'Why do you get sick if you are a Christian?' Well, there's sickness so that people will pray and God will give miracles and heal them, and then they will believe."

The Catholic Church is part of the healing landscape as well, with basilicas, shrines, and *cuartos de milagros*—miracle rooms, festooned with saints draped in thousands of miniature representations of ailing body parts. Altars are smothered in photos of the ill and recovered, punctuated by letters from physicians attesting to cures.

GUADALUPE AND ELENA'S STORY: SAINTS, PRAYERS, AND EMPTY PILL BOTTLES

We turn off the highway to meet Guadalupe and Elena in their *colonia*— a low-income neighborhood built outside the town limits by developers taking advantage of the desire of Mexican immigrants to purchase homes and put down roots in America. It lacks paved roads, a school, or any other normative public services. A lake of sewage pumped from a nearby town is being dumped into the backyards of the houses along one edge of the *colonia*.

Guadalupe, twenty-seven years old, is mentally ill and unable to work. Her mother, Elena, a widow, is the sole support of Guadalupe and her other children. Elena, her neighbors tell us, runs herself ragged working as a nurse's aide while worrying about Guadalupe, who spends her days home alone.

Elena and Guadalupe's house, surrounded by a substantial metal fence, is built right up next to the rutted and rocky road that runs around the edge of their hastily constructed *colonia*. Opening up a series of padlocks, bolts, and chains, Elena ushers us into a living room that is surprisingly comfortable. Tastefully furnished with inexpensive "finds" from the flea markets and yard sales that Elena loves to visit, their living room showcases an eclectic Mexican and American aesthetic: assorted pictures of birds, blessed palm leaves left from Palm Sunday, a painting of a black guardian angel, a portrait of St. Ignatius of Loyola, an exquisite Virgin of Guadalupe, and Our Lady of Sorrows dressed in black.

The locks and the saints, Elena confides, give her peace of mind when she is at work. She departs each day at 5:00 A.M., leaving her eleven-year-old son, Juan, alone with Guadalupe until he goes to school at 7:30 A.M. "Then she stays alone until I return in the afternoon. Who takes care of them for me? I tell her, 'Never leave the door open—because a lot of itinerants pass this way—because anyone could come in.' On my way to and from work, I am always praying to the saints who have always protected me, every day. From here to the corner, I have already called upon all my saints and leave them all here in the house."

Even the saints, however, are not able to help Elena arrange reasonable and consistent medical care for Guadalupe. The young woman has suffered with severe psychological problems since about the age of two, when her father was killed in an accident at work. Although Guadalupe has had many years of therapy, Elena does not know her exact diagnosis. She does know that depression is part of the problem and that she has a personality disorder. Most difficult for Elena to handle are the frequent fits of rage and violence that overcome her daughter. Guadalupe is unable to work; she has tried several times, but after a week or two, she starts to fight with everyone around her.

Both Guadalupe and Elena are U.S. citizens, with strong ties to Mexico. Elena's husband worked for a large petroleum company in Mexico. When he died, the company hired Elena. Those were good years: the company provided health insurance for Guadalupe until she turned eighteen. Though Elena had to work hard to raise her three children, and though Guadalupe's condition did not seem to improve, Elena felt somewhat secure in the knowledge that she could get help for her.

Then, ten years ago, Elena was injured in an accident at home. After she had surgery on her knee, her employer refused to let her come back to the company, claiming that she could no longer do the same amount of work. Elena decided that the time had come to move Guadalupe and her youngest son, Juan, to the United States, where, she felt, Guadalupe might get better care. With settlement money provided by her former employer, and with some money from her father, she purchased her small house in the Texas *colonia*, enrolled Juan in school, signed on as a nurse's aide, and set out to find medical care for Guadalupe.

At first, things went well. Guadalupe was eligible for Medicaid, and she received treatment from a psychologist and a psychiatrist who gave her medication that, for the first time since she was two, brought her fits of rage under control. In Mexico, Guadalupe had received extensive "talk therapy," which was a bit helpful but didn't seem to make fundamental changes in her behavior. Elena explains that, without the medicine, "when Guadalupe is not well, she screams a lot, and one cannot say anything to her, because she gets very angry and says all kinds of mean things. Before, she used to say that it would be better if she were to die. With the medicine, she does not say that to me anymore." Guadalupe is taller and heavier than her mother and younger brother; both Elena and Juan appreciate the respite from violence that the drugs provide.

A few months after Guadalupe began the therapy and medication, her file was reviewed by Medicaid, and the family received some very unwelcome news: a ruling that Guadalupe was not eligible for benefits because she had never worked, was not a single mother, and was not pregnant. She was told to apply for Social Security disability payments, but she was turned down. Elena and Guadalupe are currently appealing the denial. In the meantime, Medicaid will not cover Guadalupe while the Social Security appeal is pending.

The crux of the problem, as far as Elena and Guadalupe can make out, is that even though Guadalupe is a U.S. citizen, she does not have a Social Security number. Elena has been trying to straighten this out for a year, but for some reason that she does not understand, the matter has not been resolved. Compounding her troubles with the bureaucracy, Elena has been told that she does not have sufficient proof that Guadalupe is truly disabled. In fact, Guadalupe has many papers from Mexico documenting her psychiatric history (which we saw), but those papers are not recognized in the United States.

Guadalupe also showed us a document prepared by a government-appointed psychologist who evaluated her for U.S. Social Security disability eligibility. Folded and refolded for perusal by various government clerks, the document seems to make little sense. The clinician who completed the form described Guadalupe as retarded and drooling. In the full morning we spent in Guadalupe's company, we observed nothing resembling drooling, and we saw no hint of mental retardation. Guadalupe reads in two languages, makes appropriate jokes, uses and understands irony, follows the conversation going on around her, takes a lively interest in her own treatment, and proudly shows off the complicated crafts projects she pieces together out of soda can tops and bits of taffeta.

Did the clinician who filled out the form confuse Guadalupe with another patient? Did he or she believe that Mexican Americans are likely to be retarded? Did the clinician even meet Guadalupe? Or was this psychologist valiantly trying to work the system on Guadalupe's behalf by giving her a diagnosis that might allow her to be accepted by Social Security?

The last time Guadalupe tried to visit the psychologist and the psychiatrist, they wouldn't see her because she lacked insurance. Elena recalls, "The other times we went to see the counselor, he would get medications from the doctor and would give us a lot of free samples. But this time, he did not even see us because we did not . . . have a paper that qualifies us to receive services." Elena, like other uninsured Americans, is grateful for the samples physicians sometimes give her. Yet she is not blind to the downside of the patchwork school of pharmacology: "One time, a doctor kindly gave Guadalupe samples, but the only samples she had in her office weren't the right strength. So the doctor gave her 300 instead of 200 milligrams. It completely knocked her out, and she slept around the clock."

When we last meet them, Guadalupe has only a few days' worth of pills left, and the family is in a bind. They have not yet received notice that Guadalupe will receive Social Security disability payments, so they are unable to refill the prescription in the United States. And though they can cross the border into Mexico to buy many other medicines over the counter, they cannot buy Guadalupe's psychiatric medications in Mexico because they are considered controlled substances and need a prescription.

Like that of other family caregivers, Elena's path is not an easy one. "I start work at five o'clock in the morning. I purposely took the morning shift because Guadalupe would hit her brother a lot. . . . When I was working from two in the afternoon to ten at night, Guadalupe would be with him all afternoon, and she would hit him a lot. Since he was very young, he did not know how to defend himself, and she would pinch him.

"I spoke to my manager at work to see if she could change me to the morning shift. That way, when I leave for work at five or five-thirty, I leave his clothes out and the alarm clock on so that he can get up at six-thirty to shower and change and go to school. Guadalupe only opens the door for him, and she locks herself in again. I have a neighbor at the corner house who waits for him and sees him get on the bus."

We ask Elena whether she has a church community that can help her out. "The truth is that here I don't go anywhere, because after I leave work, I am very tired when I get home. I get here and go to sleep because I get up at three in the morning or three-thirty in order to fix my lunch and go to work. . . . I don't like to be late for work. We start work at five-thirty, but I always arrive between five-fifteen and five-twenty. So I get up very early.

"And also the job is very draining. Lifting the elderly is hard. Sometimes my arms hurt right here, and sometimes I get shooting pains here." She points to her shoulders and wrists. "Sometimes the individuals are very heavy, and at times there are only two of us to lift twenty-four men and women. Some can get up, but we have to change all of them. I have to bathe six in the morning. From five-thirty in the morning, which is my schedule, to seven, I must have them bathed and ready for breakfast in the dining room."

Elena's employer offers "no benefits whatsoever." But even more galling to her is management's lack of concern for the well-being of either the employees or the residents. "When we are short of personnel, they move us from one area to another" instead of bringing in substitute workers, she says. When that happens, "they don't pay us extra. The only thing is that they make us sign this paper, and they give us half an hour overtime pay. Half an hour—and, between us, we do the work of the person that is absent."

Elena suffers from high blood pressure, which seems to be under control, though she has stopped taking her blood pressure medication because the clinic she uses no longer has drug samples to give her. In addition, her old leg injury still bothers her. Right now, Elena is barely scraping by. It is unclear what she will do in a couple of years when she can no longer lift the old people at the nursing home. How will she support herself? How will she support Guadalupe?

If Guadalupe had been suffering from a physical ailment rather than mental illness, would she have found it easier to access competent care? Will Guadalupe be able to refill the prescriptions that had been so helpful? If she cannot access consistent medication, will she truly harm her brother or her mother some day? If Guadalupe could get systematic psychiatric and psychological help, including proper medication, would she be able to work and help support herself and her mother? Guadalupe is good with her hands, bright, and sociable. Will she spend the rest of her days behind the locked door and fence, holding on to empty boxes of pills the same way her mother holds on to pictures of saints and rosary beads?

Guadalupe and Elena risk slipping into the death spiral through any of several portals. Elena is burning out from the stress of constant family caregiving; she has work-related injuries that are not being addressed by workers' compensation; she is a widow trying to get by on her meager salary in a society in which men generally earn more than women; she is working in a service-sector job where health insurance isn't even a topic of conversation; and, like other members of minority groups, she must deal with the subtle and not-so-subtle racism that is pervasive in the social service system (for example, Social Security's refusal to recognize Guadalupe's extensive medical documentation because it comes from Mexico).

Compounding and amplifying all these risks is the particular health problem with which Guadalupe lives. Her psychiatric disability has sentenced Guadalupe, and her mother as well, to membership in the caste of the ill, infirm, and marginally employed.

THE STIGMA OF MENTAL DISABILITIES

> For those who have lived and experienced discrimination [because of psychiatric diagnoses] the events are cumulative and interrelated. It is not only that people are rejected by their family and shunned by their friends; dismissed from school; scrutinized uneasily or fired at work; patronized by doctors and refused coverage by insurance companies; denied custody of their children by judges; and threatened by family, friends, and doctors with institutionalization, but also that all of these things happen in interrelated and long-term ways. . . . Thus, individual acts of discrimination combine and continue to have an effect on the individual that is far greater than the sum of its parts: exclusion from a graduate program or college on the basis of a diagnosis affects family relations, health care, employment, and self-confidence; loss of employment affects health care, housing, and self-confidence; each of these affects the other in a continuing cycle.
>
> Susan Stefan, *Unequal Rights: Discrimination against People with Mental Disabilities and the Americans with Disabilities Act*

Guadalupe and Elena daily confront the stigma that is attached to psychiatric disabilities in our society. This stigma typically is expressed through the persistent pattern of treating mental illness as a moral weakness rather than a legitimate medical condition. In this way, mental health and illness, much like race, have always constituted a castelike social ethos in our country.

Ambivalent public attitudes and policies lead to a multitude of problems for those struggling with psychiatric disabilities. For example, Medicare generally pays only half the cost of outpatient mental health visits, compared with 80 percent payment for visits related to physical problems. It also allows fewer days of inpatient care for mental health problems than for a physical illness. Many states outsource their mental health coverage for Medicaid, forcing patients into behavioral health managed-care plans, which severely restrict access to care. In most states, Medicaid reimbursement rates for mental health providers are so low that very few providers agree to accept Medicaid patients at all.

This ambivalence is reflected in inconsistent workers' compensation policies around the country as well. States have different guidelines regarding workers' comp coverage for emotional injuries or mental illness. In some states, conditions arising from predictably stressful jobs are covered, whereas in other states the same condition resulting from the same job is not covered precisely because stress is an inherent part of such employment.

One of the clearest examples of institutionalized ambivalence is the 1996 Social Security Act amendment that excludes individuals from eligibility for SSI (Supplemental Security Income) or SSDI (Social Security Disability Insurance) benefits if drug addiction or alcoholism is material to the disability determination. In most states, the loss of SSI benefits means the loss of Medicaid, and the loss of SSDI means the loss of Medicare coverage.* This amendment ignores the standard judgment of

*At the time the Social Security Act was amended, the Social Security Administration expected that 70 percent of SSI recipients whose coverage was terminated for alcohol- or drug-related reasons would still qualify for Medicaid under SSI or another eligibility category. As of 2000, however, only about 35 percent had done so (National Health Care for the Homeless Council 1999, p. 7).

the vast majority of mental health professionals that substance abuse is a psychiatric disorder, as it is listed in the standard diagnostic manual used by psychiatrists *(Diagnostic and Statistical Manual IV)*. In this case, Congress allowed old prejudices about the moral implications of drug use to trump the medical definition of alcohol or drug addiction as a psychiatric condition.

Egregious as these public policies may be, insurance company practices are even worse, as Susan Stefan, a renowned disability attorney, writes: "The most explicit discrimination on the basis of mental disabilities is done by private insurance companies, which provide differential and distinctly disadvantageous coverage for mental health conditions in both health insurance and disability benefits. In addition, private insurance companies deny people with histories of mental health treatment insurance for life, disability, and property or charge them substantially inflated rates, simply because they are receiving mental health treatment or even counseling or therapy."

Stigmatized conditions such as mental illness particularly disrupt employment opportunities and are thus especially likely to reduce access to employment-based health insurance—a situation that reinforces our argument about the workings of the death spiral. As a presidential commission on mental health reported in October 2002: "Undetected, untreated, and poorly treated mental disorders interrupt careers, leading many into lives of disability, poverty, and long-term dependence. Our review finds a shocking 90 percent unemployment rate among adults with serious mental illness—the worst level of employment of any group of people with disabilities. Strikingly, surveys show that many of them want to work and report that they *could* work with modest assistance."

In a recent survey, Stefan and her research team found that, despite the 1990 Americans with Disabilities Act, people with psychiatric disabilities continue to experience employment discrimination. Many are denied jobs; others are fired when they reveal their disability. Some are dismissed when they indicate that they are taking medication or during periods when their medication is being adjusted. Others endure condescending or demeaning attitudes on the part of supervisors and co-workers.

Although our health insurance system cannot be held responsible for all the employment woes faced by those with psychiatric diagnoses, the system does play an important part in perpetuating and institutionalizing discriminatory practices. Stefan documents numerous testimonials from people who were denied jobs because employers claimed that hiring disabled workers would make insurance rates go up. In other instances, insurance companies refused to insure employers who hired too many people with disabilities.

Stefan further explains that both case law and survey respondents underscore the causal relationship between discrimination at work and emotional breakdowns. Discrimination has an enormous and detrimental impact on people with psychiatric disabilities, often triggering or exacerbating acute episodes of disability. Most Americans with psychiatric disabilities want to work and see work as improving their mental health by providing an identity, friends, social contacts, and a purpose to life, in addition to money and health benefits.

And so, in typical death spiral fashion, job loss and continuing unemployment as a result of psychiatric challenges further impair mental health, leading to harsher challenges, worse access to health care, and so on. This scenario is a frightening one: as chapter 10 shows, psychiatrically disabled Americans are greatly overrepresented among the homeless and the incarcerated.

CHAPTER NINE

RACE MATTERS

HEALTH CARE STORIES FROM BLACK AMERICA

RACE AND CASTE

Throughout this book, we argue that links between employment and health care are key components of the political and economic policies that are creating a caste of the ill, infirm, and marginally employed. Issues of race are critical to this argument for two reasons: racial discrimination strengthens the pull of the death spiral; and race itself has always been the basis of a caste system in America.

Considering the experience of African Americans historically as well as today, Indian anthropologist Ursula Sharma convincingly argues for applying the notion of *caste*—as opposed to *ethnicity* or *class*—to the racial categorization of black people in the United States. First, she points out, use of the word *caste* distinguishes the situation of African Americans from ethnic groups such as Poles and Italians, who, though originally distinct as immigrants with well-defined cultures, over time became assimilated in America. Rigid racial boundaries are quite different from those facing white immigrant groups. Second, because of entrenched racism, African Americans experience few opportunities for class mobility. Even when they become affluent, they are still "black" and do not enjoy the same status and privileges as white Americans.*

---

*Other scholars, including Michael Byrd and Linda Clayton (2002) and Douglas Massey and Nancy Denton (1993), identify the persistent, pervasive, and castelike features of America's racial hierarchy.

Other scholars emphasize the biological, sexual, and marital ideologies that underpin racial categorization in America. John Dollard, writing in 1937, argues: "American caste is pinned not to cultural but to biological features—to color, features, hair form, and the like. This badge is categorical regardless of the social value of the individual." Moreover, Dollard clarifies, "class conflict centers around economic position and advantage, whereas the caste conflict centers around social, and ultimately sexual contact."

Picking up on these insights, this chapter draws attention to some of the ways in which our racialized health care system has contributed to the construction of physical markers that reinforce ideologies of immutable racial difference.

In their landmark study of race, medicine, and health care in the United States, Michael Byrd and Linda Clayton show that "legally sanctioned medical and environmental neglect of enslaved Africans and the institutionalization of an inconstant, often inferior, 'slave health subsystem'—processes that began in the seventeenth century—had future implications and dire consequences for Black people. A 'slave health deficit' transmitted from Africa by the Atlantic slave trade became institutionalized in English North America. Race in the embryonic health system became a marker almost as important as it was in the institution of slavery."

Writing about the historical processes that led to the creation of a "Black health and health care underclass,"* Byrd and Clayton write: "Caste, race, and class problems distorted the nation's hospital system from its beginnings. The nation's early hospitals discriminated against and sometimes medically abused Black patients. . . . The foundations of the American health delivery system were built on a class-stratified, racially segregated, and discriminatory basis." As is typical in caste systems, ideology was invoked to justify social hierarchies: "The professional assumption of poor health as 'normal' for Blacks remained in-

*This phrase, coined by Byrd and Clayton (2002), was inspired by the insights of Dr. M. Alfred Haynes.

grained in the minds of White American physicians—who went so far as to create a lexicon of 'Negro disease' and alternate physiological mechanisms based on race—well into the twentieth century."

Moreover, these racial hierarchies proved resistant to change, another trait common to caste systems. Along with Medicare and Medicaid legislation, the passage of the 1964 Civil Rights Act, which desegregated hospitals, helped to improve the health status of African Americans through the mid-1970s, as federal funding increased access to medical care. In 1975, however, Byrd and Clayton note, health progress for black Americans "virtually stopped . . . as the commitment, political support, and funding for the special programs" waned. After 1980, these authors argue, the health status of African Americans actually deteriorated relative to that of whites.

Increasing residential segregation has been a key factor in this deterioration. Other factors include continuing discrimination in hiring practices, welfare reform policies that have led to large numbers of African American women losing their Medicaid enrollment, and a growing political inclination to incarcerate African American men.

TIMOTHY'S STORY: "NO BENEFITS, NO MEDICAL"

Denise's potent voice resonates through the small but crowded Pentecostal church in Decatur, Illinois, where she and her husband, Timothy, are part of the prayer team that stands in front of the pulpit, charged with the sweet duty of inviting the all-black congregation to feel the presence of the Holy Spirit. Timothy, small of build and soft of voice compared to his statuesque wife, more than makes up for his slight stature by choosing an array of ultra-stylish clothes. Dressed in a spiffy white suit jacket cut well below his hips and adorned with shiny gold buttons, Timothy looks as if he shops at a boutique that caters to televangelists or soul music stars. They are, indeed, a striking couple on the Sunday that we meet them for the first time.

At our second meeting, we have to do a double-take in order to recognize them. Shepherded to our house after work by a local pastor, they seem to have none of the personal power that had beamed from their faces at church. Instead, their bearing proclaims nervousness, timidity—the psychic act of shrinking down in order to take up less space that so many African Americans learn to execute when they enter white neighborhoods.

Denise and Timothy were born in southern Illinois. Both have worked at a variety of blue-collar jobs since 1970, when they left high school. This is a second marriage for both of them. They wed after living together for a number of years. Looking at Denise with obvious affection, Timothy explains, "Couldn't find no one else to put up with me, and she couldn't find no one else either, so we stayed with each other. We figured we'd been together so long we might as well get married."

Timothy has never worked at a job that offered health insurance. At all his jobs, "even the job that I have now, the work is strenuous and the work is hard, but yet still, they don't have no health insurance."

Timothy's current job is at an animal feed plant in the countryside outside Decatur. The plant is exposed to the elements—no heat in the freezing Decatur winters and no air conditioning in the boiling Decatur summers.

The work involves stacking up bird seed and dog food, lifting sacks that weigh anywhere from twenty-five to sixty-five pounds, day in and day out. We ask Timothy how many sacks he lifts in a day.

"Whoa, I mean, there's no end to it. Putting them on pallets. Stacking up pallets with forklifts. Sometimes we're stacking them ten high, sometimes we're stacking them sixteen high. The feed comes down a machine into the sack, it goes on the conveyor belt, and the machine sews it. Then we stack it. When the stack is over our heads, we throw the sacks up. You get it up there the best you can."

Standing five foot nine (in platform shoes), Timothy finds this work physically demanding. Denise tells us that he is "wore out" from the work and that his health has deteriorated in the past year.

For this work, Timothy is paid $7 an hour, with no benefits. Much to our surprise, he tells us that there is not much turnover on the job, "because they know folks want a job. They hold on to people for a good while."

The air in the warehouse where the seed sacks are stored is almost always filled with dust from wheat, oats, and other grains. Although the workers wear face masks to protect their lungs from the dust, one of Timothy's co-workers was hospitalized because of lung damage. We ask whether the employer paid for the medical care and medication. "No, no, no, no, no, no, no." Then we ask whether the injured employee received workers' compensation payments. "No, no, no, no, no, no, no. They don't have it. No benefits, no medical." None of Timothy's jobs has ever paid well or provided health insurance, but he claims that some, such as construction jobs, have been more "lenient" regarding paying for workplace injuries—although, as chapter 5 indicated, construction jobs in fact are not all that "lenient" either.

Timothy injured his knee, tearing cartilage, while on his current job. The knee became infected. The emergency room treated the infection but told him that he needed surgery to correct the torn cartilage, which required a down payment of $1,000. He also was told that without the surgery, he might not be able to use his knee later on. He does not have the $1,000 down payment and has not had the surgery.

We ask whether the hospital referred him to its charity care program.

"No, they just said they will not do nothing till we come up with the first thousand dollars." Timothy suspects that the hospital took this position because he has already incurred medical debt of about $30,000, accumulated over the years in the wake of other injuries and infections.

Both Timothy and Denise have worked their entire lives, yet they have no savings and do not own their house. Nonetheless, Timothy would take a lower-paying job if it provided health benefits. He has never received any sort of basic, ongoing health care, and, after years of hard work, his age has begun to catch up with him. He is experiencing several disturbing symptoms. Without dental care, he has lost quite a few teeth. He knows he needs glasses (he buys them without a prescription at Walgreens for a couple of dollars) but has not had his eyes checked in ten years. He also has been bothered by periodic numbness in his arms; it feels as if he is "losing circulation" in his arms.

Most distressing, Timothy has been experiencing rectal bleeding for a number of years. The bleeding is sporadic: sometimes "it comes out like a woman's period," and sometimes it will stop for a day or so. "So I know there's something that's not right." The bleeding seems to have worsened since he started his current job. He knows he needs to see a doctor. "If I can get a job with medical insurance or something where we'll pay fifty percent and they pay fifty percent, yeah, I'll go have it checked out." This rectal bleeding is particularly problematic, as it may be an early (or, at this point, not so early) sign of colon cancer or other serious illness that could be treated if caught in time but could prove fatal with delays.

RACE, HEALTH, AND HEALTH CARE

Timothy's career path is not unusual for African American men in the United States. Almost one-third of African American workers are employed in low-wage jobs, in contrast to fewer than 20 percent of white workers who hold such jobs. African Americans are three times as likely as whites to have family incomes below the poverty line. Black workers are also more likely than whites to be employed in temporary jobs, which rarely include health care benefits. Moreover, even with comparable levels of education, nonwhites earn less than whites.

Partly because of discrimination in hiring, and partly because they are stuck in low-wage or temporary jobs, black Americans are less likely than white Americans to have health insurance. African Americans make up 12 percent of the workforce but represent 16 percent of the working uninsured. Overall, in 2003, 20.8 percent of black Americans and 35.7 percent of Hispanics were uninsured, compared to 14.5 percent of white Americans (see figure 7).

The gap in insurance rates is part of a larger picture of racial disparities in health outcomes in the United States. African Americans are

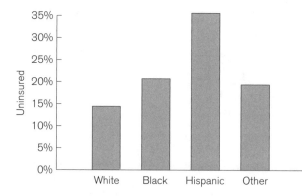

FIGURE 7. The uninsured, by race, under age 65 (first half of 2003). *Source:* Rhoades 2004.

much more likely than whites to die of cancer, heart disease, and diabetes; and the maternal mortality rate for black women is three to four times that among whites. Infant mortality among black children is more than twice that for whites. Life expectancy overall is five years shorter for African Americans, and this disparity is even more marked in poorer areas of the country. African American women are more than twice as likely to die of cervical cancer as white women and are more likely to die of breast cancer than women of any other racial or ethnic group. Overall, 40 percent of black men die prematurely, often from strokes, as do 37 percent of Hispanic men, compared to 21 percent of white men.

Although many factors account for differences in health status, experts agree that good access to appropriate health services could reduce many of these disparities. In spite of their higher mortality and morbidity for cardiovascular disease, African Americans and Hispanics are less likely to receive treatment for these conditions and are especially less likely to receive high-tech cardiac procedures such as cardiac catheterization and coronary revascularization. African American women are diagnosed more frequently than white women with late-stage breast cancer—

probably related to barriers that prevent them from accessing life-saving diagnostic services and treatment.

DENISE'S STORY: "THEY ARE SO PREJUDICED"

For Denise's part, the best job she ever had was at the Caterpillar plant, where she worked for eight years. During that time, she enjoyed excellent benefits, including good health insurance with dental care and full coverage for her three children.

When she became pregnant in 1991, she was working in the Caterpillar paint shop. The work involved cleaning out the inside of large iron vats. Leaning into a vat, she bumped her abdomen on a handle, causing a miscarriage. At the same time, the ongoing strain of the paint shop work injured her back.

She went to a doctor, who told her to stay off work until she felt fully recovered from both the miscarriage and the back injury. But before the doctor released her for work, Caterpillar insisted that she return to the plant. She was fired when she told Caterpillar that she was still unable to work. Denise explains, "I didn't understand these things at first, like people do now. I didn't know then about getting a lawyer or anything about that. So that was just it."

After the Caterpillar experience, Denise worked at a series of jobs as a nurse's assistant. But these jobs typically involved lifting patients, and she was unable to stay for very long at any one nursing home. None of these jobs offered health insurance.

In the mid-1990s, after her children were grown and out of the house, Denise became involved with drugs and alcohol. In 1999, as she puts it, the Lord helped her leave that behind. Since then, she has been an active member of her church community and has learned that she needs to take responsibility for her own life.

At the time of our meeting, she was enrolled in Medicare, receiving disability payments. But she told us that the Medicare would be cut off soon—she just didn't know when. Denise has a number of nagging medical problems with her eyes and her feet and knows she should take care of them before the Medicare runs out, but she is not quite sure how to go about this. In any case, Medicare does not cover prescription medication, so she isn't really convinced that going to the doctor will do much good.

Compounding her anxiety about her health is the fear that she will never again be able to find a good job. Over the past year, she has picked up some casual work at a beauty parlor, but nursing jobs seem to have dried up, and she believes that she has no hope of landing the kind of job that will provide long-term employment or health benefits. Denise's assessment of her job prospects is probably correct, for two somewhat different reasons.

First, when the large manufacturing plants in Decatur close or move abroad, the government and the unions provide job retraining programs for the workers who are laid off. One of the most popular programs offers certification as a hospital aide or a certified nurse's aide (CNA), work that had not previously required formal training or certification, at least in the Decatur area. Given the long history of racial and gender discrimination in the town's factories and labor unions, this kind of service-sector work had been an extremely important job niche for African American women, who were unlikely to land the higher-paying manufacturing jobs with union contracts.

But the new job training programs available to "displaced" manufacturing employees now are turning out large numbers of white men and women who have received free training and certification, giving them an advantage in the health service–sector job market. African American women we spoke to in Decatur told us, in puzzlement, that it had always been easy to find jobs as a nurse's aide but that all the jobs have now begun to demand certification. Like Denise, these women didn't know what this certification was or how to go about getting it. (They would not have been eligible for the job retraining programs, in any case, since they were not officially classified as "displaced workers.")

A second issue that affects Denise's chances of landing a good job is her felony history (drug related). This record will make it impossible for her to work at a nursing home or hospital

With the three-strikes-you're-out policy and tougher drug laws (an issue we return to in chapter 10), U.S. prisons increasingly are filled with minorities who have been arrested on minor drug charges. These charges are now classified as felonies, making it nearly impossible for people like Denise to find a job. As Marc Mauer notes, "Prisons in the United States are increasingly serving as institutions of the poor and minorities. Half of all prison inmates today are African American and 16% are Hispanic; their median annual income prior to incarceration was less than $10,000."

We ask Denise and Timothy what it is like for an African American family to try to arrange health care, without insurance, in the mostly white towns of southern Illinois. "Well, if they ain't got no money, black people ain't going to get nothing," Denise asserts. "With white people, they overlook [medical bills], but some, a lot of them here in Decatur, they're so prejudiced. They are so prejudiced."

Denise recalls an incident from a couple of years ago. "I called for a job that I saw advertised. And they told me that they need a person right then, right then, right then. I was talking on the phone. I guess I talk like I'm not a black person. And I was talking, and he said, 'Oh, come on. I need somebody right away. I'll guarantee that I'll hire you. Come on in.' Well, I went in, sit down, and talk to him, and he said, 'Oh, I'm sorry, I've already filled that position.' Now that really hurt me. He had told me to come on in, yes, because I had experience in that job. When he seen the color of my skin, that was it."

Denise's experience is not unique. A number of large-scale studies document that when well-matched pairs of black and white job applicants apply for the same advertised jobs, the black applicant is less likely to be offered the job.

Denise and Timothy are not interested in public aid. As Denise says,

"I'd rather work and make my own money with the strength that God gave me." They also do not relish the paperwork and personal questions that people must answer in order to receive public aid. But they would like the government to make health care available to people like themselves who don't have a lot of money but are not (yet) "flat-out" broke.

CHAPTER TEN

DESCENT THROUGH THE DEATH SPIRAL

CASTE IN AMERICA

Throughout this book, we use the word *caste* to describe an emerging group of Americans who are stuck in a stigmatized cycle of illness and marginal employment. The characteristics, beliefs, and restrictions that both define and reinforce the idea that such a caste system exists include the following:

- Commonly acknowledged and easily recognized distinctions between different levels of the caste hierarchy. We argue, for example, that rotten teeth and obesity often distinguish members of America's lower caste.

- A belief that caste status is passed on from parents to children. In the United States, this belief is sometimes expressed in terms of contempt for pregnant teenagers and "welfare mothers." On a more concrete level, one might argue that caste status is passed on via poor educational opportunities, deficient prenatal care, and substandard pediatric care.

- Differential evaluation and rewards associated with different castes. Castes are ranked in terms of their "intrinsic worth." We think here of America's traditional valorization of hard work and good jobs and negative stereotypes such as "welfare queens."

- Attribution of moral stigma or physical "pollution" to members of the lower caste. In American society, moral stigma is frequently attached to psychiatric diagnoses, and physical illness often is construed as polluting.

- Stigmatization of sexual contact between castes. Historically, legal restrictions were imposed in terms of race. Nowadays, sexual contact may be stigmatized in terms of the spread of HIV/AIDS.

- Restricted mobility within the caste system. The link between employment and health care traps individuals within the death spiral.

Some scholars and journalists have used the term *underclass* in much the same way we use the term *caste* in this book.* Sociologist Herbert Gans argues that the term *underclass* typically is invoked as a pejorative label invented to describe poor people who are accused, rightly or wrongly, of "failing to behave in the 'mainstream' ways of the numerically or culturally dominant American middle class. This behavioral def-

---

*We prefer the term *caste* because it references the entire social system rather than one group of people. For close to a century, scholars have debated whether the designation *caste* makes sense only in reference to the particular religio-social organization of traditional Indian society or whether the term can be used more broadly to describe highly stratified societies found around the world. Among those who argue for the former position are Edmund Leach (1960) and Louis Dumont (1980). Those who take the latter position include Fredrik Barth (1969), George De Vos (1967), Gerald Berreman (1967), and Lucile Duberman (1976). Ursula Sharma cogently suggests that we think of "castification" as a social and political process by which ethnic or other groups become part of a ranked order: "If we think in terms of process rather than form we do not have to get bogged down in the problem of whether a group is a 'caste' . . . but can focus on the more constructive question of the direction in which current change is moving" (1999, p. 93).

inition denominates poor people who drop out of school, do not work, and, if they are young women, have babies without benefit of marriage and go on welfare. The behavioral underclass also includes the homeless, beggars and panhandlers, poor addicts to alcohol or drugs, and street criminals."

Gans and other sociologists explain that the existence of an underclass serves as a warning that keeps "mainstream" Americans in line. The visibility of the underclass in settings such as homeless shelters and prisons is a powerful encouragement to the rest of "us" to abide by normative values, standards, and life practices in order to avoid such a fate.

This observation helps us understand why American society is doing so little to combat the process of caste formation. *Inasmuch as the association between employment and health coverage conjoins core American beliefs in the merit of work and the virtue of health, the possibility that unemployment can serve as a "punishment" for poor health and poor health can serve as a "punishment" for unemployment is compelling indeed.* The strength of these beliefs has reached new heights in modern U.S. society, as the moral value of work has become legislated, through the welfare reform of the 1990s, and as theories assigning ultimate responsibility to the ill for falling sick have surged in popularity. This discourse is most explicit in regard to HIV/AIDS, but it is also invoked in regard to obesity, mental illness, tooth decay, cancer, and many other diseases.

WEIGHT AND TEETH AS CASTE MARKERS

Loretta and Greg, the Mississippi family whose story opened this book, embody the life experiences of the new American caste of the ill, infirm, and marginally employed. In a series of conversations, Loretta talked about how her part-time job did not provide health insurance, how her husband's small business could not possibly allow them to pay for health coverage, how poor living conditions damaged the health of her entire family, and how the meager patchwork care available to working-poor families like hers really did not solve any of their health problems.

But of all the experiences she shared with us, the one we simply cannot erase from our minds is how she pulls out her own teeth when the pain becomes unbearable. Not able to afford a visit to the dentist, on more than one occasion Loretta has grabbed hold of an aching tooth, closed her eyes, told herself that once it's over she'll feel some relief, and yanked hard.

Most of our interviewees raised the issue of their teeth. Gina, the young hair stylist we met in Idaho, covered her mouth with her hand during our entire interview because she was embarrassed about her rotting teeth. Daniel, the Mississippi construction worker, used his pliers to yank out decayed and aching teeth. Almost every time we asked interviewees what their first priority would be if the president established universal health coverage tomorrow, the immediate answer was "my teeth."*

All over the country, we heard that untreated dental problems can be incredibly painful, leading people to the medicine cabinet, the liquor cabinet, or both in search of relief. And we learned that overuse of medication or alcohol leads to further obstacles to employability, health insurance, and access to medical and dental care—a pattern typical of the death spiral.

Dental problems frequently mix and match with other chronic diseases to create illness cycles that prove especially difficult to break. Because they affect the ability to chew, untreated dental problems tend to exacerbate conditions such as diabetes or heart disease. Being limited to soft foods is particularly problematic for people with diabetes, who must be careful to eat well in order to control blood sugar levels. Missing and rotten teeth make it painful if not impossible to chew fruits, whole-grain foods, salads, or many of the fiber-rich foods recommended

*Almost no state Medicaid programs cover dental services for adults, and very few free clinics provide dentistry. As a result, there is a notable shortage of dentists in most poorer parts of the country. Some counties that we visited in Mississippi, for instance, do not have a single dentist willing to take Medicaid or uninsured patients.

by doctors and nutrition experts. Typical daily diets for those who cannot chew tend to include large quantities of processed lunch meats, mashed potatoes, and cream soups—food choices that are particularly bad for people with diabetes. To make matters worse, healthy foods also tend to be more expensive, priced out of reach of families such as Loretta's.

Like Loretta, many of the women we interviewed look heavier than current standards of beauty or fitness would dictate. As sociologists Peter Freund and Meredith McGuire explain, weight has become a marker of socioeconomic status in the United States. Studies show that poorer women are far more likely to be obese than wealthy women (six times more likely in one study), that opportunities to consume a healthy diet and to exercise are more abundant for the well-to-do, and that different groups in American society assign different social and moral meanings to body size. The stigma associated with obesity, as signifying a lack of impulse control, echoes the well-entrenched belief among the affluent that poor people are less capable of governing their impulses. "Dieting and fitness rituals are primarily a middle- and upper-class phenomenon. . . . [I]n middle-class American culture fat symbolizes loss of self-control . . . [and] obesity is strongly stigmatized," argue Freund and McGuire.

They cite a study in which ten- and eleven-year-old children indicated less interest in forming friendships with obese children than with children who were unable to walk or children with facial disfigurements. Negative feelings toward obesity continue into adulthood: other studies document discrimination against overweight people in education, rental housing, and—in keeping with the workings of the death spiral—employment.

Obesity is a health risk (though not necessarily to the extent that middle-class Americans have come to believe) and has been linked to high blood pressure, stress on the musculoskeletal system, and complications of diabetes. Although members of the medical community disagree about the extent to which weight problems are to blame for a long list of medical problems, there is consensus that obesity is not optimal for health. Thus, one would expect, in a rational system health care services would be more available to those who are at high risk because of their weight. The opposite seems to be the case, however. Following the logic of the death spiral, obesity—like rotted teeth—has become a caste marker, making Americans like Loretta less employable and thus less likely to have the ongoing access to health care that they need in order to "escape" their caste label.

When we recall the many times we heard comments about the physical appearance of people like Loretta, one conversation stands out. One day in rural Idaho, we sat down in the playground with a group of mothers, health care professionals, and teachers. This group, called the Read to Me Coalition, organizes a variety of programs to encourage families, clinics, and schools to be more attentive to early childhood development. As happens often at coalition meetings, the conversation came around to "those people" (members of what we call the caste of the ill, infirm, and marginally employed) who don't do the things they "should" to raise their children "properly."

"A lot of people around here have untreated dental [problems]. And they actually need care, starting with the kids. The mothers just stick bottles in their mouths all the time. The mothers are just unable to take care of their kids. They're stretched beyond their limits. They might be working. They're just not educated enough. The kids get bottle rot. And they're not covered by any kind of insurance, so their teeth rot. The kids eventually, then, might need oral surgery. In any case, because of the rotten teeth, the kids end up having delayed speech and needing developmental help, which they might or might not get, depending on the circumstances [of the school and family]."

These middle-class women identified bad teeth as a sign of poor parenting, low educational achievement, and slow or faulty intellectual development. Loretta, Gina, and many other people we interviewed know very well what rotten teeth signify in America today. They may not use the same words, but they understand that teeth have become one of the clearest outward markers of caste, presenting to the world the "face of poverty." Dale Maharidge and Michael Williamson report the words of Debbie, a working-class woman in Alabama in the 1980s, who described this face vividly: "There are two classes: those with rotten teeth, with no sign of ever having had any professional dental care, and those whose teeth are perfect. . . . Some of the rotten-teeth people have accents that set them apart even from other southerners."

Set apart—that is the essence of caste. Set apart in low-wage jobs with no possibility of advancement. (Though poor teeth or obesity may not cause someone to lose a job, either condition can certainly interfere with getting a good job.) Set apart in crowded emergency rooms and low-income clinics. Set apart in homeless shelters, which our interviewees understand as the bottom of the death spiral. Set apart in prisons that are overpopulated with the chronically ill, the mentally ill, and the poor.

RESOURCES AND THE RATE OF DESCENT THROUGH THE DEATH SPIRAL

Not everyone descends through the death spiral at the same rate, and not everyone who enters through one of its portals becomes a permanent member of the caste of the ill, infirm, and marginally employed. Broadly put, the resources one can muster serve as handholds, slowing down or breaking one's fall. These resources can include a healthy spouse, homeownership, strong community networks, insider knowledge about how to access free or low-cost care, and hearty mental health, which comprises good coping skills, resourcefulness, persistence, and the ability to fight off the stress and depression that often accompany unemployment and physical illness. Nevertheless, for the overwhelming majority of Americans, if enough disasters strike all at once, those handholds quickly become slippery indeed.

At the time we interviewed them, the people introduced in this book were at different points in the death spiral. Dave and Judy, described in chapter 1, illustrate what we have come to see as a crucial tipping point, right in the middle of the death spiral. Although many things have gone very wrong for them—both in their personal lives and in the economy of the Rust Belt—they do have some important resources that have kept their descent relatively gradual: for example, a loving marriage, a middle-class demeanor (both are slim and have teeth that look "nice" to a casual observer), and some possessions that can be sold to pay the bills (at least for the time being). Most notable in the credit column is that they own their home. Most notable in the debit column is that they need to sell their home in order to give Judy a chance to heal her emotional pain. But property values have declined precipitously in their community; if they sell their house and leave town, they could end up homeless—at the terrifying bottom of the death spiral.

Several other people we met have substantial handholds. Rachel, the young dancer/day care center worker/typist, can go to her physician parents for financial assistance, a place to live, and connections to medical providers if her cervical dysplasia develops into cancer. Jamie, the young Illinois mother with a special-needs son and a high risk of diabetes, is happily married to a healthy and hard-working man; is blessed with exceptional organizational and managerial skills, which she applies to her household budgeting and other domestic tasks; and has purchased a home for a reasonable price (next to the railroad tracks and a highway) at a good commuting distance from Champaign-Urbana. She also is physically attractive and verbally articulate and has an associate degree in early childhood education. All of these advantages serve as buffers to the death spiral's gravitational pull.

Many more of the people we met have access to resources that may turn out to be too precarious or too weak to slow their descent significantly. Rae and Martin are well-educated professionals and loving parents. Yet Martin's severe coronary disease and their son's chronic mental health problems are likely to be too much for the family to handle. Roberta, the divorced professor in Illinois, knows how to advocate for herself and has rich community networks. Still, with her insecure employment status as an adjunct professor and the enormous costs of cancer treatment, Roberta may descend more quickly than she ever would have dreamed. Denise and Timothy have two important hand-holds: a loving marriage and a strong church community. But these key resources are unlikely to be enough to offset the accelerating impact of racism, Denise's past felony conviction, the toll taken on Timothy's body by decades of hard physical labor, and the absence of high-placed connections who can help them find better-paying or more secure jobs.

Others have even fewer resources. Guadalupe's severe mental illness is off-putting to neighbors and employers alike, and Elena's poor English skills limit her ability to advocate on her daughter's behalf. It is hard to imagine their descent slowing. They do own their home, but it is in a *colonia*. They are immigrants and thus do not have deep social networks in the United States. And Elena is a widow, which, as chapter 3 suggests, places her at greater risk for a quick slide down the spiral. Annette, the Mississippi woman who continues to suffer from visual impairment and chronic head pain as the result of abuse by her former husband, has no specific job skills, no parents or other family members to support her, and no strong community networks (she moved to Mississippi to get away from her husband). She does not own a home, has few prospects for good employment in post-NAFTA Mississippi, and is less than savvy about accessing public assistance and otherwise managing her money.

For the vast majority of the people we interviewed, emotional or psychological distress—of one sort or another—added to and magnified all their other struggles and canceled out the possibility of using many of the resources that might have been available to them. For almost all (Guadalupe actually is an exception), this distress was not what initially pulled them into the death spiral but rather was acquired as they began their slide. Once acquired, however, it became part of their personal journeys, adding to the stigma of being members of the caste of the ill, infirm, and marginally employable and making it more difficult for them to put the brakes on their descent. Psychiatric disabilities function like chemical catalysts, intensifying the pull of the death spiral, opening additional portals, and generally hastening an individual's fall.

The trajectory experienced by many of our interviewees (Dave and Judy are good examples) reflects this course of events: employment problems (downsizing, low wages, loss of a job), poor access to health care, rising stress over the job situation and the health care situation, emotional/psychological distress, decreasing employability, more severe emotional/psychological distress, and so on.

A surprisingly large number of those we interviewed, including Dave and Judy, had been given prescriptions for an antidepressant, either paying to fill the prescription themselves or receiving the medication at no charge from a free clinic. Therapy or counseling, however, was not available to them. To our minds, it seems unlikely that Prozac or Zoloft will stop anyone's descent through the death spiral. It certainly did not seem to be helping Dave and Judy. Instead, it contributed to their feeling that something was wrong with them (after all, their long-time family physician wrote the prescriptions for both of them) rather than wrong with our society. Taking a broader view, one of the union organizers in Danville, Illinois, told us, *"People around here need jobs, not Prozac."*

WHERE ARE THE BODIES? THE FINAL DESCENT

When we began work on this book, we saw ourselves as cartographers, mapping the portals into a death spiral that seems to be drawing in increasing numbers of Americans. Our research was not aimed at understanding the experiences of those who had hit bottom, but rather at learning about those who had "done all the right things" but still found themselves pulled in.

Yet we felt unable to end our journey without asking the next logical questions: What is the next step down for Judy and Dave? What will happen if he gets sicker (which is likely, considering his multiple chronic health problems and his inability to buy the medication to control them) and if Decatur's economy does not pick up (also likely, since none of the plants show any sign of reopening)? Will Kim decide, against her better judgment, to get pregnant in order to be eligible for Medicaid? Will Edna's mother and daughter end up institutionalized? Will Steve and Mary Ann's "self-medication" cross the line into full-fledged alcoholism?

Quite simply, we couldn't close this book without peering a bit further down the death spiral. Here, then, we move beyond the stories of our own interviewees and explore how the issue of health insurance fits into the wider picture of caste creation in America today.

Homelessness

> It is clear to experienced homeless providers and advocates that far too much effort is expended in this country in trying to keep "unworthy" people from obtaining public health insurance, and that not enough resources and energy are devoted to increasing access to comprehensive health care.
>
> Patricia Post, *Casualties of Complexity: Why Eligible Homeless People Are Not Enrolled in Medicaid*

For many Americans, medical problems raise the specter of homelessness. Although none of our interviewees were homeless at the time we spoke to them, at least one had a lien taken out against his home by the county indigent committee (the social welfare arm of the county government, which had helped pay his hospital bills). Several had experienced periods of homelessness previously, and several others had just barely managed to avoid homelessness for the time being. (In one case, a woman in her late fifties was allowed to live in a municipal senior citizens' housing complex that had vacant apartments, but there was no guarantee that she would be allowed to stay if "legitimate" senior citizens wanted to move in.) Other individuals had disappeared from their homes when we went back to visit them a second or third time.

The frequency with which our interviewees spoke of the fear of losing their homes points to a live link between lack of insurance and homelessness. Dave and Judy are holding on to their house near the railroad tracks, even though the train whistles are driving Judy out of her mind. John, the Idaho bartender, sands down the bones in his feet because he'd rather pay rent than pay the doctor—in his words, he doesn't want to "sleep out in the street." Misty and Nathaniel, Loretta and Greg—both families were gone from their homes when we went back to talk to them a few months after our initial interviews.

Homeless individuals are sicker than other Americans. Rene Jahiel, who has summarized a number of local studies, writes that 33 percent of homeless respondents report their health as poor, compared to 18 percent of the general population; 48 percent of homeless respondents describe their health as fair, while only 21 percent of the general population do so. Rates of arthritis, asthma, diabetes, elevated blood pressure, and myriad other chronic conditions are far above the average in homeless populations. According to research conducted by the Community Health Advisory Information Network at Columbia University's School of Public Health, one out of four people living with HIV in New York City is homeless or marginally housed at any given time. Interestingly, several studies have documented extraordinarily high rates of dental disorders (up to 50 percent), including missing teeth, in a large-scale sample of homeless men and women in Baltimore.

Newspapers and academic studies typically attribute the poor health of homeless individuals to the unhealthy living conditions on the street and in shelters and to the paucity of available health care services.* While these observations are at least in part correct, our research points to a

---

*One might expect that Medicaid—the health care safety net—would serve the needs of homeless Americans. In reality, the complexity and diversity of state Medicaid programs, and a variety of limitations on eligibility, present significant barriers for impoverished people who lack residential stability, especially for those without the capacity to document their eligibility in prescribed ways. In two Los Angeles studies, more than 80 percent of homeless people had no medical coverage of any kind, and fewer than 10 percent were covered by Medicaid. In another California study of homeless people, only 22 percent of those with severe mental disorders and 9 percent of others were enrolled in MediCal (the state's Medicaid program). See Post 2001.

somewhat more complex chicken-and-egg scenario. *Adding to the conventional notion of causality—that homelessness leads to poor health—we suggest that poor health leads to unemployability, weakened coping abilities, diminished social support and resources, and medical debt and bankruptcy, which lead to homelessness.* Being homeless then leads to worse health and a more problematic outward appearance (it's hard to be well groomed when living in a shelter), which in turn reduces the chances of finding a good job with insurance, causing even worse health and continued homelessness. The final outcome is starkly reflected in the statistic cited in the introduction to this book—a mortality rate among the homeless that is four times higher than the death rate among the general U.S. population.*

THE MENTAL HEALTH FACTOR   While only 4 percent of the U.S. population overall has a serious mental illness, five to six times as many people who are homeless (20 to 25 percent) have serious mental health problems. Their diagnoses encompass the most personally disruptive and serious mental illnesses, including severe, chronic depression; bipolar disorder; schizophrenia; and severe personality disorders.

The popular press often attributes the rise of homelessness in America to the deinstitutionalization of hospitalized psychiatric patients during the 1960s. Yet the relationship between psychiatric disabilities and homelessness is far more complex. The number of inpatient treatment beds that were lost accounts for only a tiny portion of the vast increase in the number of homeless individuals. Numerous studies demonstrate that only about 5 percent of those who are currently homeless may actually need institutionalization. Most are capable of functioning with varying levels of community support.

*Jahiel (1992) notes substantial evidence of the special health risks encountered by the homeless, including an unusually high frequency of cellulitis (a complication of untreated or poorly managed trauma or local infections); a high rate of other trauma-related diagnoses such as lacerations, fractures, and head traumas; and a frequency of rape victimization that in some areas is reportedly fifteen times higher than in the general population.

Deinstitutionalization was never meant to deprive mentally ill people of medical services; rather, the intent was to provide services that were more humane and less likely to infringe on personal freedom and dignity. The deinstitutionalization movement assumed that community mental health services would grow and serve more people. Unfortunately, however, cuts in mental health and other social services have severely limited the availability of community-based treatment and support. Local communities often have compounded the problem by resisting the establishment of community-based mental health facilities, especially group homes, in their neighborhoods.

The United States is the only Western nation that attributes homelessness to mental illness. European scholars, studies, and homeless advocacy groups explain homelessness in terms of governmental housing policies, the housing market, lack of government-sponsored support services that help to normalize employment situations, and a paucity of organizations offering legal protection for the homeless. For example, Brian Harvey, an Irish scholar and executive board member of FEANTSA (European Federation of National Organizations Working with the Homeless), writes that homelessness is "associated with and linked to much larger issues of social exclusion, poverty, unemployment and the appropriate role of the state in the late 20th century."

The contrast between this European analysis and the U.S. analysis that identifies homelessness with mental health problems suggests that particular attitudes and policies in the United States turn mental illness into a death spiral mechanism that leads downward to homelessness. Chief among these attitudes and policies, as we argue, are the normative link between employment and health care and pervasive discrimination against people with psychiatric disabilities. Specific government policies also reinforce these attitudes and institutions. In a recent study, the National Health Care for the Homeless Council surveyed 193 clients who had lost their SSI or SSDI benefits in the preceding twelve months. Slightly more than half had lost benefits because of the new alcohol and substance abuse elimination provisions (discussed in chapter 8). This study found that 76 percent of individuals who had been paying for their own housing before losing their benefits had subsequently lost their housing and were living in shelters, on the streets, with friends and relatives, or in a treatment facility.

THE SPECIAL CASE OF VETERANS   Veterans of military service are overrepresented among homeless men. According to the National Coalition for Homeless Veterans, as of January 2004 approximately 33 percent of homeless men are veterans, although veterans represent only 23 percent of the general adult male population.

Linda Boone, executive director of the National Coalition for Homeless Veterans, shared her thoughts about why the rate of homelessness among veterans—a group that our society claims to honor and respect—is so high. Boone notes that aspects of the military experience itself may lead to impaired independent functioning in the civilian world. She traces a trajectory that resembles our own understanding of the death spiral: mental health problems (sometimes related to post-traumatic stress disorder) that lead to self-medication and substance abuse, which lead to homelessness and its attendant physical health problems—and end with no way out.

The Veterans Administration operates a health care system that is intended to meet the special needs of those who have served in the military. Although, in many ways, the VA medical system comes closer than any other American institution to the kind of publicly guaranteed universal health care system that we endorse, multiple problems beset it. First, the VA system has a complicated scale of ranking priorities for use of their facilities, and many veterans find themselves excluded. In addition, personnel shortages and deteriorating physical facilities mean that not even all eligible veterans can access the care they need.

Second, the system has, over the years, become oriented toward long-term institutionalization and the care of chronic illness, primarily for the elderly. In our interviews, we found that many younger and middle-aged veterans did not know that they might be eligible for care through the

VA. Moreover, many were unable to use the VA services in a meaningful way, especially for acute problems, because no VA facility was located nearby.

Third, the VA system has not been particularly successful at dealing with mental health problems, especially in the post-Vietnam era. In fact, studies have shown that extraordinarily high percentages of Vietnam-era veterans have sought discharge from VA psychiatric facilities against medical advice. Linda Boone specifically notes the negative impact of recent reductions in the VA's mental health system. Finally, the ambivalence with which the VA medical system relates to drug-related problems and to contested issues such as Gulf War Syndrome and the effects of Agent Orange reduces its effectiveness in providing adequate health care and housing solutions for many veterans.

Most of today's homeless veterans served during the Vietnam era. They returned home from an unpopular war at a time of high unemployment, and only a relatively small percentage found jobs that utilized skills they had acquired in the military. They also returned home with rates of health problems unknown in previous wars. Rapid helicopter evacuation and sophisticated medical science combined to save thousands of soldiers who would have died in earlier wars. "But," according to Paul Starr, author of *The Discarded Army: Veterans after Vietnam*, "progress in reducing deaths has not been matched by progress in restoring health. More men come home, but more come home with severe and permanent injuries." This includes both amputations and paralysis as the direct result of combat injuries, the effects of widespread drug use among soldiers serving in Vietnam, and the impact of chemicals that were used as part of military operations in Southeast Asia.

Fred Milano, author of "Gulf War Syndrome: The 'Agent Orange' of the Nineties," explains that from 1962 to 1971 the United States sprayed nineteen million gallons of herbicides over five million acres of South Vietnam to defoliate the jungle. Approximately three hundred thousand Americans and uncounted thousands of Vietnamese were exposed to significant levels of dioxin, the primary ingredient in Agent Orange and an extremely powerful carcinogen. These U.S. veterans returned home with a disturbing array of physical disorders: cancer; liver and kidney malfunctions; skin problems; vision and hearing impairments; and degenerative nerve diseases.

The response by the U.S. government was largely one of denial and delay. Eventually, veterans and veterans' organizations sued the makers of dioxin and received a $180 million out-of-court settlement, the largest mass damage award ever negotiated. But eligible and surviving veterans received an average of less than $6,000 each, clearly not enough to preclude future homelessness.

Milano further reports that, in the aftermath of the Persian Gulf war, more than one hundred thousand of the seven hundred thousand U.S. troops who served in the region reported a mysterious cluster of severe health problems that came to be called Gulf War Syndrome. Symptoms include chronic fatigue, memory loss, headaches, joint and muscle pain, bleeding gums, numbness in limbs, dizziness, night sweats, and disorientation. Initially, the Pentagon dismissed the complaints and ruled out systematic investigation. Under pressure, some preliminary studies were conducted; they concluded that most of the symptoms could be attributed to post-traumatic stress syndrome, a finding that was quickly challenged by veterans' groups.

In 1996, the Pentagon finally admitted that more than twenty-five thousand troops had been "in the vicinity" when arms depots were blown up in Kamisiyah in March 1991. These explosions released huge clouds of mustard gas and the deadly nerve gas sarin. In addition, U.S. soldiers had been given experimental drugs to protect them against anticipated chemical and biological warfare. One of the drugs, pryidostigmine bromide, which was given to four hundred thousand military personnel, is known to cause extensive neurological damage. Moreover, during Operation Desert Storm, the U.S. military for the first time used munitions made of depleted uranium, which is also a probable cause of a variety of kidney, liver, and bone marrow problems.

As of this writing, the existence of Gulf War Syndrome and the need for these veterans to receive comprehensive health and other support services are still being contested by medical experts and the Pentagon. And, while these veterans remain caught in the death spiral, Linda Boone reports that the National Coalition for Homeless Veterans is already seeing homeless veterans of the latest Iraq war.

Incarceration

> On any given day, at least 284,000 schizophrenic and manic depressive individuals are incarcerated, and 547,800 are on probation.
>
> Representative Ted Strickland of Ohio, 2003

The United States has the highest incarceration rate in the world, a rate that has increased significantly over the past twenty years: as of June 2003, 2.1 million people were incarcerated in U.S. jails and prisons, with African American men being incarcerated at a rate seven times higher than that of white men.* America's prisons have become a vast, if seldom discussed, domicile for the sick and dying.

The single most important factor contributing to the growth of prison populations since 1985 has been the enormous rise in the number of drug offenders sentenced to prison. Approximately 23 percent of

---

*At midyear 2003, there were 4,834 black male prisoners per 100,000 black males in the United States, and 681 white male inmates per 100,000 white males (U.S. Department of Justice 2003). Michael Katz writes (1989): "Two groups— black teenage mothers and black jobless youths—[have] dominated the images of the underclass. The former received the most attention, and antipoverty policy, redefined as welfare reform, came to mean intervening in the alleged cycle of dependency in which young, unmarried black women and their children had become trapped. Black males became less a problem for social welfare and more one for the police. Instead of training and employment, public policy responded by putting more of them in jail."

inmates of state prisons and 60 percent of inmates of federal prisons currently are incarcerated on drug-related offenses. Even more prisoners
are addicted to drugs or alcohol, though their incarceration is not officially drug related. According to estimates, more than half of prisoners
have a diagnosable drug use disorder, and one-quarter have an alcohol
use disorder.

The rationale behind incarcerating drug users is that locking them up
will reduce the demand for drugs, thus making drug trafficking less profitable. However, most regular drug users are unable to break their habit
without substantial and continual medical, psychological, and social
assistance, which they do not receive in prison. An estimated 70 to 85
percent of inmates currently need substance abuse treatment services,
but only 10 to 13 percent actually receive them. If, as mental health and
public health experts have been saying for decades, addictions are diseases, then we, as a society, are filling our prisons with citizens whose
"crime" is illness and who may well have turned to drugs in the first
place in order to self-medicate physical, emotional, or social pain.

Drug addicts are far from the only ill Americans sitting in jails. Prisoners have higher rates of HIV infection, hepatitis C infection, chronic
lung disease, musculoskeletal disorders, and sexually transmitted diseases than Americans who are not incarcerated. Tuberculosis is a striking case in point: of all Americans with active TB in 1996, an estimated
35 percent served time in a correctional facility that year.

The health profile of women prisoners is particularly distressing.
More than 40 percent report having been physically and/or sexually
abused before incarceration. Two-thirds report using drugs regularly
before their incarceration, and more than 40 percent used drugs daily.
Compared to male prisoners, women inmates have higher rates of HIV
infection and other sexually transmitted diseases and are in greater need
of mental health services. It might sound far-fetched to claim that
women are being punished for being physically or sexually abused, but
if we recall the discussion of the long-term health problems faced by
women victims of violence (recall Annette's headaches and distorted

vision), we begin to see a trajectory that goes from abuse to physical and emotional distress to self-medication via drugs or alcohol to unemployability to jail.

Andrea Weisman, a nationally recognized mental health researcher, writes that among people who are seriously mentally ill in the United States today, more than twice as many receive services in jails and prisons as in public psychiatric hospitals. According to estimates, as many as 40 percent of all seriously mentally ill people in the United States may be incarcerated.

Once in jail, the mentally ill are more likely than other prisoners to be physically harmed and to be placed in administrative segregation or solitary confinement. Indeed, the conditions of brutality and confinement in jail are likely to make even healthy men and women experience symptoms of mental illness. What these conditions do to those who already are mentally ill is horrifying to contemplate.

Upon release from prison, matters do not improve. Liz Lipton, a medical and legal journalist and researcher, explains that when inmates with mental illness begin their jail terms, they often lose eligibility for Medicaid or federal disability benefits. When they are released, restoring that eligibility takes a substantial amount of time, leaving many without health care coverage for long periods. Without SSI, SSDI, or Medicaid, they are more likely to end up in the emergency room or back in jail, according to the Bazelon Center for Mental Health Law.

The picture we have painted here is one in which incarceration is used punitively to punish Americans who have been branded by stigmatized medical conditions or social identities. Similarly, denial of access to social services is used to punish those who are deemed to be, in some way, unworthy. Thus, in 1980, Congress denied SSI benefits to convicted criminals. In 1994, Congress further denied SSI benefits to people who had been accused of crimes punishable by imprisonment for more than one year but who were found not guilty by reason of insanity.

Americans who need but cannot access medical treatment in the outside world are more likely to end up in jail than healthier Americans.

Once inside the prison system, they sometimes (temporarily) receive the medical care that might have lessened their chances of being incarcerated in the first place. In the long run, however, incarceration strengthens rather than breaks the clutches of the death spiral, both because of the unhealthy living conditions inside prisons and because a record of incarceration limits employment possibilities. In language evocative of the death spiral, Andrea Weisman notes, "One third of all individuals in jails and prisons today—more than half a million people—are parole or conditional release violators. Perhaps the only sure result of being incarcerated is being reincarcerated."

A final irony of the death spiral: across the country in communities where plant closures have resulted in massive job loss, prisons offer a thriving new economic niche. In Danville, Illinois, interviewees told us that the only significant new jobs are in the prison that has just been built to accommodate young men, most of them African American, shipped downstate from the Chicago area. In the town of Berlin, New Hampshire—population one hundred thousand, down from a booming two hundred thousand in the wake of closure of paper and lumber mills—a new federal prison currently is under construction. In a radio interview on National Public Radio on March 31, 2004, the mayor of Berlin extolled the benefits that the new prison would bring to the town. Hundreds of workers who had been laid off in the manufacturing sector and had lost their health insurance will have their coverage resume if they are hired to work in the prison. In a ripple effect, the mayor announced, this will also open up employment at the local hospitals, giving many who had been laid off from the paper and lumber mills new hospital jobs caring for those lucky enough to land the new prison jobs.

CHAPTER ELEVEN

MOVING FORWARD

Florence Nightingale was one of the first people to understand the importance of good nutrition, fresh air, and cleanliness in medical recovery. And that was really her revolution in medicine—if you want patients to recover, give them good food, give them fresh air, give them a clean place to be. She believed that hospitals just cannot be kept clean enough over the long term, so that every twenty years, they just need to be burned down and rebuilt, so that there can be a clean and healthy facility. And that's what I have to say about the health care system. It needs to be burned down and rebuilt.

Katherine, uninsured emergency room nurse, Mississippi

PRINCIPLES FOR REFORM

We completed work on this book during the 2004 election year and spent many hours thinking about how the proposals floated by various candidates and other groups might affect the uninsured men and women we had met across the country.

The United States has a long history of attempts at structural health care reform. Nearly every modern president, both Democratic and Republican, from Teddy Roosevelt through Richard Nixon and Bill Clinton, has proposed changes to at least part of the health care system. Incremental alterations have indeed been implemented, some of which—the institution of Medicaid and Medicare, for example—are quite significant, but systematic and structural change continues to elude our society.

At this time, dozens of proposals for health care reform have been put on the table by political parties, advocacy groups, unions, foundations, academics, and think tanks. Our goal in this book is not to add another detailed proposal to this mix. Rather, based on our understanding of what it means to be uninsured in America today, we offer these six principles for reform.

1. INCREMENTAL SOLUTIONS TO EXPAND THE SAFETY NET, WHILE BENEFICIAL IN THE SHORT RUN, ARE WHOLLY INADEQUATE TO SOLVE THE PROBLEM IN THE LONG TERM.

Most current proposals designed to address the problems of the uninsured come down to widening the existing safety net. Many suggest expanding eligibility for public insurance programs—lowering the eligibility age for Medicare from sixty-five to fifty-five, for instance, or expanding Medicaid/SCHIP (State Children's Health Insurance Program) to cover young adults up to age twenty-five. Others would increase the income limits for Medicaid and SCHIP to 200 or 300 percent of the federal poverty line or use the programs to cover parents as well as poor children. Still other proposals seek to expand the number of federally qualified health centers to serve the uninsured or encourage the formation of more church-based or other charity clinics.

These proposals, while helpful to some of the uninsured in the short term, would not eliminate the structural barriers that both consumers and providers face in giving and getting adequate care. Many groups, such as the caregivers of both the young and the old (described in chapter 4), would still fall through the cracks. Nor does expanded eligibility solve the problem, faced by almost all our interviewees, of gaining and losing benefits whenever their personal situation changes or their state's rules are altered.

Andrew Bolton, an outreach worker at Boundary Community Health Center in Idaho, put it well: "I feel like all the programs that we talked about, community access programs, the community health center system, all the volunteer clinics—and they're all staffed by people that are very passionate and committed to the idea of providing health care to everyone—but for all of that, we've only scratched the surface of the demand and the need. And when you start talking about things like dental care, then we don't even begin to scratch the surface. In mental health care, it's a very similar situation.

"So I think, from a national level, we're getting Band-Aid approaches, and we're supplementing those on the state and the regional and the local level. But what we end up with is a network of bandages, and it's not a real efficient way or a thorough way of delivering health care. A lot of people, even within our system, end up falling through the cracks in various areas such as mental health and dental and chronic disease management. And the people who don't find our systems fall through, literally to the point of death sometimes.

"I think it's something that needs to be addressed in a comprehensive, national manner—purely comprehensive, beyond just things like the president's five-year initiative to double the size of the community health center system. So that's my personal opinion. And, you know, it might put me out of a job, but it would be nice to see."

2. MANDATING PARTICIPATION IN THE CURRENT SYSTEM MAY MARGINALLY INCREASE THE NUMBER OF INSURED INDIVIDUALS, BUT IT WILL STILL EXCLUDE THE VAST MAJORITY OF THE MOST VULNERABLE.

Another popular set of proposals focuses on mandating coverage, either by employers or by consumers themselves. The state of Hawaii, for instance, requires all employers except the smallest to provide health insurance for their employees or else pay into a state fund to provide coverage. The state of California in 2003 passed a similar proposal, though, at this writing, opponents are gathering signatures for a ballot initiative to reverse this decision. A variant proposal, modeled after auto insurance mandates, puts the burden of getting coverage on consumers themselves by requiring all Americans of sufficient means to provide proof of adequate insurance when they file their taxes each year; those who cannot do so would be charged an additional tax.

These proposals would not help most of the people we interviewed. Although some of the uninsured, particularly some of the young, intentionally choose not to purchase coverage, the vast majority of those who are uninsured simply cannot afford to pay the premiums. Mike Wilson, a retired business executive from Idaho and head of a Chamber of Commerce committee looking into health care in Boise, explains: "If the average individual policy costs three thousand dollars a year, and the family policy costs eight thousand dollars a year, then obviously people can't afford that. You can't afford it. That's an issue that even the most conservative people in the world, I think, agree with. They have come to the realization that you can't fix this by telling people to disconnect the cable TV and go out and buy health insurance. It doesn't work. The arithmetic doesn't work."

Nor would the employer mandate help many of the people we met. Most of the larger employers who would be affected by a mandate already offer insurance to their employees. It is the smaller employers, who are exempt from most proposals, who typically do not offer benefits.

In addition, as we pointed out in chapter 2, many uninsured people work in low-wage jobs, where the cost of coverage would be a significant part of their compensation. Given that the full-time salary for someone making the federal minimum wage is a bit over $9,000 a year, one can see why it might be difficult for even a large employer to provide insurance to these workers (at an average employer cost of $3,000 for an individual policy and $8,000 for family coverage). Many argue that employer insurance mandates would increase labor costs to a point that would cause many of these jobs to simply disappear or, more likely, go offshore. Mandates might even further discourage employers from hiring chronically ill or disabled employees.

Finally, our interviewees who do work for large companies, including state universities, attest to the creativity these companies use in finding ways to deny health benefits to many employees. It is unlikely that any of the proposals for incremental change or mandated participation in the insurance system would prevent these large employers from defining certain workers as seasonal, temporary, or part-time and thereby denying them benefits.

3. THE ONLY WAY TO TRULY BREAK THE DEATH SPIRAL IS TO SEVER THE LINK BETWEEN EMPLOYMENT AND HEALTH INSURANCE.

As the introduction explained, the link between employment and health insurance developed as a result of the shortage of civilian labor during World War II and subsequent decisions by the War Labor Board to allow unions to bargain for health care benefits, in an attempt to attract and retain employees.

What served us well in World War II, however, is not appropriate for today. Employment-based insurance worked well when most people lived in stable, two-parent households, with one breadwinner who spent an entire career at a large, established, profitable company with strong union representation—firms like Ford, Lockheed, or, later, IBM. But the structure of the nuclear family, the nature of employment, and the system of health care have all changed radically.

Now people live in a variety of family structures, which change not infrequently. Issues of divorce, same-sex partners, and elderly dependents are much more prominent than they were when the system first started. Also, most employment today is through small businesses, which are only sometimes profitable. Unions are on the decline, and people typically change jobs several times during their career. Dave, introduced in chapter 1, is a good example of someone who used to have a stable, industrial career but now bounces from job to job, trying to accumulate enough hours to get insurance benefits.

A growing number of people work for employers who intentionally define employees' status as transitory in order to deny them insurance coverage; Kim, for instance, described in chapter 7, works at Walgreens, which reduced her hours just as she reached the twelve weeks of full-time work that would have given her access to health insurance. We heard these stories again and again, from construction workers, shopping clerks, teachers, and others. Indeed, most of the young people we met—Rachel and Heather, for example—seemed to face a world where almost all the jobs they could find were defined as temporary, substitute, or part-time.

As long as our system continues to make employment the dominant way to receive health care benefits, we are all just one illness, one family change, one pink slip away from potentially sliding down the death spiral.

4. PURELY MARKET-BASED APPROACHES TO BREAKING THE LINK BETWEEN EMPLOYMENT AND HEALTH INSURANCE WILL NOT SOLVE THE PROBLEM FOR THOSE MOST HURT BY THE CURRENT SYSTEM.

One way to weaken the link between employment and health insurance, advocated by some conservatives, is to encourage employers to simply provide their workers with a cash benefit equal to what the employers now pay for health insurance. Employees then would be free to buy any policy on the market to meet their individual needs and would not be forced to change policies or providers each time they change jobs. To encourage this sort of arrangement, the tax deductibility of insurance premiums could be extended to individuals (or, even more radically, it could also be removed from corporations). The resulting change would be similar to the now-prevalent change in retirement benefits, from defined benefits (pensions) to defined contributions, such as 401K or 403B plans.

Although this change in tax law would help break the link between employment and health care, it would not benefit most of the people we met in our travels. Individual insurance costs money, and many Americans do not have the savings to pay for insurance when they are not employed. In particular, those who are poor, such as Nathaniel, Loretta, and Timothy, would not fare well under a purely individual-based insurance market.

Some propose giving tax credits to low-income Americans to help alleviate this problem. Unfortunately, even with such subsidies, most members of the working-poor and middle classes would still not be able to purchase insurance. Total premiums for a family cost close to $10,000 in most parts of the country. A $3,000 family tax credit, proposed by President George W. Bush in 2001, would still leave a huge gap for most families. One advocacy group likens it to throwing a ten-foot rope to a person who is stuck in a twenty-five-foot hole.

In addition, those who are chronically ill, such as Edna, Guadalupe, and Kim, would have trouble finding affordable premiums, no matter how much money they made. Because they would no longer be part of a large risk pool, their premiums would be rated based on their health history. And new genetic tests on the horizon will only heighten the ability of insurers to match premiums with a patient's expected risk.

5. THE ONLY APPROACH THAT WILL SERVE ALL THE PEOPLE WE INTERVIEWED IS TO MAKE THE PROVISION OF BASIC, COMPREHENSIVE HEALTH CARE FOR ALL AMERICANS A PUBLIC RATHER THAN A PRIVATE RESPONSIBILITY.

Our conversations with uninsured individuals and medical providers across the country have convinced us that the only way to truly break the grip of the death spiral, which locks numerous Americans into a caste of the chronically ill, infirm, and marginally employed, is to make the provision of health care for all a public responsibility. This concept does not require nationalizing all hospitals and doctors; rather, it simply means that the federal government would mandate and guarantee adequate resources to provide all Americans with access to basic, comprehensive health services, including primary and specialty care, appropriate prescription drugs, diagnostic tests, mental health services, hospitalization, home care, and hospice care.

The system we envision has a close analogy with the U.S. public school system. As a nation, we believe that providing primary and secondary education to all Americans results in both individual and collective benefits. Thus, we make education a public responsibility and provide a public school system that is open to all. We do not leave it up to employers, and we do not offer it only for certain groups of people (based on income levels or family status, for example). There is a strong consensus that providing education is the right thing to do both from a moral standpoint and for the well-being of our society.

Just as an educated public helps everyone, so a healthy public helps us all. We can envision a publicly financed system of health care that is open to all Americans, just as the public schools are. One would be eligible purely by being a resident of the country. This system would offer a package of basic, comprehensive services—comprehensive enough to meet basic health needs, yet not inclusive of everything pushed by every special interest group. Premiums could be funded through the income tax system and could be proportional to income and ability to pay.

Such a system of government-guaranteed, comprehensive coverage is far from a new idea. Indeed, almost every other developed country in the world has chosen to adopt this basic structure for its system of health care financing. The Canadian system is perhaps the closest model for what might be possible in the United States. Each province guarantees the provision of health care to its residents, funded by tax revenues. Although many other factors outside the health care system are at play, the Canadian system, when compared to the current U.S. situation, has been able to achieve similar or better measures of health (such as life expectancy and infant mortality) with much less disparity within its population, at a much lower cost. The Israeli system, with which Susan is familiar, also ensures comprehensive coverage for all its citizens, which includes a complete program of prenatal and well-baby care (immunizations and developmental assessments, for instance).

An objection often voiced warns that any sort of comprehensive coverage proposal will cost too much. In the short run, it almost certainly will cost money to provide services to people who currently are not receiving them. But the amount is not as much as many fear. Our society already provides a great deal of care to the uninsured, but in a very inefficient and costly manner. We pay for care in the most expensive settings, such as emergency rooms, and pay for the most expensive complications, such as kidney dialysis, which we do not pay to prevent.

Urban Institute researchers Jack Hadley and John Holahan estimate that it would cost $33.9 billion a year to provide comprehensive coverage for the forty-one million uninsured residents of the United States. Although this is a substantial cost, it is significantly lower than estimates of lost productivity because of lack of insurance, which run from $65 billion to $130 billion a year. It also pales in comparison to the $100 billion in tax breaks that subsidize employer-sponsored insurance each year.

6. UNIVERSAL COVERAGE SHOULD ENSURE CHOICE AND INNOVATION.

Many of our interviewees expressed concern with choice in securing health care. It is important that our health care system allow individuals to obtain services outside the publicly financed system, in much the same way that some seek private tutoring or private schools to meet educational needs. Such options may not be egalitarian, but they are likely to be part of any American solution. What is crucial is that the public plan be funded adequately to provide for basic care for all and that everyone continue to pay their fair share of the common burden.

One way to do this would be to abolish the tax deduction for private health insurance. If the government is providing a health care option, it should not be subsidizing other options, although it should not ban them either. Ending this tax deduction would result in well over $100 billion in extra funding available to the federal government for health care.

It is also important that any health care system maintain the incentive to innovate, thereby improving both the technology and the processes of health care. Continuing with our public school analogy, some health care might be delivered by agencies modeled on charter schools, which are privately and independently run but publicly financed and must compete for enrollees based on service and quality. Alternatively, additional services might be offered for those who wish to pay privately, much as after-school tutoring is offered in the educational model. The key would be to carefully structure the system to discourage "cherry-picking" only the healthiest patients and to maintain equity along with innovation and freedom of choice.

EFFECTS OF REFORM

What would such reform mean to the people we met? It would not restore Dave's factory job, but it would help him maintain his health so that he would be able to work if and when the job market improves. He could afford his cholesterol-lowering medication and reduce his risk of a heart attack. His wife, Judy, could get the therapy she needs to pull her life back together. Kim, the young woman from Champaign who works at Walgreens, would be able to control her diabetes without getting pregnant in order to be eligible for Medicaid.

Jonathan, the young musician we met in chapter 7, could get definitive treatment for his kidney stones and not risk losing his kidneys. Guadalupe, the young woman in Texas, would get the medication and counseling she needs to stop terrorizing her family and might even improve enough to go out of the house, go back to school, and get a job. And Alisha, the young mother in Mississippi, would find a diagnosis and treatment for her abnormal uterine bleeding, which may be the sign of a serious, potentially malignant condition.

Justin, Jessica, Roberta, and Timothy would not fear more medical debt and the collection agency harassment, liens, and bankruptcies that follow. They would also be able to maintain their credit ratings and seek care without fear of being turned away because they owe money. Steve,

Mary Ann, and Daniel, all of whom we met in Idaho, could get definitive treatment and rehabilitation for their injuries and would no longer need to spend time and money on lawyers fighting to prove that their problems are job related.

Jamie, whom we met in chapter 4, could stay home with her special-needs son without fearing for her own health. Edna could take care of her own health problems so that her mother, daughter, and grand-daughter can stay out of nursing homes, prisons, or residential schools for problem kids. Belle could grow her acupuncture business without fear of losing her health care, and young people such as Rachel, Heather, and Jonathan could start building the careers and families they dream about.

Government-supported, universal health coverage will not eradicate the need for prisons, the fear of homelessness, or the struggle to make ends meet for millions of Americans. Corporate America's preference for nonunionized and contingent labor, cutbacks in social welfare programs, growing gaps between the rich and the poor, continued racial segregation and discrimination, unrealistic drug laws, domestic and nondomestic violence, and a culture that is loath to fund prevention (as opposed to miracle cures, high-tech treatments, and punishments) will continue to keep our emergency rooms, prisons, and homeless shelters busy.

Breaking the link between employment and health care will not fix all that is broken or right all wrongs. It will, however, help stop current inequalities from being irrevocably marked on our bodies and help prevent current injustices from hardening into a permanent caste structure.

SEVERAL YEARS LATER

"As you get older and see how little access the average person has to health care—it's disgraceful!" Rachel, the twenty-something teacher *cum* singer *cum* law student exclaimed when we called her in December 2005 to ask how she had been doing in the three years since our initial interview. Steve of Idaho put it a bit less delicately when we trekked out to his trailer to speak to him a second time: "Our country has got to get their heads out of their asses and take care of our people. The line between the rich and the poor, the space in between, has just gotten wider. Congresspeople don't have a clue, they are not common people. You got people out there dying because they don't have health care, they can't afford it."

In the fall of 2005 we set out to partially retrace our steps and see how the past couple of years had been treating the people whose stories we've reported in this book. We knew that the numbers were worse: when we had begun our research in 2003, "forty million uninsured" was the figure everyone seemed to know; just a few years later the number quoted in the media had become forty-five million. Good manufacturing jobs are still disappearing from the Rust Belt, the calamitous hurricane season of 2005 has left large numbers of Louisiana and Mississippi residents homeless and jobless, and welfare-to-work policies continue to expose too many women to the low-wage job market in which health insurance isn't even on the table. At the same time, big corporations are becoming more vocal about their inability to compete on the global market because of their health care costs; Wal-Mart has become a target of righteous anger because so many of its employees are receiving health care "at the taxpayers' expense" through Medicaid; and small businesses have all but given up on providing health coverage to their employees.

For all of these reasons, we expected to hear that our interviewees were still uninsured and that only a few—at best—would have made their way out of the death spiral. In fact, the landscape we encountered on our second round of research was far more complicated than we expected.

TOO LITTLE, TOO LATE

Jonathan (chapter 7), the young musician who originally told us that he didn't have any health problems except that "I'll probably lose a kidney someday," was happy to hear from us. He is doing great, things are good with him, he said. "Oh, and since I last spoke with you I was diagnosed with Crohn's disease."

Looking back at the transcript of our original interview, we can see that the symptoms already were there—the rectal bleeding, the nausea, the kidney stones. If Jonathan had been treated by anyone even remotely functioning as a primary care physician, his condition probably would have been identified before he became critically ill.

This is what happened: "When I saw blood when I wiped I assumed it was hemorrhoids since I'd had the internal abscess. So I didn't pay attention. In about April 2004 it became more. More blood. I began to worry. I went to the doctor right before a concert tour I had planned. The doctor at the emergency room said, 'It's probably internal hemorrhoids. Your blood work is fine.' I went on tour and it got worse. I got back and did research. I went to the emergency room again and told them that before this I hadn't been to a doctor in seven years and that this was my second visit there in a short time. The emergency room didn't diagnose the problem. It kept getting worse. I was getting sicker. So I went to a [government-funded] sliding-fee-scale clinic. They were really good there. I became sicker. They made me an appointment at the state hospital for a colonoscopy in two months. But in the next ten days I lost about twenty pounds. So the clinic doctor used her connections for a quicker colonoscopy appointment. By then I had lost thirty pounds altogether. The colonoscopy diagnosed colitis. They gave me medicine but it didn't work and it made me sick. I got so anemic and dehydrated and malnourished that I stayed in bed for the summer. I could barely sit up."

No doctor was in charge of him or managing his care at that time. "I applied for Community Free Care at the hospital. The doctor there said, 'You should be able to eat whatever you want as long as you are on the right medicine.' But the medicine cost $300 a month and didn't really help. I was going to the bathroom ten times a day. The doctor was not helpful. So I read and researched and little by little figured out it was Crohn's disease [a serious autoimmune condition that affects a number of organ systems, primarily the intestines]. Finally someone at the hospital got my earlier medical history and saw the kidney stones and diagnosed Crohn's.

"I was put on Prednisone [a steroid that acts as an immuno-suppressant] and got nearly asymptomatic within two days, after being sick for months. That was more than a year ago. I never saw the doctor again." Not liking the side effects of Prednisone, Jonathan decreased the dosage and now manages his condition through diet, multivitamins, and acidophilus.

Jonathan's reality—that he has an incurable and fairly incapacitating condition and that he had to give up his musical career (he can't tour anymore)—doesn't seem to fit his self-presentation, that he is doing much better than the last time he saw us. Edna (chapter 4), the African American Illinois woman caring both for her elderly mother, who is suffering from early dementia, and for her developmentally delayed granddaughter, helped us understand what Jonathan meant. She, like Jonathan, was delighted to see us again and eager to tell us how much better she was doing.

"I'm great, feeling much better. I have full-blown diabetes now and they amputated a toe," is how Edna began our conversation. Edna was not being sarcastic. She really is feeling better now that her diabetes is under control, the pain in her foot has been taken care of, and she has become integrated into the health care system. When we first met she had borderline diabetes for which she could not access care, and pain and swelling in her foot for which no doctor seemed willing to treat her. Shortly after that conversation she went to the emergency room several more times for her foot. "It was swollen and painful and killing me." But the emergency room doctors brushed her off and told her to go home and elevate her foot. "But I don't have time for that with my mama and baby."

Finally, the last time she went to the emergency room because the pain was so bad she couldn't stand it anymore, they rushed her up to the operating room. "Poison was backing up in my system. It was touch and go for a while." Apparently the medical staff had ignored the diabetes-related infection that had been causing her foot pain until it reached the point at which her toe had to be amputated.

Since then they have been treating her well. While she was in the hospital "it must have been my lucky day, I was treated like royalty." They also provided home care to help her with the dressings and pain medication afterwards and physical therapy at home to help her walk.*

The hospital did bill her $22,000. Seeing that Edna no longer is able to work outside the home, we ask her how she will pay it. "I'm not paying it. They're going to sue me. I feel bad, since they took such good care of me. I'm sorry that I can't pay this."

Edna needs ongoing medical services, which she now receives through the Community Health Center in a neighboring town. This came about

---

*Her rave reviews lead us to wonder whether part of the reason she received such good care is that the hospital that treated her, a hospital that has come under a great deal of community fire lately, is afraid of a lawsuit.

when the hospital that carried out her surgery introduced her to the public aid office, which arranged her treatment at the Community Health Center. The treatment is very low cost, and Edna is happy to pay for it. (She has applied for both Medicaid and Social Security but has been denied.)

We discuss why she is getting good care now at the same Community Health Center that was not a usable alternative for her when we first met her. She reminds us that before the amputation, she could never get an appointment when she actually needed one. The other barrier she used to face was the long wait to see a doctor. The center is the only facility in the area that serves uninsured patients as well as the many Medicaid patients who can't find providers willing to take them, as well as the growing number of insured patients who can't afford their deductibles or co-pays. As a result, the center is overenrolled and patients typically have to schedule appointments so many months in advance that the center is not an option for any sort of urgent care. In Edna's case now however, she knows what is wrong with her and what she needs to do, and she has become part of the system with a regular doctor and regular appointments. She no longer depends on last-minute urgent care and now finds that the center works well for her.

As we finish up talking, Edna blurts out, "I feel terrible for all of the negative things I said last time you were here about [the hospital and the health center]. Now I'm on top of the world. I'm feeling much better now. I was being poisoned by my own toe. Now I can run around the block. Two years ago I was sick and didn't know I was sick."

Edna, like Jonathan, was suffering from a serious yet undiagnosed medical condition. The sporadic trips to the emergency room did not lead to proper medical assessments, diagnosis, or treatment plans. Now Jonathan has Crohn's disease and has lost his career hopes, while Edna has full-blown diabetes, has lost her toe, and will never again work outside the home for pay. But the conditions are being managed properly, and both feel "great." One wonders whether they would have been feeling even better if these conditions had been diagnosed and treated before life-threatening complications had set in.

ESCAPE FROM THE DEATH SPIRAL

Several of the people we interviewed seem to have escaped the death spiral's centrifugal force, at least for now. We offer their stories as evidence that consistent access to health care really does make a difference in people's lives and that the kind of health care that can keep American men and women able to function and work is not necessarily tremendously expensive.

For the most part, those who elude the death spiral are fortunate enough to receive timely help: they have reasonably affluent families, they have good self-advocacy skills, they are lucky enough to have someone to advocate for them, and/or they live in states with policies that offer reasonable protection for their residents.

Despite the poor health coverage prognosis for those dealing with mental health issues, Heather and Samantha (chapter 7) were the most obvious winners in the health care sweepstakes. Young college graduates, daughters of affluent families, both were uninsured and struggling in 2003, and both now have good health insurance. Heather, still living in Boston, reports that since landing a job that offers health insurance she has been going to therapy. "It's remarkable to me how much a difference it makes to me in my abilities as an employee. Without therapy I miss more sick days and am less reliable at work. With coverage I'm able to focus more at work and work harder and things like that." Samantha, now living in California, also has "full benefits that cover everything." It turned out that the depression that she had seen as situational when we first met her actually was cyclical and severe. But with a job that provides good mental health coverage, she is being treated properly with therapy and antidepressants. "It changed my life, it stabilized me. I feel more even." Most important, she no longer experiences the depression-related fatigue that was making it difficult for her to work or look for work.

Guadalupe (chapter 8) turned out to be perhaps the most surprising success story. As a result of her mother, Elena's, dedicated advocacy and willingness to deal with endless bureaucratic inquiries and forms—not to mention their family's membership in an active grassroots community organization—Guadalupe now is covered by Medicaid and Social Security. When we met her in 2003 she was vacillating between episodes of aggression (when she did not have medication) and periods of being lethargic and confused (when the doctors she sporadically saw over-sedated her). When we met her in November of 2005, she was lucid, articulate, happy, working, and planning her upcoming wedding.

Elena explains that because Guadalupe's Mexican medical records were not recognized in the United States, it took several years to coordinate her coverage. At the time we first met them, Elena had been trying to get Guadalupe on Medicaid or Social Security but could only arrange temporary help. It was during that time of erratic coverage that things seemed to be particularly bad with Guadalupe.

Once Guadalupe made it into the health care system she was assigned a social worker, and according to both daughter and mother that is what turned her life around. The social worker hooked her up with an adult day care center, where she loves the camaraderie and the handicraft programs. It turned out that the social isolation of staying in the house all day while her mother was at work and brother at school played a part in Guadalupe's unmanageable behaviors and depression. At the center, the socializing and the opportunities for creative expression through crafts projects have contributed to her newfound calm and positive sense of self. The social worker also suggested that she enroll in Goodwill's employability program—a program that teaches basic work skills (punctuality, etc.) and then helps with job placement. Guadalupe is thrilled to be working and earning money (she works four hours a day cleaning offices) and no longer needs most of her medications. Still, when she does need "something for her nerves," her mother knows that she can take her to a doctor who knows their history and that Guadalupe will receive an appropriate prescription.

TREADING WATER:
THE EMPLOYMENT-HEALTH CARE LINK

As writers, we love sharing the most dramatic narratives. As researchers, however, we are more interested in the repeating patterns, the patterns that are widespread—normative, even if they are less remarkable. In fact, most of the people we spoke to were dealing with more or less the same sets of challenges that they had described three years earlier. Our national policy of linking health care access to good jobs means that most of our interviewees are in one sort of holding pattern or another, sometimes slipping a bit further down the death spiral, sometimes finding a temporary handhold to slow down their passage. This observation carries with it a certain optimism, but even more it carries a call to action. It is not yet too late to turn things around for these individuals, for this society.

Small business owners—and those employed in small businesses—continue to bend and break under the employment-based health care system. After much soul-searching and number-crunching, Collective Home Care (chapter 6) indeed stopped offering insurance to its employees. "Expenses for health insurance kept going up. We couldn't afford it." Sue, the community-activist owner, decided to sell the company to an investor who had the cash to keep the business going. The new owner set a cap to the number of full-time employees—that is, employees who could be offered insurance. The cap is fifteen employees, out of a total workforce of sixty.

Sue explains that though she was sad to have to leave Collective, she has moved on to direct a small nonprofit organization that in many ways fulfills an even deeper dream of hers: the new organization is involved in training and advocacy for family caregivers. The downside is that she no longer has insurance for herself. Forty-nine years old, she had a heart attack last summer. While she did receive free care for the initial heart attack at one of the Massachusetts hospitals, she has accumulated some medical debt and now spends more than she can afford on the medication that she will continue to need for the rest of her life.*

*On April 4, 2006 the Massachusetts House and Senate approved legislation that will expand Medicaid coverage and benefits, make available sliding fee subsidies for health insurance for low income residents, create financial incentives to purchase insurance, and create a financial penalty for some employers who do not offer insurance. The annual income limit for an individual to receive the sliding fee subsidy has been set at approximately $29,000, which means that Sue

The uninsured state of the part-time Collective employees is indicative of a pattern growing throughout the country. A 2005 Commonwealth Fund study showed that while 75 percent of regular full-time employees receive health benefits from their employers, just 20 percent of the thirty-four million "nonstandard" workers (that is, temporary, seasonal, part-time, contingent, or supplemental workers) in the United States are covered. And, for the most part, these workers find that even the low wages they earn make them ineligible for Medicaid.

Annette, the woman dealing with blinding pain from a head trauma caused by her former husband (chapter 3) spent much of the past year caring for her mother, who was dying of cancer. "Things happen for a reason," Annette believes. It turns out that after she lost her last job (Annette frequently loses jobs because her migraines cause her to miss work) all she could find were "temp" jobs, none of which provided insurance. These were not the kind of jobs she was willing to take, especially if it meant not being available to tend to her mother. Ironically, not working provided Annette with certain benefits. First, her government-subsidized rent is calculated on the basis of her income, and with no income she now pays no rent. Second, with no income she became eligible for Medicaid, and as a result her migraines are under better control. Though Annette's mother has since passed away and Annette is eager to go back to work, she is being careful in her job search. With a salary, even a very low salary, she will lose her Medicaid and rent subsidy, but the temporary jobs she has been offered will not provide health benefits or possibilities for career advancement. In the meantime she is scraping by on child support payments and prayers, a house of cards that already had begun to wobble at the time of our last conversation.

Jamie, the preschool teacher with the disabled toddler (chapter 4), still is committed to staying home with her son, though she does plan to

---

probably will not qualify for a health insurance subsidy under the new system. It remains to be seen how the new legislation will affect people like Sue who earn a bit too much to receive a subsidy but who cannot possibly afford to pay the full cost of insurance.

go back to work next year when he starts school. The child is doing well: for the past two years he has been covered steadily by KidCare, Illinois' expanded Medicaid program for children. This has allowed Jamie to arrange the speech therapy and other treatments he needs. As for herself, the picture isn't quite as good. She has applied for Medicaid several times but has been turned down. At the local public health department she asked how she could get covered and was told, "If you get pregnant you'll get Medicaid." In light of the gestational diabetes she was diagnosed with during her previous pregnancy, Jamie wisely declined. She has not been to the doctor since her last postpartum check: That was four years ago.

The men and women whose health had deteriorated from years of hard physical labor are not doing any better than when we first met them. Joe, the construction worker in chapter 5, continues to suffer from work-related injuries to his shoulders and knees. For the most part, Joe receives minimal treatment for these injuries, and often not before long-term damage develops. He explains that the expectation of employers and employees in his line of work is that if you get hurt on the job you don't claim it against the job, you just work through it and get it fixed later. His shoulder, in his words, is "toast."

Joe elaborates, "It hurts every minute of every day. The doctor said there is nothing left, the joint is down to bone on bone." The shoulder needs replacement but the doctor advised against it, saying that the new shoulder would wear out too fast with the work he does, especially using the jackhammer. Joe plans to have his shoulder replaced once he retires, which hopefully will be in eight years. His dilemma is that if he stops working before age fifty-five, he will not get medical benefits or a pension. But, he explains, "Working eight more years is unfathomable. I should do something else, that is what everyone says, but I'm forty-seven and I'd have to start all over again and I wouldn't be able to retire until who knows when. It's scary, and there are lots of guys like me out there."

Timothy's (chapter 9) work situation—lifting huge sacks of seed at a warehouse—has not changed. "Each and every year gets worse and worse, harder and harder." In the five years he has been at his current job his wages increased by all of $1 an hour, from $7 to $8, with no benefits. Like Joe, he continues to suffer from work-related injuries. His employer has not changed the company "policy"—the company does not pay for the medical care employees receive, even for injuries incurred on the job. One of Timothy's injuries led to a serious infection in his thumb that necessitated hospital visits, IV antibiotics, and finally surgery. From this and other injuries he accumulated a great deal of medical debt, about $47,000. The hospital sent bills and repeatedly harassed him with phone calls. Timothy and his wife Denise decided to hire a lawyer, whom they paid $500 to arrange bankruptcy, and that "took care" of almost all of the medical bills. Ironically, even before they received a letter from the court saying that their bankruptcy had gone through, they began receiving letters from car dealerships saying they were eligible to buy a car. Apparently, the dealerships monitor bankruptcy proceedings and hasten to offer great "deals" to families like Denise and Timothy, who now own a heavily financed 2004 car.

Timothy is determined to improve his life and in the evenings is studying to take the GED exams. "In June I'll get my robe and go across that stage." Unfortunately, however, his rectal bleeding continues (though not as heavily as before). Without medical care, it is impossible to tell if the bleeding is due to a benign condition like hemorrhoids or something more serious like Jonathan's Crohn's disease or, more likely given his age, colon cancer.

Despite all they've been through, Denise is optimistic about their situation. "God blessed me to get a waiver to get my certificate to go back to nursing [her Certified Nurse Assistant certificate, which had been revoked because of her felony conviction]. I prayed and my pastor's wife wrote a recommendation [to the certification board], and God has turned my life around." Denise was starting on the afternoon shift the very day of our conversation. She believes she will have health coverage with the new nurse's aid job, a nice change after five years of scraping by on temporary and part-time work.

EVICTED: THE HEALTH CARE–HOUSING LINK

During our initial interviews in 2003, we were surprised by how many people—including those who seemed to be middle class—expressed fear of losing their homes. These fears, it turns out, were not without cause. In a recent study of low- and moderate-income earners in seven locations across the United States, more than one-quarter of respondents with medical debt reported housing problems resulting from that debt. These problems include being unable to qualify for a mortgage, being unable to make rent or mortgage payments, being turned down from renting a home, and being forced to move to less expensive housing. A small but not insignificant portion of the respondents also reported having been evicted in the past or being homeless at the time of the study. Finally, while some of the study's respondents had amassed large medical debt, even some respondents with medical debt of less than $500 found that the debt had harmed their credit.

When we returned to Decatur, Dave and Judy (chapter 1) told us that since we had last spoken they had indeed lost their home. They had to declare bankruptcy, and since they hadn't paid their mortgage for a year, the bank repossessed their house. Then a lawyer who worked for the bank during the bankruptcy proceedings encouraged them to fire the lawyer who had been handling the $1 million lawsuit against the railroad for the death of Judy's daughter. The new lawyer negotiated a settlement of $100,000 (he got 10 percent and they ended up with about $80,000). Though the settlement allowed the railroad company to escape taking liability and gave Dave and Judy much less money than they probably should have received, it made it possible for Dave and Judy to put a down payment on a new house. This was important to them: during the first year after they lost their old house they had to rent an apartment and were racking up even more debt. The new house isn't quite as nice as their old house, and Judy has no desire to decorate it—"It doesn't feel like home." But at least they are not on the streets.

The good news is that Judy has begun working in an office as a receptionist and Dave now has a steady job at a local manufacturing plant, though not in as high-paying a position as he had previously. "It pays about $10 less an hour, but it has insurance." Dave needs the insurance—he is not at all well. When we met them at one of their favorite coffee shops, we barely recognized him. Dave had lost forty pounds over the past few months and looked gaunt and pale. He is seeing a new doctor who seems to be taking his health concerns more seriously than the doctor he went to previously when he was sporadically (un)insured. The new doctor is concerned about his lungs and, Dave told us, made him an appointment with a lung specialist. Between the stress that causes him to chain-smoke and the chemicals that he inhales daily both in his job as a welder and in the ambient air of this Rust Belt city, Dave is not surprised that problems have developed in his lungs.

Across the country in Idaho, Steve and Mary Ann (chapter 5) now live in a trailer at the end of an unpaved track. The trailer is narrow—a single-wide, packed wall-to-wall with furniture. With Steve unable to work, they had to sell their house before they lost it to the bank. The good part is that they were able to sell it to his daughter. The bad part is that they sold it for well below market value. Still, it was enough to pay off the mortgage and their credit card debt. They had bought the trailer a number of years ago for $350 while they were still living in their house. The trailer had been intended for storage and for use as a workshop—they never dreamed that they would be living in it.

Steve and Mary Ann's friend John (chapter 5) is not yet homeless but seems to be at great risk for becoming so. We found John at the bar in his cowboy hat and black leather jacket sitting on a stool holding a bottle of Rainier beer and smoking a Camel. It was about 10:00 a.m.

John is one of the few interviewees who did not remember us, but then John tends not to remember much since he had a stroke in 2004. When he first suffered the stroke he was seen by a doctor. After this initial care, however, he received a letter saying the doctor would not see him again until he paid his bill. John explains, "I couldn't afford anything insurance-wise." He was given a prescription for medication, but he can't afford to have it filled. As of this writing, he has applied for Social Security Disability Insurance to pay for his stroke-related expenses, but his case is still "pending." He does have a lawyer helping him; as is customary, the lawyer will get a part of the disability claim when it comes through.

Despite severely impaired functioning on the right side of his body, John receives no poststroke care. His arm is weak and he often drops things; he can't walk very well—his right side drags; and he fell down a few days ago, hit his head, and broke his glasses. Now they are wired together and he can't afford new ones. John would like to go back to work as a bartender, but with glasses slipping out of his hands and legs that don't hold him up, that is not an option. He is frustrated. "I can't work, can't do anything. How can I pay the doctor? I'm waiting for the government to do something, but they aren't doing it. I've paid [taxes] all these years, why don't they give something back? All these years, and I'm sitting here stuck."

John describes himself as stressed; his compatriots at the bar say his memory is gone. When we last spoke with him, John was living with a girlfriend who was paying the rent. Unfortunately, we suspect this situation will not last.

Of course, we couldn't find most of the people who lost their homes; they'd moved on to other cities, other jobs, other sets of problems. Loretta and Greg (Prologue) already were gone from their Mississippi home when we returned less than a year after our initial interview. A year after that, Loretta's best friend Robin and her family also were gone, and the gas station Robin's husband rented had changed hands three times. Perhaps even more disturbing, in the course of the two-year interval almost the entire low-income rental neighborhood seemed to have turned over; when we knocked on neighbors' doors and asked if they knew where Loretta or Robin had moved to, the answer we heard most often was "I just moved here a couple of months ago myself."

Misty and Nathaniel (chapter 5) were getting ready to leave Idaho when we first returned to talk to them early in the summer of 2003. Things were not going well for them and they couldn't get the health care that Nathaniel needed for his serious and painful medical conditions. They decided to move to Oregon, where state policies are more generous. In June they held a lawn sale, selling everything they own, and were planning to buy a camper (the type that is mounted on a truck) and live in that with their four kids while Misty looked for work and saved some money. The final time we met them they had spent what little savings they had on a truck with defective brakes. By late summer of that year, they were gone.

Misty is a warm and engaging person and certainly could count on friends to help as best they could. However, her closest friend, Brittany, had just been told by the landlord that she and her family had one month's notice to move out. The last time we saw Brittany, she was unsure where they would go. Shortly afterwards, another neighbor did tell us that Brittany was quite ill with a chronic cough "that I can hear from across the street" and had lost an alarming amount of weight. Neighbors think she has hyperthyroidism, but the local doctor won't do the diagnostic lab test to confirm this because she can't pay for it. In December 2005 we were unable to locate Brittany and her family.

These are not the only original interviewees who have moved on. Alisha (chapter 2) had been living in a family-friendly Section VIII housing neighborhood in Mississippi but was gone when we tried to find her again. We made many phone calls, one to a local family of the same last name. The woman who answered the phone asked if we were from a collection agency. Then she complained bitterly that collection people and loan people keep calling her looking for Alisha. "I don't know her." Our best guess is that Alisha left town with some serious debts and probably with some real reluctance. She had loved her neighborhood and had been committed to building strong networks with other mothers in the neighborhood so that they could help look after one another's children. We did find an Alisha with the same last name in Georgia, the state that her friend Althea believes Alisha moved to. At that number we found a recording saying the number has been disconnected.

We also couldn't find any trace of Kim (chapter 7), Daniel (chapter

5), and Gina (chapter 2). While there is no absolute pattern describing those we couldn't find, we do note that it was much harder to track down our African American interviewees than our white or Mexican American interviewees (Daniel, Alisha, and Kim are African American). Not only had more African Americans left (or lost) their homes—probably reflecting the lower rate of home ownership among African Americans—but we also found that neighbors and relatives were more reluctant to pass along information that might lead us to these interviewees. They clearly had been burned in the past by official-sounding strangers trying to track down people they knew. In fact, quite a few of the lower-income interviewees had abandoned landlines altogether because so many of the phone calls they received were harassing calls from collection agencies.

"NO DOGGONE GOOD" INSURANCE

When we set out on our mission to hear how people were doing two or three years later, we certainly did not expect to find that many of our originally uninsured interviewees would now be insured. However, almost a third of the people we reinterviewed told us that they actually do have health insurance at this time.

Upon reflection, this probably should not have surprised us. The "forty-five million uninsured Americans" statistic is misleading. That number refers to Americans who were uninsured for the entire past year. At least as many Americans were/are uninsured for parts of the year. Put differently, while there certainly are many people who are permanently excluded from the normative system of health care coverage in the United States, there are even more people who are sporadically excluded. Thus, because our initial research protocol required that interviewees were uninsured at the time of the study, we were catching people on the "outside" segment of the insured-uninsured churn. This time around, some of them were on the "inside," though an even greater number of Americans overall were now on the "outside." Our interviewees' current insured status offers little comfort; rather, it illustrates the reality that "the uninsured" are not a self-contained "Other" and that most Americans are at risk of being without health care coverage and thus unable to access medical services.

But even these numbers tell only a small part of the story. Most of our newly insured interviewees told us that the insurance they have is "crappy," "lousy," or "useless" and that it does not cover their dependent family members. In the words of Alisha's friend Althea, "After the electronics plant moved [out of Mississippi] I lost my insurance. Now I'm working at the chicken plant and I got insurance through United Health, but it's not worth a doggone." With a $500 annual deductible, $50 co-pays for doctor appointments, $90 co-pays at the emergency room, and 30 percent coinsurance for many procedures and treatments, her insurance is indeed useless.

Althea's experience is part of a growing trend. Over the past several years insurance that does not kick in until an annual deductible is paid out of pocket has become increasingly common. About half of covered workers now face annual deductibles. In 2004, the average deductible for preferred provider services in PPO plans (the most common type of plan) was $410, significantly higher than in previous years. Other expenses for consumers have increased as well: co-payments have gone up, out-of-pocket costs for prescription drugs have risen sharply, and many plans limit payments for physical therapy, psychotherapy, and other treatments.

Rachel (chapter 7), the daughter of an upper-middle-class household, shares Althea's frustrations. The moderately priced insurance she purchased through her law school last year (she actually had dropped it and was uninsured when we spoke in November 2005, though she was planning to re-enroll) "was nothing but a hassle. The way the plan works is that you have to pay up front for medicines and some other things, and then send in receipts and forms. And claim forms have to be sent in for every office visit, treatment, everything. Everything requires a claim form that you send them with the bill, and then you have to pay the difference between what they pay and the amount billed. This is particularly ridiculous for students who may not be so organized. I'm bad at logistical stuff, and they make money off people's disorganization. They bank on that."

Making matters worse, the plan paid only a small fraction of the costs of the throat specialist that Rachel, who still is striving to build a career as a singer, needed to see in order to treat the nodules on her vocal cords. In words that may sound odd coming from a student at a prestigious law school, Rachel added, "I don't understand how this plan works."

Several of the now-insured people we spoke to in Texas offered more details of how these "not worth a doggone" plans work. Isabel, who works at the community organization that has helped out Elena and Guadalupe (chapter 8), had to pay 50 percent of the cost of her gall bladder surgery. That left her funds so low that she cannot afford the second breast biopsy her doctor told her she needs (two of her brothers died of cancer). Sylvia, her co-worker, still owes $3,000 for a hysterectomy she had in 2000 (she has a history of cervical cancer) and another $3,000 for assorted other treatments. She can't afford the $750 co-pay for the kidney MRI her doctor ordered (she has a cyst in her kidney), and she is living with knee pain so severe that her movements have slowed down and she no longer can kneel in church. She does not have money for the MRI co-pay needed to diagnose the cause of the pain, but in any case the diagnosis wouldn't be all that helpful since she wouldn't be able to afford the co-pay for whatever treatment is indicated. Her doctor did tell her that it might help if she would lose some weight. She'd like to, but her insurance does not cover a nutritionist.

This situation typically is referred to in newspaper articles and the rhetoric of politicians as "being underinsured." None of our interviewees used that term, for reasons that became increasingly clear to us. *Underinsured* implies that one *has* insurance but that it's not quite enough. Think of the term *underdressed*, for example, as in the sentence "I think I was underdressed at the Christmas party; I wore a suit but most of the other men were wearing tuxedos." *Underdressed* does not mean "exposed" or "excluded"; rather, it means not quite well dressed enough. Althea, Isabel, and Sylvia however, *are* exposed and excluded. They are not underinsured in any functional sense of the word; rather, they have useless insurance that requires deductibles and co-payments that they cannot possibly afford. Despite being counted in the official tally of the insured, they still cannot go to the party.

MOVING FORWARD, REVISITED

We finished this second round of interviews feeling deeply uncomfortable. We are troubled by the absence of meaningful national initiatives to expand health care access and by cuts to the already insufficient federal Medicaid budget. We are troubled by the realization that current state-level initiatives to expand access mostly are framed in terms of developing so-called "affordable" policies. These policies are affordable in the sense that monthly premiums are comparatively low. The lower premiums, however, are more than offset by higher payments in the form of deductibles or coinsurance down the line. Indeed, these are the exact same plans that our interviewees consistently called "crappy" or "useless." Many of these, like the Association Health Plans targeted at small businesses, also remove significant consumer protections and mandates that currently exist.

Experts predict that the fastest-growing insurance products over the next few years will be so-called "consumer-directed health plans," which include deductibles of over $1,000 (and sometimes as high as $5,000 or $10,000), often linked with a medical savings account. Many employers and politicians support this trend because, supposedly, consumers will behave more economically if they have to pay out of pocket for medical services. In fact, the only costs automatically reduced by these "consumer-directed plans" are the premiums, which mostly are paid by employers in any case.

A recent study found that 17.6 million Americans—one in six *insured* adults, largely from middle-class families and holding full-time jobs— have substantial problems paying their medical bills. Not surprisingly, insured people with medical debt were found to have fewer benefits in their health plans; that is, they had lousier insurance. Echoing the cycle that we have become well acquainted with, medical debt is associated with decreased access to health care—in this study those with medical debt were more likely to skip recommended tests, treatments, and medication because of the cost. Decreased access to health care, in turn, is associated with poorer health outcomes. And the cycle goes on.

None of the people we interviewed make recreational visits to the doctor or frivolously demand more expensive medications. High deductibles and co-payments present barriers to necessary services far more often than they serve as gentle deterrents to unnecessary care. In fact, the high medical care costs incurred by many of our interviewees—Dave and Judy come to mind here—result directly from their having had to delay care because they could not afford the annual deductibles or high co-payments. In the absence of affordable care, health problems that probably could have been managed at a modest price escalated into full-blown crises.

Between the high deductibles that discourage many Americans from seeking primary care for budding or chronic illnesses and the high co-insurance that exposes many Americans to debt, bankruptcy, and even home loss, these plans do not seem to offer any real solutions to the national health care crisis. In our more cynical moments we see these plans as not much more than a financial bonanza for the already profitable insurance industry and a political prize for politicians who can claim to have tackled the problem of the uninsured.

We also are disturbed by the recent move to open low-cost clinics at Wal-Marts and various pharmacy chains around the country. These clinics do provide needed acute services for sore throats and ear infections, especially during the evening and weekend hours when they may be the only doctors available—or the only doctors accessible—in many communities. Yet when we think about the issues our interviewees cope with—chronic pain, diabetes, asthma, allergies, arthritis—walk-in clinics that do not provide preventive, ongoing, and family-centered care are not very useful. In fact, they may even be harmful in cases where medications are prescribed without knowledge of the patient's full history. Jonathan and Edna, whose serious illnesses went undiagnosed until they came close to hitting the bottom of the death spiral despite their having been seen at clinics and emergency rooms, exemplify the inherent weakness of this kind of arrangement. In the context of short, one-shot appointments, doctors are unable to do more than write prescriptions. Our interviewees, however, especially in Texas and Illinois, already have drawers full of medicine, much of which they can't identify or use properly. Again, in our more cynical moments we see these clinics as not much more than a financial bonanza for the already profitable pharmaceutical industry.

We have come to realize that there is a fundamental disconnect between the reality of the lives of most Americans and the health care policies enacted by our leaders. Public debates remain framed in individualistic and economic terms: experts count the number of uninsured individuals and talk about the costs of providing some of them with medical services. Annette and Edna, however, know that their own well-being is inseparable from the health of their families and communities, and that the costs of illness cannot be measured solely in dollars and cents. Our more religiously inclined interviewees explain that it is a moral duty to help those who are suffering—when Jesus healed the sick, he never asked to see anyone's insurance card. Our more politically inclined interviewees explain that life is a basic human right, and that the right to life necessarily entails adequate health care for all members of society. And our more pragmatically inclined interviewees wonder who is going to staff the factories and the supermarkets and the nursing homes when working- and middle-class Americans have become too sick to stand up to the demands of the workplace. When Sue, the founder of Collective Home Care, told us about her recent heart attack, we asked her, "Aren't you scared to be without insurance, isn't that uncomfortable, don't you feel insecure?" Sue answered slowly, thoughtfully, in words that helped put into focus the sense of unease that had been building for us throughout this project. "I'm scared being in our culture, we're all in trouble. It's not 'comfortable' for me to work with people who don't have a living wage and don't have health insurance. That's not 'security'—even if I have insurance for myself."

NOTES TO AFTERWORD

A study of current and former welfare recipients found that parents who met the goals of welfare reform (that is, who were working, had married, and were less dependent on welfare) actually were *less* likely to be insured than those who were still receiving welfare. Only 30 percent of employed former welfare recipients received employer-sponsored health insurance. See Illinois Family Studies Policy Briefs, July 2002 and September 2005.

The Commonwealth Fund study of "nonstandard" workers is Ditsler, Fisher, and Gordon (2005).

Seifert (2005) is an excellent study of housing, homelessness, and health costs. Information regarding current insurance policies and their costs can be found in Kaiser Family Foundation (2005), Exhibit 4.4, Average Annual Deductibles for Covered Workers, by Plan Type, 2000–2004. Also see Cover the Uninsured Week (2005).

For information on medical debt, see Hoffman, Rowland, and Hamel (2005).

A PRIMER ON THE U.S. HEALTH CARE SYSTEM AND THE SAFETY NET

> Our "system" is a system in name only. It is really a patchwork
> of public and private programs with widely differing eligibility
> criteria. And many people end up falling between the eligibility
> requirements of the programs and many others have benefits
> only loosely connected to their needs.
>
> Stuart Butler, Heritage Foundation

The United States has by far the highest per capita spending on health care of any nation, more than $5,400 per person per year. This figure is more than 80 percent higher than per capita health care spending in Canada, and 134 percent higher than the average of other industrialized nations.

Of the $1.6 trillion spent on health care in the United States in 2002, $486 billion (30 percent) went to hospitals, $340 billion (21 percent) to physician services, $162 billion (10 percent) for prescription drugs,* and

---

*The pharmaceutical industry has been one of the most consistently profitable economic sectors in the United States, often receiving kudos from *Fortune* magazine and other business publications for having the highest profit margins of any industry in a given year (Public Citizen 2002). Although it receives substantial government subsidies to develop new drugs, the industry has excelled at creating new demands for new products and guarding its patents. As a result, Americans pay close to twice as much for the same medications as people in other countries (see Anderson et al. 2004).

$139 billion (9 percent) to nursing home and home health care. It is especially notable that the health care insurance industry and other administrative bodies absorb more than 30 percent of all health care spending in the United States, as a review of 1999 spending indicated. Even routine interactions with the system, such as an uncomplicated case of appendicitis, can cost well over $10,000. Complex cases such as organ transplants can run in the hundreds of thousands of dollars.

Because most individuals are not able to bear the high costs of a serious illness, a system of spreading the risk of medical costs has evolved into a system of financing care, as it has elsewhere in the world. In most countries, the cost of health care is spread among the entire population by making it a public responsibility with a strong government role in either financing care (as in Canada) or directly providing care (as in Great Britain).

INSURANCE

The American system of risk spreading is somewhat unique among industrialized countries. Most Americans receive health insurance for themselves and their dependents (usually defined as spouse and children under the age of nineteen living at home) through their employers, typically at some direct cost to the individuals. Offering insurance coverage is a purely voluntary feature of the system; there is no requirement at the state or federal level that employers provide insurance for their workers. As a result, larger employers are more likely to provide coverage, and higher-paid employees are more likely to be covered.

The traditional form of insurance is called *indemnity*, a system in which the employee can see any doctor or go to any hospital, and these providers are paid reasonable and customary charges for their services. Over the past few decades, however, most employees have come to be covered by managed-care plans, which include health maintenance organizations (HMOs), preferred provider organizations (PPOs), and point-of-service (POS) plans. All of these managed-care plans attempt, in varying degrees, to coordinate care and control costs by restricting enrollees to a network of contracted doctors and hospitals, limiting drug choices to an approved formulary, and requiring pre-approvals for specialist referrals and for expensive tests and procedures. Employers are increasingly requiring their employees to assume a greater share of the costs through higher deductibles (the amount an individual must spend out of pocket before benefits start), co-payments (a share of the costs when benefits are being paid), and exclusions.

A small number of people buy health insurance in the private market. These insurance policies tend to be quite expensive because they attract sicker members and often contain significant restrictions on coverage. Whereas coverage for a twenty-five-year-old healthy adult might cost a few hundred dollars a month, coverage for a fifty-five-year-old with a preexisting condition such as diabetes could be as high as several thousand dollars a month. Some people who are between jobs purchase private insurance through a federal law commonly known as COBRA (named for the health benefit provisions of the 1986 Consolidated Omnibus Budget Reconciliation Act), which mandates that employers offer their employees a chance to continue their health coverage after employment is terminated. Unfortunately, the employees must pay the full, unsubsidized rate, which typically puts the cost of COBRA out of reach for low-wage workers.

There are two situations in which health insurance generally does not cover health care costs. For injuries related to motor vehicle accidents, automobile insurance is expected to pick up the cost. For work-related conditions, workers' compensation insurance provides coverage. While this division may make sense for acute injuries, it can become problematic when the health consequences of the car accident or workplace injury are delayed.

Although historically somewhat cyclical in nature, the current fortunes of the insurance industry are quite good indeed. Profit reports show that 2003 was a banner year for both for-profit insurers (such as Aetna, which made a profit of $933 million) and not-for-profit ones (such as Massachusetts Blue Cross/Blue Shield, which made $215 million). This profitability should not be surprising, as insurers in some ways resemble the house in a Vegas casino. At the end of the day, they simply structure the game—that is, premiums and benefits—to ensure that they always win.

MEDICARE

A variety of public coverage options are designed to help strictly defined subgroups of the population. Philosophically based on the Victorian Poor Laws first enacted in Britain more than five hundred years ago, these programs offer government-sponsored health insurance for certain groups of the "deserving."

The largest such program is Medicare, which provides coverage to all residents over the age of sixty-five, to the disabled receiving Social Security benefits (this is commonly referred to as "disability" or "SSI disability"), and, in a strange quirk of history and lobbying effort, to those with end-stage kidney disease. Medicare is a federally funded program with several parts: Part A, which is a hospital benefit financed by employer and employee payroll taxes; Part B, which provides voluntary coverage for physician services financed by premium payments from beneficiaries and general tax revenues; and a recently enacted complex coverage plan for pharmaceuticals.

Although Medicare pays for a significant portion of all doctor and hospital bills, and now for some pharmaceutical bills, enrollees are responsible for a reasonable degree of costs themselves—for instance, an approximately $850 deductible for hospital stays, 20 percent of doctor bills, and some of the costs of prescription drugs. Some larger companies provide their retirees with insurance to cover such costs. Other seniors are able to purchase private "wraparound" policies to cover these expenses. The poorest elderly (called the "dually eligible") are able to qualify for Medicaid as well as Medicare to cover these excess costs.

DISABILITY

Although most Americans think of Medicare primarily as paying for care for the elderly, the disabled are the fastest-growing group within the program. Many of the people interviewed for this book spoke about negative experiences in applying for disability benefits. The Social Security Disability Insurance (SSDI) system officially defines disability as an "inability to engage in substantial gainful activity" that is expected to last for at least a year or result in death. Benefits are provided only for people who cannot engage in "any kind of work that might exist in the national economy." The disability system, which requires a lengthy and complex application process, makes its own determination about whether an individual meets these criteria. Many law firms specialize solely in helping people make disability claims. Since 1981, the eligibility requirements for disability benefits have been progressively tightened, leaving many disabled people outside the system and with nowhere else to turn for medical benefits.

Susan Stefan, a disability attorney, notes that the disability application process is unwieldy and often impossible, especially for psychiatrically disabled people. The appeals process is worse. The average time for review of an adverse decision in fiscal year 1998 was 850 days, almost two and a half years.

MEDICAID

Medicaid, the second largest public insurance program, is a joint federal-state program that is meant to supply essential health services to federally designated categories of the poor—principally those who also receive federal cash assistance, which means primarily women and children. Each state receives federal matching funds for money it spends on the program (these funds are calculated to roughly reflect the state's overall wealth) and has latitude to determine what level of benefits it will offer above those that are federally mandated.

In addition, Medicaid pays for long-term care (nursing homes) for those who are poor or spend down their assets. Nationally, although children make up 52 percent of Medicaid beneficiaries, they account for only 15 percent of the costs. Conversely, the aged and disabled make up only 17 percent of beneficiaries but account for close to 40 percent of costs. In the late 1990s, the federal government enacted the State Children's Health Insurance Program (commonly known as SCHIP or CHIP), an expansion of Medicaid to cover near-poor children up to the age of nineteen. Although every state signed up to provide such coverage, some are more aggressive than others about enrolling people in the plan. SCHIP has a variety of names from state to state; many, including New Jersey, Illinois, and Alaska, use some variant of "KidCare."

THE UNINSURED

People who do not receive coverage through their employer or through a spouse or parent's employer, through a public payer such as Medicare or Medicaid, or through private purchase fill the ranks of the uninsured. Nowadays, few people work uninterruptedly for the same employer their entire lives. For that reason, and because of the complex eligibility requirements for public plans, many people move in and out of coverage throughout their lives. "Far from being a static group, the uninsured population is constantly changing," says Douglas J. Holtz-Eakin, director of the Congressional Budget Office. "While many people are chronically uninsured, many more are uninsured for shorter periods of time."

Because of this dynamic nature, it is hard to get an exact count of how many Americans are uninsured. The Congressional Budget Office completed a study in May 2003 showing that 57 to 59 million people, about a quarter of the nonelderly population, lacked insurance at some point in 1998 (the most recent data available). During that same period, the CBO estimated that 21 to 31 million of these people lacked coverage for the entire year. Thus, the number of uninsured varies from about 20 to 60 million people, depending on how one asks the question. The number most often reported is the figure for those uninsured for the entire year, which rose to about 47.3 million in 2003.

In addition to the uninsured, a large number of Americans are underinsured, meaning that they lack coverage for some critical illnesses or procedures. For instance, many insurance plans either do not cover preexisting conditions or else require long waiting periods before these conditions are covered. Many policies mandate severe limitations on benefits for mental illnesses, and almost none provide for long-term care. Many policies expect large co-payments for other medical care, including outpatient and hospital services. It is estimated that at least as many Americans are significantly underinsured as are uninsured.

THE SAFETY NET

In a 1999 poll, 57 percent of Americans surveyed believed that those without health insurance were "able to get all the care they need from doctors and hospitals." This belief in a "safety net" that provides care for the uninsured unfortunately does not reflect the reality on the ground. For those who lack health coverage, seeking medical care is a complex and variable process. Mary Helen Mays, executive director of Community Voices in El Paso, Texas, likened it to playing the video game Donkey Kong, trying to weave in and out of constantly moving programs and avoiding barriers.

For primary care, the federal government funds a number of sliding-scale fee clinics in poorer rural and urban areas. Known as federally qualified health centers (FQHCs), these facilities tend to operate as large walk-in clinics, where everyone seeking care lines up in the morning and waits several hours before seeing whichever provider happens to be available. These clinics are typically understaffed and overworked, and clients rarely see the same provider twice. Patients are charged a sliding-scale fee, depending on their income. Some private charitable organizations operate free clinics, usually staffed by volunteer providers, often in church basements or other donated space and sometimes operating only one evening a week. In both these settings, some free medications may be available, donated by pharmaceutical companies. Some clinics may help patients navigate the ever-changing maze of free care programs offered by the drug companies.

Most not-for-profit hospitals offer some amount of free care in their ambulatory clinics as part of their mission (and their justification for not paying taxes). This is highly variable, however. A few not-for-profit providers have recently been called to task by advocacy groups for inadequately providing services for the uninsured.* In many localities, a public hospital funded by local property taxes serves as the provider of last resort, meaning that it theoretically takes all comers, especially those unable to get care elsewhere. Many of these public facilities, like the FQHCs, are stretched to capacity and occasionally need to turn patients away or delay a patient's care because they are too full.

Some counties have active public health departments that provide some screening services, prenatal care, and immunizations. As the number of uninsured individuals increases, some public health departments are rerouting their resources from classic public health (preventive) measures to offering medical treatment, particularly for chronic diseases such as hypertension and diabetes that are not addressed well by the existing safety net systems.

Almost everywhere, for many of the uninsured, the most reliable source of care is the local emergency room. A federal law called the Emergency Medical Treatment and Active Labor Act (EMTALA) obligates hospitals to provide "medical screening" to all patients who come to their emergency rooms in order to determine whether an emergency medical condition exists and, if it does, to stabilize the patients as best they can before transferring them to another facility. Some hospitals also provide other sorts of diagnostics and treatment for the uninsured as

*The *Wall Street Journal* reported that a hospital in Champaign, Illinois, was stripped of its tax-exempt status because of the way it treated its uninsured patients (Lagnado 2004).

charity care; some refer the uninsured to a local free clinic for further management; others simply discharge patients after stabilizing the emergency.

Those who are admitted to hospitals, as well as those seen in emergency rooms, are billed by the hospital, almost always at a much higher cost than the prices negotiated by insurance companies. Some hospitals are willing to negotiate long-term payment plans, but often these bills are turned over to collection agencies, leading to harassment at best, liens on property and bankruptcy at worst.

HOLES IN THE NET

In the course of our research, we met many dedicated people who work for FQHCs, private charitable clinics, and public health departments. They work long hours in poor conditions for little or no pay, usually out of a deep sense of mission and a desire to help those who are less fortunate. This personal dedication, however, cannot make up for the very limited resources with which they try to meet enormous needs. Almost all free, sliding-scale, and low-cost clinics have long waiting lists for appointments, or even urgent visits, and cannot consistently provide specialty care, advanced testing, a full range of medications, or other needed services such as mental health or dentistry.

In addition, a deeper problem is that the system is structurally rigged against both the doctors and the clinics. The Medicare system demands that physicians charge Medicare the same rate that they charge their lowest-paying patients. Thus, if a physician agrees to see a poor, uninsured patient for a discounted rate, Medicare will pay only that rate for all Medicare patients. A physician who undercodes a visit in order to charge less (claiming to have spent less time with the patient than was in fact the case) can be prosecuted for Medicare fraud.

Even when doctors treat patients for free, bill them at low rates for their visits, or arrange extended payment plans, they may be unable to obtain lab tests or medications to carry through with diagnostic and treatment plans. Researchers at the New York Academy of Medicine and the International Longevity Center–USA report that fewer than one-quarter of internists can often get medications at lower prices for their uninsured patients, and fewer than one in ten can often get reduced-cost lab tests or diagnostic procedures.

RESOURCES FOR HEALTH CARE

If you or someone you know is uninsured and needs help obtaining health care, there may be some sources of aid. Unfortunately, the available resources are extremely variable, fragmented, and incomplete. Most programs are targeted at specific populations and cover only specific services. Both eligibility and benefits tend to change frequently. Often, your best chance of finding resources is through a knowledgeable (and dedicated) local social worker.

The following sources might also be useful:

- Covering Kids and Families is an initiative in forty-five states and the District of Columbia intended to help eligible children and adults sign up for public coverage. Information is available online at http://coveringkidsandfamilies.org/.

- For information on free or low-cost coverage for children, see www.insurekidsnow.gov or call 1-877-543-7669.

- To find the nearest Community Health Center (which sees all patients regardless of ability to pay and charges based on a sliding-scale fee schedule), visit the Web site http://ask.hrsa.gov/pc/.

- For assistance in finding programs that provide free or low-cost medications for those who cannot afford them, consult www.needymeds.com or www.rxassist.org.

- To find a free clinic near you, visit www.freeclinic.net.

We argue that only through large-scale structural reform will we ever be able to serve the needs of those who are currently uninsured. A number of local and national advocacy groups are involved in trying to implement such structural change. To volunteer or get involved, you can contact these organizations:

- To find a list of local advocacy groups actively involved in expanding access to health care, visit the Web site www.accessproject.org.

- National advocacy groups include Community Catalyst (www.communitycatalyst.org) and Families USA (www .familiesusa.org).

NOTES

PROLOGUE

For information on migraines, see Stewart et al. 1992. For more on the link between stress and health status, see Brunner 1997; Ruberman et al. 1984.

INTRODUCTION

For Medicaid statistics, see Kaiser Family Foundation Commission on Medicaid and the Uninsured 2004. For a report on the number of people with low family incomes who lack health insurance or Medicaid, see Short and Graefe 2003. The Institute of Medicine report *Care without Coverage* (2002a) summarizes studies concerning insurance and health status. On the number of young adults who lack health insurance, see Collins et al. 2004. On the formation of the link between health insurance and employment, see Fein 1986; Hacker 2002, p. 7.

Grumbach and Bodenheimer (2002) emphasize the medical importance of continuity of care. Burstin, Lipsitz, and Brennan (1992) discuss the substandard care received by the uninsured, and an Institute of Medicine report (2002a) compares the treatment received by insured and uninsured individuals; see also Kerr and Siu 1993.

Lagnado (2003b) compares the cost of an appendectomy for insured and uninsured patients. For comparative costs of emergency room visits, see Forrest and Starfield 1996. On the tactics used by collection agencies against the uninsured, see Daly et al. 2002. For bankruptcy statistics, see Sullivan, Warren, and Westbrook 2001. The *Wall Street Journal* ran several articles on the topic of body attachment; see, for example, Lagnado 2003a.

On caste, see Sharma 1999 and Seabrook 2002.

For in-hospital death rates for insured and uninsured patients, see Hadley, Steinberg, and Feder 1991. On death rates in homeless shelters, see Barrow et al. 1999. Jaffee and Zdanowicz (1999) write in the *Washington Post* about prisons as treatment facilities for the mentally ill.

1. FROM WORKING CLASS TO WORKING POOR

Naomi Klein's remarks are taken from Klein 1999, p. 231. On job loss in Illinois, see Crump and Merrett 1998. Comments on corporate restructuring are quoted from Harrison and Bluestone 1988, p. 22. On outsourcing, see Lewin and Johnston 2000; Pottruck 1996. Rifkin (1996) describes job loss among mid-level management in the 1980s. For information on such job losses in the 1990s, see Greenglass and Burke 2001, who cite Uchitelle and Kleinfield 1996; also see Feldman, Leana, and Bolino 2002; Fagiano 1996. Hagevik (2001) discusses the continuing disappearance of jobs in the new millennium. For more on the debates over the extent of job loss, see Downs 1996.

2. MEDICAID, WELFARE REFORM, AND LOW-WAGE WORK

Collins et al. 2003 is an excellent overall report on low-wage workers and health insurance. For data on the number of Americans whose wages put them below the federal poverty line, see Shulman 2003b. On who is likely to hold a low-wage job, see Shulman 2003a, p. 70. Collins and colleagues (2003) present data on rates of uninsurance among low-wage workers at various income levels.

For more on the link between socioeconomic status and health, see Adler and Newman 2002; Pincus et al. 1998. The Philadelphia Department of Public Health study is cited in Robbins 2003. On higher mortality rates among low-income residents, see Pappas et al. 1993. Pamuk and colleagues (1998) report data on lead exposure. Nemeroff and colleagues (1992) provide data on stress and the immune system.

Comparative income data for Mississippi are from the U.S. Bureau of Economic Analysis (epodunk.com 1999). For U.S. mortality and morbidity rates, see Kaiser Family Foundation 2001. International comparisons are from Organization for Economic Cooperation and Development 2001.

Hays 2003 is a useful source on welfare reform; for Hays's comment on the fate of former welfare clients, see p. 8. See Greenstein and Guyer 2001, pp. 335–336, 340, on families who failed to receive Medicaid or food stamps after leaving the welfare rolls. See Hays 2003 on the work requirements and time limits of TANF (p. 22) and on the relation of the Personal Responsibility Act of 1996 to the "family ideal" (pp. 17–18); Hays reports the findings of the General Accounting Office study on p. 165. On SSI's disability definition, see Zedlewski and Loprest 2001, p. 312. On lack of insurance after leaving welfare, see Seccombe 2002, p. 293.

3. FAMILY MATTERS

For statistics on women's marital status and lack of insurance, see Ohio Department of Health 2001; Berk and Taylor 1984; Institute of Medicine 2002b, p. 49. On rates of poverty among women who are widowed, separated, or divorced, see Morgan 1991, pp. 94, 97. On women who lose their health benefits after divorce, see Weitzman 1985, p. 135.

For statistics on rates of domestic violence, number of physician visits, outpatient expenses, long-term physical and emotional repercussions of domestic violence, and difficulties in diagnosing the causes of long-standing problems, see Koss 1994 and Koss et al. 1994, esp. p. 182.

For an analysis of the role of domestic violence in the lives of women on welfare, see Governor's Commission on Domestic Violence, State of Massachusetts 1997, esp. the conclusion. On financial support as a factor in leaving abusive relationships, see Brandwein 1999. Davis (1999, pp. 22–23) describes the challenges that victims of domestic violence face in trying to hold down jobs.

4. WHO CARES FOR THE CAREGIVERS?

Hooyman and Gonyea (1995) provide an in-depth discussion of the issues involved in family caregiving; see esp. pp. 1, 127, 144, and 146; for the prediction that the nursing home population would triple without family assistance, see p. 2. This volume also describes how difficult it is for mothers of children with disabilities to return to work (p. 127) and reports data about the number of adults with chronic disabilities who depend on others for care (p. 1). Statistics from the National Family Caregivers Association were presented by Suzanne Mintz, president and cofounder of the association, in her testimony before the U.S. Senate Special Committee on Aging (Mintz 2001). The health risks of family caregiving are described in Schulz et al. 2003. On the likelihood that a family caregiver will be female, see Hooyman and Gonyea 1995, p. 3. Hooyman and Gonyea (1995, p. 142) also discuss the health problems faced by women caregivers and cite the study of older mothers caring for adults with mental retardation. For the NFCA members survey, see National Family Caregivers Association 2001.

5. THE FOX GUARDING THE HENHOUSE

On laws requiring workplace safety standards, see Schlosser 2001. Leigh and colleagues present data showing that the actual coverage workers receive is often not commensurate with the actual costs of their injuries (2000, pp. 2, 11). On insurance companies denying payment of workers' compensation claims ("starving them out"), see Cullen 2002, p. 27; for discussion of the firewall between health insurance and workers' compensation, see pp. 21, 59. Messing 1998 is an excellent source of information about occupational hazards that particularly affect women. On the number of Americans who die each day from occupational disease and work-related injuries, see Leigh et al. 2000, pp. 1–2.

6. RISKY BUSINESS

For statistics on the number of new small businesses and the demographics of small business owners, see Blackford 1991, p. 117. On the economic contributions of small businesses—including the percentage of private-sector workers employed, new jobs generated, patents produced—see Small Business Administration 2004, which contains figures supplied by the SBA's Office of Advocacy.

Blackford's argument that governmental policies have favored big business over small is explicated in Blackford 1991, pp. xiv–xv. On the difficulties faced by small businesses in obtaining insurance for employees, see Glover et al. 2000, p. 5. The Kaiser Family Foundation (2003a) analyzes the rates of uninsurance in small businesses. On the high insurance costs faced by small firms, see Small Business Administration 2004. On the rise in health care costs between 2000 and 2003, see Mercer Human Resources Consulting 2001 and 2003; also see Scorza 2001. The epigraph in which Mansel Blackford describes some of the core characteristics of small businesses is quoted from Blackford 1991, pp. xii–xiii.

7. YOUNG, SICK, AND PART-TIME

Collins et al. 2004 is an excellent review of the lack of insurance among young people. On the increase in the number of contingent workers, see Hooyman and Gonyea 1995, p. 67. For a discussion of economic mobility and young adults, see Bernhardt et al. 2001.

On insurance plans marketed to young adults, see Windham 2003. Collins and colleagues (2004) cite statistics on pregnancy rates among young women. For data on the injury rate among young adults, see Quinn, Schoen, and Buatti 2000. On the effects of delay of care, see

Collins et al. 2004. For health care statistics from Massachusetts, see Kaiser Family Foundation 2001.

Furstenberg (2003) discusses the diminished employment prospects of poor and minority youth; see pp. 211–212, 218, 221, 223, 226–227.

8. MENTAL HEALTH MATTERS

On poverty rates among Texas Hispanics, see Kaiser Family Foundation 2003b. Families USA 2004 provides statistics on uninsured Hispanics in Texas.

Both Stefan 2001 and Stefan 2002 are excellent sources concerning discrimination on the basis of mental illness. The epigraph on the cumulative effects of discrimination is taken from Stefan 2001, p. 4. On the issue of inadequate mental health coverage by Medicare and Medicaid, see Stefan 2001, pp. 202–205. For a discussion of explicit discrimination on the basis of mental disabilities by private insurance companies, see Stefan 2001, p. 249. For an analysis of the impact of a mental disability on employment, including the various types of employment discrimination faced by individuals with such disabilities, see President's New Freedom Commission on Mental Health 2002; Stefan 2002, esp. p. 15.

9. RACE MATTERS

On caste and race, see Sharma 1999. Dollard (1937) describes caste conflict in America; see pp. 63, 91.

For a historical perspective on race and health care, see Byrd and Clayton 2002, esp. pp. 9, 13, 14, 17. The Institute of Medicine report titled *Unequal Treatment* (2003) offers an excellent general review of the subject of racial disparities in health care (including insurance coverage). On race, education, and wages, see Shulman 2003a, pp. 70, 76. Rhoades (2004) analyzes rates of uninsurance by race. For statistics on mortality among African Americans, see Institute of Medicine 2003, esp. chap. 1. On racial disparities in health outcomes, as well as the implications of delayed diagnosis and treatment of minorities, see Brown et al. 2000; Institute of Medicine 2003.

On difficulties in landing a job after a felony conviction, see Bushway 2000. See Mauer 2000, p. 47, on the racial makeup of prisoners in the United States. On racial discrimination in hiring practices, see Riach and Rich 2002.

10. DESCENT THROUGH THE DEATH SPIRAL

See Gans 1995, p. 2, for his behavioral definition of the underclass. On weight as a marker of socioeconomic status, see Freund and McGuire 1999, pp. 49–50. Debbie in Alabama is quoted in Maharidge and Williamson 1989, p. 148.

Patricia Post's statement on homelessness and access to health care comes from Post 2001, p. 31. Our primary sources on health problems among homeless people include Curry 2000; Jahiel 1992; National Health Care for the Homeless Council 1999. Jahiel (1992) summarizes various local research projects on homelessness and health, including the New York and Baltimore studies; see esp. pp. 135–137.

On the extent and types of mental health problems in the homeless population and estimates of the percentage of homeless individuals who might need institutionalization, see National Coalition for the Homeless 1999. Brian Harvey is quoted in Hutson and Clapham 1999, p. 71. See National Health Care for the Homeless Council 1999 on loss of benefits, substance abuse elimination provisions, and homelessness.

For information about homelessness among veterans, see National Coalition for Homeless Veterans n.d. On the issue of Vietnam veterans seeking discharge from psychiatric hospitals against medical advice, see Starr 1974, p. 73; on the increasing numbers of returning veterans with permanent injuries, see p. 54. For information on Agent Orange and Gulf War Syndrome, see Milano 2000.

Representative Ted Strickland is quoted in Human Rights Watch 2003. Cohen (2000, p. 98) presents data on incarceration rates. On racial understandings of the underclass, see Katz 1989, p. 195. On the number of drug offenders sentenced to prison and the percentages of prisoners with substance abuse problems, see Anno 2000; Cohen 2000. For numbers of prisoners actually receiving treatment for substance abuse, see Peters 2000. Cohen (2000) also discusses the incidence of medical problems, including tuberculosis, in prisons. Anno (2000) describes the health profiles of women prisoners. On the incarcerated mentally ill, see Weisman 2000; McGarrahan 1991. On mentally ill individuals who lose their eligibility for Medicaid or federal disability benefits, see Lipton 2004. Weisman's comment on reincarceration is found in Weisman 2000, p. 108.

11. MOVING FORWARD

For a useful review of the history of attempts to reform the health care system in the United States, see Fein 1986. The advocacy group report on Bush's proposed tax credits is Families USA 2002. Woolhandler, Campbell, and Himmelstein (2003) compare costs of the U.S. health care system to costs of the Canadian system. Hadley and Holahan (2003) provide an estimate of the cost of providing comprehensive coverage. On subsidies for employer-sponsored health insurance and estimates of lost productivity resulting from lack of insurance, see Williams 2003; Salisbury 1999. The estimate of government revenue added by removing the tax deductibility of insurance is from Salisbury 1999.

APPENDIX 1. A PRIMER

Stuart Butler is quoted from his testimony before the Senate Special Committee on Aging (2003). The estimates and breakdown of 2002 U.S. health care spending are detailed in Levit et al. 2004, pp. 147–159. The estimate of administrative costs is found in Woolhandler, Campbell, and Himmelstein 2003. Profit statements of Aetna and Massachusetts Blue Cross/Blue Shield are contained in the companies' respective annual reports. Friedman (1996) offers an interesting review of Medicare's coverage of end-stage renal disease. Hays (2003, p. 167) discusses the tightening of disability eligibility. The review time for disability claims is reported in Stefan 2001, pp. 221–222. See Liska 1997 for a breakdown of beneficiaries and costs for Medicaid.

Douglas Holtz-Eakin is quoted in Pear 2003, which also describes the Congressional Budget Office study. The poll asking whether Americans believe that the uninsured can get adequate care was conducted by the Kaiser Family Foundation; see Blendon, Young, and DeRoches 1999. On the difficulties internists face in caring for their uninsured patients, see Fairbrother et al. 2003.

BIBLIOGRAPHY

Access Project. 2003. "The Consequences of Medical Debt: Evidence from Three Communities." February. Available online at www.accessproject.org/downloads/med_consequences.pdf (accessed August 11, 2004).

Adler, Nancy E., and Katherine Newman. 2002. "Socioeconomic Disparities in Health: Pathways and Policies." *Health Affairs* 21, no. 2 (March/April): 60–76.

Allard, Mary Ann, M. E. Colton, R. Albelda, and C. Cosenza. 1997. "In Harm's Way: Domestic Violence, AFDC Receipt, and Welfare Reform in Massachusetts." John W. McCormack Graduate School of Policy Studies, Center for Social Policy. Available online at www.mccormack.umb.edu/csp/publications/harms%20way.pdf (accessed April 9, 2004).

Anderson, Gerard F., Dennis G. Shea, Peter S. Hussey, Salomeh Keyhani, and Laurie Zephyrin. 2004. "Doughnut Holes and Price Controls." *Health Affairs* Web exclusive, July 21. Available online at http://content.healthaffairs.org/cgi/content/full/hlthaff.w4.396/DC1 (accessed August 30, 2004).

Anno, B. Jaye. 2000. "Inappropriate Prison Populations." In *Building Violence: How America's Rush to Incarcerate Creates More Violence*, edited by John P. May, pp. 76–81. Thousand Oaks, Calif.: Sage.

Badley, E. M., and P. P. Wang. 2001. "The Contribution of Arthritis and Disability to Nonparticipation in the Labor Force: A Canadian Example." *Journal of Rheumatology* 28, no. 5 (May): 1077–1082.

Barlett, Donald L., and James B. Steele. 1996. *America: Who Stole the Dream?* Kansas City: Andrews and McMeel.

Barrow, S. M., D. B. Herman, P. Cordova, and E. L. Struening. 1999. "Mortality among Homeless Shelter Residents in New York City." *American Journal of Public Health* 89, no. 4 (April): 529–534.

Barth, Fredrik. 1969. *Ethnic Groups and Boundaries: The Social Organization of Culture Difference*. Boston: Little, Brown.

Bartley, M., and C. Owen. 1996. "Relation between Socioeconomic Status, Employment, and Health during Economic Change, 1973–1993." *British Medical Journal* 313 (August 24): 445–449.

Berk, Marc L., and Amy K. Taylor. 1984. *Women and Divorce: Health Insurance Coverage, Utilization, and Health Care Expenditures*. Rockville, Md.: U.S. Department of Health and Human Services, National Center for Health Services Research.

Bernhardt, Annette, Martina Morris, Mark S. Handcock, and Marc A. Scott. 2001. *Divergent Paths: Economic Mobility in the New American Labor Market*. New York: Russell Sage Foundation.

Bernstein, J., and H. Heidi. 2000. "The Low-Wage Labor Market: Challenges and Opportunities for Economic Self-Sufficiency." U.S. Department of Health and Human Services Publication. Available online at http://aspe.hhs.gov/hsp/lwlm99/bernhart.htm (accessed October 13, 2003).

Berreman, Gerald D. 1967. "Stratification, Pluralism, and Interaction: A Comparative Analysis of Caste." In *Caste and Race: Comparative Approaches*, edited by Anthony De Reuck and Julie Knight, pp. 45–73. Boston: Little, Brown.

Blackford, Mansel G. 1991. *A History of Small Business in America*. New York: Twayne.

Blendon, Robert J., John T. Young, and Catherine DeRoches. 1999. "The Uninsured, the Working Uninsured, and the Public." *Health Affairs* 18, no. 6 (November/December): 203–211.

Boushey, Heather, Chauna Brocht, Bethney Gunderson, and Jared Bernstein. 2001. *Hardships in America: The Real Story of Working Families*. Washington, D.C.: Economic Policy Institute.

Brandwein, Ruth A. 1999. "Family Violence, Women, and Welfare." In *Battered Women, Children, and Welfare Reform: The Ties That Bind*, edited by Ruth A. Brandwein, pp. 3–16. Thousand Oaks, Calif.: Sage.

Brown, E. Richard, Victoria D. Ojeda, Roberta Wyn, and Rebecka Levan. 2000. "Racial and Ethnic Disparities in Access to Health Insurance and Health Care." UCLA Center for Health Policy Research and Henry J. Kaiser Family Foundation. April.

Brown, Karl, and Elizabeth Herbert. 2002. "Health Status Report: Infectious Diseases in Corrections." *HEPP Report* (HIV and Hepatitis Education Prison

Project) 5, no. 10, October. Brown Medical School Office of Continuing Medical Education.

Brunner, E. 1997. "Socioeconomic Determinants of Health: Stress and the Biology of Inequality." *British Medical Journal* 314 (May 17): 1472–1476.

Burstin, H. R., S. R. Lipsitz, and T. A. Brennan. 1992. "Socioeconomic Status and Risk for Substandard Medical Care." *Journal of the American Medical Association* 268, no. 17 (November 4): 2383–2387.

Bushway, Shawn D. 2000. "The Stigma of a Criminal History Record in the Labor Market." In *Building Violence: How America's Rush to Incarcerate Creates More Violence*, edited by John P. May, pp. 142–148. Thousand Oaks, Calif.: Sage.

Butler, Stuart. 2003. "Laying the Groundwork for Universal Health Care Coverage." Testimony before the U.S. Senate Special Committee on Aging. March 10. Available online at http://aging.senate.gov/_files/hr95sb.pdf (accessed August 30, 2004).

Byrd, W. Michael, and Linda A. Clayton. 2002. *An American Health Dilemma: Race, Medicine, and Health Care in the United States, 1900–2000.* New York: Routledge.

Cohen, Robert L. 2000. "Mass Incarceration: A Public Health Failure." In *Building Violence: How America's Rush to Incarcerate Creates More Violence*, edited by John P. May, pp. 95–99. Thousand Oaks, Calif.: Sage.

Collins, Sara R., Cathy Schoen, Diane Colasanto, and Deirdre A. Downey. 2003. "On the Edge: Low-Wage Workers and Their Health Insurance Coverage." Commonwealth Fund Issue Brief, April. Available online at www.cmwf .org/programs/insurance/collins_ontheedge_ib_626.pdf (accessed June 28, 2004).

Collins, Sara R., Cathy Schoen, Katie Tenney, Michelle M. Doty, and Alice Ho. 2004. "Rite of Passage? Why Young Adults Become Uninsured and How New Policies Can Help." Commonwealth Fund Issue Brief, May. Available online at www.cmwf.org/programs/insurance/collins_riteofpassage_ib_649 .pdf (accessed June 29, 2004).

Cook, Thomas D., and Frank F. Furstenberg. 2002. "Explaining Aspects of the Transition to Adulthood in Italy, Sweden, Germany, and the United States: A Cross-Disciplinary Case Synthesis Approach." *Annals of the American Academy of Political and Social Science* 580 (March): 257–287.

Crump, Jeff R., and Christopher D. Merrett. 1998. "Scales of Struggle: Economic Restructuring in the U.S. Midwest." *Annals of the Association of American Geographers* 88 (3): 496–515.

Cullen, Lisa. 2002. *A Job to Die For.* Monroe, Maine: Common Courage Press.

Curry, Jen. 2000. "Homelessness and HIV." *ACRIA (AIDS Community Research Initiative of America) Update* 9, no. 3 (Summer). Available online at www .criany.org/treatment/treatment_edu_summerupdate2000_homeless.html (accessed January 1, 2004).

Curtis, J. R., W. Burke, A. W. Kassner, and M. L. Aitken. 1997. "Absence of Health Insurance Is Associated with Decreased Life Expectancy in Patients with Cystic Fibrosis." *American Journal of Respiratory and Critical Care Medicine* 155, no. 6 (June): 1921–1924.

Daly, H. F., L. M. Oblak, R. W. Seifert, and K. Shellenberger. 2002. "Into the Red to Stay in the Pink: The Hidden Cost of Being Uninsured." *Health Matrix* 12, no. 1 (Winter): 39–61.

Davis, Martha F. 1999. "The Economics of Abuse: How Violence Perpetuates Women's Poverty." In *Battered Women, Children, and Welfare Reform: The Ties That Bind,* edited by Ruth A. Brandwein, pp. 17–30. Thousand Oaks, Calif.: Sage.

De Reuck, Anthony, and Julie Knight, eds. 1967. *Caste and Race: Comparative Approaches.* Boston: Little, Brown.

De Vos, George. 1967. "Psychology of Purity and Pollution as Related to Social Self-Identity and Caste." In *Caste and Race: Comparative Approaches,* edited by Anthony De Reuck and Julie Knight, pp. 292–315. Boston: Little, Brown.

Dollard, John. 1937. *Caste and Class in a Southern Town.* Garden City, N.Y.: Doubleday.

Doty, Michelle. 2003a. "Hispanic Patients' Double Burden: Lack of Health Insurance and Limited English." Findings from the Commonwealth Fund 2001 Health Care Quality Survey. February. Available online at www.smwf .org/usr_doc/doty_hispanicdoubleburden_592.pdf (accessed August 30, 2004).

———. 2003b. "Insurance, Access, and Quality of Care among Hispanic Populations: 2003 Chartpack." October. Commonwealth Fund. Available online at www.cmwf.org/usr_doc/Doty_chartpack_pdf_684.pdf (accessed August 30, 2004).

Downs, Alan. 1996. "The Wages of Downsizing." *Mother Jones* 21, no. 4 (July/August): 26–31.

Duberman, Lucile. 1976. *Social Inequality: Class and Caste in America.* Philadelphia: J. B. Lippincott.

Dumont, Louis. 1980. *Homo Hierarchicus: The Caste System and Its Implications.* Rev. English ed. Chicago: University of Chicago Press.

Edin, Kathryn, and Laura Lein. 1997. *Making Ends Meet: How Single Mothers Survive Welfare and Low-Wage Work.* New York: Russell Sage Foundation.

epodunk.com. 1999. "Mississippi: Income." Available online at www.epodunk .com/cgi-bin/incomeOverview.php?locIndex=25 (accessed August 11, 2004).

Fagiano, David. 1996. "Employment Contract Myth." *Management Review* 85 (7): 5.

Fairbrother, Gerry, Michael K. Gusmano, Heidi L. Park, and Roberta Scheinmann. 2003. "Care for the Uninsured in General Internists' Private Offices." *Health Affairs* 22, no. 6 (November/December): 217–224.

Families USA. 2002. *A 10-Foot Rope for a 40-Foot Hole: Tax Credits for the Uninsured.* Update, Publication Number 02-102. May. Available online at www.familiesusa.org/site/DocServer/taxcreditsreport2002update.pdf?docID =281 (accessed August 11, 2004).

———. 2004. "The Uninsured: A Closer Look—Texans without Health Insurance." June. Available online at www.familiesusa.org/site/DocServer/Texas .pdf?docID=3697 (accessed August 14, 2004).

Fein, R. 1986. *Medical Care, Medical Costs.* Cambridge, Mass.: Harvard University Press.

Feldman, Daniel C., Carrie R. Leana, and Mark C. Bolino. 2002. "Underemployment and Relative Deprivation among Re-employed Executives." *Journal of Occupational and Organizational Psychology* 75 (4): 453–471.

Forrest, C. B., and B. Starfield. 1996. "The Effect of First Contact Care with Primary Care Clinicians on Ambulatory Health Expenditures." *Journal of Family Practice* 43:40–48.

Franklin, Stephen. 2001. *Three Strikes: Labor's Heartland Losses and What They Mean for Working Americans.* New York: Guilford Press.

Freund, Peter E. S., and Meredith B. McGuire. 1999. *Health, Illness, and the Social Body: A Critical Sociology.* 3rd ed. Upper Saddle River, N.J.: Prentice-Hall.

Friedman, Eli. 1996. "End-Stage Renal Disease Therapy: An American Success Story." *Journal of the American Medical Association* 275, no. 14 (April 10): 1118–1124.

Fronstin, Paul. 2001. "Sources of Health Insurance and Characteristics of the Uninsured: Analysis of the March 2001 Current Population Survey." Employee Benefit Research Institute. December, no. 240. Table 2, "Non-Elderly Americans with Selected Sources of Health Insurance, by Age and Own Work Status, and Work Status of Family Head, 2000." Available online at www.ebri.org (accessed August 11, 2004).

Furstenberg, Frank F. 2000. "The Sociology of Adolescence and Youth in the 1990s: A Critical Commentary." *Journal of Marriage and the Family* 62 (November): 896–910.

———. 2003. "Growing Up in American Society: Income, Opportunities, and Outcomes." In *Social Dynamics of the Life Course: Transitions, Institutions, and Interrelations*, edited by Walter R. Heinz and Victor W. Marshall, pp. 211–233. New York: Aldine de Gruyter.

Gans, Herbert J. 1995. *The War against the Poor: The Underclass and Antipoverty Policy*. New York: Basic Books.

Garrett, B., L. M. Nichols, and E. K. Greenman. 2001. "Workers without Health Insurance." Research Report of the Urban Institute. September 1. Available online at www.urban.org/UploadedPDF/310244_workershealthins .pdf (accessed April 9, 2004).

Glover, Saundra H., Carleen Stoskopf, Thomas E. Brown, Fran Wheeler, Yang Kim, and Sudha Xirasagar. 2000. "Small Business and Access to Health Insurers, Particularly HMOs." U.S. Small Business Administration Office of Advocacy, Small Business Research Summary 202. October. Available online at www.sba.gov/advo/research/rs202tot.pdf (accessed August 30, 2004).

Goffman, Erving. 1963. *Stigma: Notes on the Management of Spoiled Identity*. New York: Simon and Schuster.

Governor's Commission on Domestic Violence, State of Massachusetts. 1997. "Safely Toward Self-Sufficiency: Battered Women's Path through Welfare Reform." Available online at www.mass.gov/gcdv/safely.htm (accessed August 30, 2004).

Greenglass, Esther R., and Ronald J. Burke. 2001. "Editorial Introduction: Downsizing and Restructuring: Implications for Stress and Anxiety." *Anxiety, Stress, and Coping* 14 (1): 1–13.

Greenstein, Robert, and Jocelyn Guyer. 2001. "Supporting Work through Medicaid and Food Stamps." In *The New World of Welfare*, edited by Rebecca M. Blank and Ron Haskins, pp. 335–349. Washington, D.C.: Brookings Institution Press.

Grumbach, Kevin, and Thomas Bodenheimer. 2002. "A Primary Care Home for Americans: Putting the House in Order." *Journal of the American Medical Association* 288, no. 7 (August 21): 889–893.

Hacker, Jacob S. 2002. *The Divided Welfare State: The Battle over Public and Private Benefits in the United States*. Cambridge: Cambridge University Press.

Hadley, J., E. P. Steinberg, and J. Feder. 1991. "Comparison of Uninsured and Privately Insured Hospital Patients." *Journal of the American Medical Association* 265, no. 3 (January 16): 374–379.

Hadley, Jack, and John Holahan. 2003. "Covering the Uninsured: How Much Would It Cost?" *Health Affairs* Web exclusive. June 4. Available online at http://content.healthaffairs.org/cgi/content/full/hlthaff.w3.250v1/DC1 (accessed August 30, 2004).

Hagevik, Sandra. 2001. "Dear Employee: Please Go, Please Stay." *Journal of Environmental Health* 62 (7): 48–49.

Harrison, Bennett, and Barry Bluestone. 1988. *The Great U-Turn: Corporate Restructuring and the Polarizing of America.* New York: Basic Books.

Hays, Sharon. 2003. *Flat Broke with Children: Women in the Age of Welfare Reform.* New York: Oxford University Press.

Herman, Judith Lewis. 1992. *Trauma and Recovery.* London: Pandora.

Heymann, S. J. 2000. *The Widening Gap: Why Working Families Are in Jeopardy and What Can Be Done about It.* New York: Basic Books.

Hooyman, Nancy R., and Judith Gonyea. 1995. *Feminist Perspectives on Family Care: Policies for Gender Justice.* Thousand Oaks, Calif.: Sage.

Human Rights Watch. 2000. "Punishment and Prejudice: Racial Disparities in the War on Drugs." *Human Rights Watch Report* 12, no. 2, May.

———. 2002. "Race and Incarceration in the United States." Press Backgrounder, February 27.

———. 2003. "Ill-Equipped: U.S. Prisons and Offenders with Mental Illness." October 22. Available online at www.hrw.org/reports/2003/usa1003/ (accessed September 8, 2004).

Hutson, Susan, and David Clapham. 1999. *Homelessness: Public Policies and Private Troubles.* London: Cassell Academic.

Hwang, Stephen W. 2000. "Mortality among Men Using Homeless Shelters in Toronto, Ontario." *Journal of the American Medical Association* 283, no. 16 (April 26): 2152–2157.

"Infectious Diseases in Corrections." 2003. *HEPP Report* (HIV and Hepatitis Education Prison Project) 6, no. 5, May. Brown Medical School, Office of Continuing Medical Education.

Institute of Medicine. 2002a. Committee on the Consequences of Uninsurance. Board on Health Care Services. *Care without Coverage: Too Little, Too Late.* Washington, D.C.: National Academy Press.

———. 2002b. Committee on the Consequences of Uninsurance. Board on Health Care Services. *Health Insurance Is a Family Matter.* Washington, D.C.: National Academy Press.

———. 2003. Committee on Understanding and Eliminating Racial and Ethnic Disparities in Health Care. Board on Health Sciences Policy. *Unequal Treatment: Confronting Racial and Ethnic Disparities in Health Care.* Edited by

Brian D. Smedley, Adrienne Y. Stith, and Alan R. Nelson. Washington, D.C.: National Academy Press.

Jaffee, D. J., and M. T. Zdanowicz. 1999. "Federal Neglect of the Mentally Ill." *Washington Post*, December 30.

Jahiel, Rene I. 1992. "Health and Health Care of Homeless People." In *Homelessness: A National Perspective*, edited by Marjorie J. Robertson and Milton Greenblatt, pp. 133–164. New York: Plenum Press.

Kaiser Family Foundation. 2001. *State Health Facts Online*. Data Source: Behavioral Risk Factor Surveillance System, U.S. Centers for Disease Control and Prevention, National Center for Health Statistics. Available online at www.statehealthfacts.kff.org (accessed February 1, 2004).

———. 2003a. "Employer Health Benefits 2003 Annual Survey." Available online at www.kff.org/insurance/ehbs2003-abstract.cfm (accessed November 24, 2003).

———. 2003b. *State Health Facts Online*. Available at www.statehealthfacts .kff.org (accessed June 15, 2003).

Kaiser Family Foundation and Health Research and Educational Trust. 2003. "Employer Health Benefits: 2003 Summary of Findings." Available online at www.kff.org/insurance/ehbs2003-abstract.cfm (accessed August 11, 2004).

Kaiser Family Foundation Commission on Medicaid and the Uninsured. 2004. "Health Insurance Coverage in America: 2003 Data Update Highlights." Available at http://www.kff.org/uninsured/kcmu092704pk.cf (accessed November 10, 2004).

Kaiser Network. 2003a. "Hospitals Reevaluating Billing Policies for Uninsured." June 10 Daily Report. Available online at www.kaisernetwork.org/ daily_reports/rep_index.cfm?DR_ID=18187 (accessed October 6, 2003).

———. 2003b. "Universal Health Coverage Would Help Reduce Racial Health Disparities, Congressional Black Caucus Says." June 10 Daily Report. Available online at www.kaisernetwork.org/daily_reports/rep_index.cfm?DR_ID =18189 (accessed October 6, 2003).

Katz, Michael B. 1989. *The Undeserving Poor: From the War on Poverty to the War on Welfare*. New York: Pantheon.

Kerr, E. A., and A. L. Siu. 1993. "Follow-Up after Hospital Discharge: Does Insurance Make a Difference?" *Journal of Health Care for the Poor and Underserved* 4 (2): 133–142.

Klein, Naomi. 1999. *No Logo: No Space, No Choice, No Jobs—Taking Aim at the Brand Bullies*. London: Flamingo.

Koss, Mary P. 1994. "The Negative Impact of Crime Victimization on Women's Health and Medical Use." In *Reframing Women's Health*, edited by Alice J. Dan, pp. 189–200. Thousand Oaks, Calif.: Sage.

Koss, Mary, Lisa Goodman, and Angela Brown. 1994. *No Safe Haven: Male Violence against Women at Home, at Work, and in the Community.* Washington, D.C.: American Psychological Association.

Lagnado, Lucette. 2003a. "Hospitals Try Extreme Measures to Collect Their Overdue Debts." *Wall Street Journal*, October 30.

———. 2003b. "A Young Woman, an Appendectomy, and a $19,000 Debt." *Wall Street Journal*, March 17.

———. 2004. "Hospital Found 'Not Charitable,' Loses Its Status as Tax Exempt." *Wall Street Journal*, February 19.

Leach, Edmund. 1960. *Aspects of Caste in South India, Ceylon, and Northwest Pakistan.* Cambridge: Cambridge University Press.

Leigh, J. Paul, Steven B. Markowitz, Marianne Fahs, and Philip J. Landrigan. 2000. *Costs of Occupational Injuries and Illnesses.* Ann Arbor: University of Michigan Press.

Levit, Katharine, Cynthia Smith, Cathy Cowan, Art Sensenig, Aaron Catlin, and the Health Accounts Team. 2002. "Trends: Health Spending Rebound Continues in 2002." *Health Affairs* 23, no. 1 (January/February): 147–159.

Lewin, Jeffrey E., and Wesley J. Johnston. 2000. "The Impact of Downsizing and Restructuring on Organizational Competitiveness." *Competitiveness Review* 10 (1): 45–55.

Lipton, Liz. 2004. "Mental Health Court." *New York State Psychiatric Association Bulletin* 47, no. 1 (Spring): 2–3.

Liska, David. 1997. "Medicaid: Overview of a Complex Program." Urban Institute, Policy Briefs/ANF: Issues and Options for States. May 1. Available online at www.urban.org/url.cfm?ID=307044 (accessed April 11, 2004).

Maharidge, Dale, and Michael Williamson. 1989. *And Their Children after Them: The Legacy of "Let Us Now Praise Famous Men," James Agee, Walker Evans, and the Rise and Fall of Cotton in the South.* New York: Pantheon Books.

Martell, D. A., R. Rosner, and R. B. Harmon. 1995. "Base-Rate Estimates of Criminal Behavior by Homeless Mentally Ill Persons in New York City." *Psychiatric Services* 46:596–601.

Massey, Douglas S., and Nancy A. Denton. 1993. *American Apartheid: Segregation and the Making of the Underclass.* Cambridge, Mass.: Harvard University Press.

Mauer, Marc. 2000. "The Racial Dynamics of Imprisonment." In *Building Violence: How America's Rush to Incarcerate Creates More Violence*, edited by John P. May, pp. 47–50. Thousand Oaks, Calif.: Sage.

McCluskey, Martha. 2002. "Rhetoric of Risk and the Redistribution of Social Insurance." In *Embracing Risk: The Changing Culture of Insurance and Responsibility*, edited by Tom Baker and Jonathan Simon, pp. 146–170. Chicago: University of Chicago Press.

McGarrahan, Ellen. 1991. "In Florida Prisons, Health Care Is Ailing." *Miami Herald*, August 25.

McGary, Howard. 1992. "The Black Underclass and the Question of Values." In *The Underclass Question*, edited by Bill E. Lawson, pp. 57–70. Philadelphia: University of Pennsylvania Press.

Medical Expenditure Panel Survey (MEPS). 1996. "Table 2: Health Insurance Coverage of the Under 65 Civilian Noninstitutionalized Population." Available online at www.meps.ahrq.gov/compendiumtables/96ch1/t2_b96.pdf (accessed August 11, 2004).

Mercer Human Resources Consulting. 2001. "Mercer's National Survey of Employer-Sponsored Health Plans, 2001." Annual survey.

———. 2003. "Mercer's National Survey of Employer-Sponsored Health Plans, 2003." Annual survey. Highlights available online at www.mercerhr.com/summary.jhtml/dynamic/idContent/1051300 (accessed September 8, 2004).

Messing, Karen. 1998. *One-Eyed Science: Occupational Health and Women Workers*. Philadelphia: Temple University Press.

Milano, Fred. 2000. "Gulf War Syndrome: The 'Agent Orange' of the Nineties." *International Social Science Review* (Spring-Summer). Available online at www.findarticles.com/cf_dls/m0IMR/2000_Spring-Summer/70378611/p1/article.jhtml (accessed January 1, 2004).

Mintz, Suzanne. 2001. Testimony presented to the U.S. Senate Special Committee on Aging, Hearings on Family Caregiving in the Older Americans Act: Caring for the Caregiver. 107th Cong., 1st sess., May 17. Available online at www.nfcacares.org/testimony5-01.html (accessed August 30, 2004).

Morgan, Leslie A. 1991. *After Marriage Ends: Economic Consequences for Midlife Women*. Newbury Park, Calif.: Sage.

National Coalition for Homeless Veterans. n.d. "Homeless Veterans Fact Sheet." Available online at www.nchv.org/background.cfm#facts (accessed August 11, 2004).

National Coalition for the Homeless. 1999. "Mental Health and Homelessness, NCH Fact Sheet #5." April. Available online at www.nationalhomeless.org/mental.html (accessed August 11, 2004).

National Commission on Correctional Health Care. 2002. *The Health Status of Soon-to-Be-Released Inmates: A Report to Congress.* Vol. 1. March.

National Family Caregivers Association. 2001. "Survey of Self-Identified Family Caregivers, September 2001." Available at www.caregiversmarketplace.com/ArticlesOfInterest/TCAP%20NFCA%20Study.pdf (accessed August 11, 2004).

National Health Care for the Homeless Council. 1999. "The Effects of SSI and SSD Benefits Termination as Seen in Health Care for the Homeless Projects." National Law Center on Homelessness and Poverty. April. Available online at www.nhchc.org/Publications/ssi.htm (accessed March 30, 2003).

Nemeroff, C. B., K. R. Krishnan, D. Reed, R. Leder, C. Beam, and N. Dunick. 1992. "Adrenal Gland Enlargement in Major Depression: A Computed Tomographic Study." *Archives of General Psychiatry* 49, no. 5 (May): 384–387.

Neumark, David, Daniel Polsky, and Daniel Hansen. 2000. "Has Job Stability Declined Yet? New Evidence for the 1990s." In *On the Job: Is Long-Term Employment a Thing of the Past?* edited by David Neumark, pp. 70–110. New York: Russell Sage Foundation.

Newman, Katherine S. 1999. *No Shame in My Game: The Working Poor in the Inner City.* New York: Alfred A. Knopf and Russell Sage Foundation.

NewsHour with Jim Lehrer/Kaiser Family Foundation. 2000. "National Survey on the Uninsured." April. Available at www.pbs.org/newshour/health/uninsured/highlights.pdf (accessed August 11, 2004).

Office of Applied Studies. 1999. "Substance Use and Mental Health Characteristics by Employment Status." U.S. Department of Health and Human Services, Substance Abuse and Mental Health Services Administration. Available online at www.oas.samhsa.gov/NHSDA/A10.pdf (accessed March 20, 2003).

Ohio Department of Health. 2001. "Health Insurance and the Use of Health Care Services among Ohio Women: Results from the 1998 Ohio Family Health Study." Available online at www.odh.state.oh.us/ODHPrograms/SADV/WOM_PUBS/Repts/fhs_Feb2001.pdf (accessed September 8, 2004).

Organization for Economic Cooperation and Development. 2001. *OECD Health Data 2001: A Comparative Analysis of Thirty OECD Countries.* Paris: OECD.

Pamuk, E., D. Macuk, K. Heck, C. Reuben, and K. Lochner. 1998. *Socioeconomic Status and Health Chartbook*. U.S. Department of Health and Human Services. Hyattsville, Md.: National Center for Health Statistics.

Pappas, G., S. Queen, W. Hadden, and G. Fischer. 1993. "The Increasing Disparity in Mortality between Socioeconomic Groups in the United States, 1960 and 1986." *New England Journal of Medicine* 329 (July 8): 103–109.

Pear, Robert. 2003. "New Study Finds 60 Million Uninsured during a Year." *New York Times*, May 13.

Peters, Roger H. 2000. "Criminalizing Addictions." In *Building Violence: How America's Rush to Incarcerate Creates More Violence*, edited by John P. May, pp. 28–33. Thousand Oaks, Calif.: Sage.

Pincus, T., R. Esther, D. A. DeWalt, and L. F. Callahan. 1998. "Social Conditions and Self-Management Are More Powerful Determinants of Health Than Access to Care." *Annals of Internal Medicine* 129 (September 1): 406–411.

Post, Patricia A. 2001. "Casualties of Complexity: Why Eligible Homeless People Are Not Enrolled in Medicaid." Nashville: National Health Care for the Homeless Council.

Pottruck, David. 1996. "Strategies for Avoiding the Rush toward Downsizing." *Vital Speeches of the Day* 62 (24): 752–755.

Powell, F. D., and A. F. Wessen, eds. 1999. *Health Care Systems in Transition: An International Perspective*. Thousand Oaks, Calif.: Sage.

President's New Freedom Commission on Mental Health. 2002. "Interim Report." Available online at www.mentalhealthcommission.gov/reports/Interim_Report.htm (accessed August 11, 2004).

Public Citizen. 2002. "Pharmaceutical Industry Ranks as Most Profitable Industry—Again." Press release. April 18. Available online at www.citizen.org/pressroom/release.cfm?ID=1088 (accessed August 11, 2004).

Quinn, Kevin, Cathy Schoen, and Louisa Buatti. 2000. "On Their Own: Young Adults Living without Health Insurance." Commonwealth Fund. May. Available online at www.cmwf.org/programs/insurance/quinn_ya_391.asp (accessed April 12, 2004).

Rhoades, Jeffrey. 2004. "The Uninsured in America." Statistical Brief #41. Medical Expenditure Panel Survey. Available online at www.meps.ahrq.gov/papers/st41/stat41.htm (accessed October 26, 2004).

Riach, P. A., and J. Rich. 2002. "Field Experiments of Discrimination in the Market Place." *Economic Journal* 112 (483): F480–F518.

Rifkin, Jeremy. 1996. *The End of Work*. New York: Putnam.

Robbins, Jessica. 2003. "Neighborhood Poverty and Local Mortality Rates in Philadelphia." Paper presented at the American Public Health Association Meeting, San Francisco, November. Available online at http://apha.confex .com/apha/130am/techprogram/paper_46065.htm (accessed April 12, 2004).

Rodgers, Daniel T. 1978. *The Work Ethic in Industrial America, 1850–1920.* Chicago: University of Chicago Press.

Rosenheck, Robert, Catherine A. Leda, Linda K. Frisman, Julie Lam, and An-Me Chung. 1996. "Homeless Veterans." In *Homelessness in America,* edited by Jim Baumohl, pp. 97–108. Phoenix: Oryx.

Ruberman, W., E. Weinblatt, J. D. Goldberg, and B. S. Chaudhary. 1984. "Psychosocial Influences on Mortality after Myocardial Infarction." *New England Journal of Medicine* 311 (August 30): 552–559.

Salganicoff, Alina, J. Zoe Beckerman, Roberta Wyn, and Victoria D. Ojeda. 2002. "Women's Health in the United States: Health Coverage and Access to Care." Kaiser Women's Health Survey, Henry J. Kaiser Family Foundation. May. Available online at www.kaisernetwork.org/health_cast/uploaded_files/ ACF624.pdf (accessed April 12, 2004).

Salisbury, Dallas, ed. 1999. *Severing the Link between Health Insurance and Employment.* Policy Forum Proceedings. Washington, D.C.: Employee Benefit Research Institute.

Schlosser, Eric. 2001. *Fast Food Nation: The Dark Side of the All-American Meal.* Boston: Houghton Mifflin.

Schulz, Richard, and Scott R. Beach. 1999. "Caregiving as a Risk Factor for Mortality: The Caregiver Health Effects Study." *Journal of the American Medical Association* 282, no. 23 (December 15): 2215–2219.

Schulz, Richard, Aaron B. Mendelsohn, William E. Haley, Diane Mahoney, Rebecca S. Allen, Song Zhang, Larry Thompson, and Steve H. Belle. 2003. "End-of-Life Care and the Effects of Bereavement on Family Caregivers of Persons with Dementia." *New England Journal of Medicine* 349 (November 13): 1936–1942.

Scorza, John. 2001. "Health Insurance Premiums Increase Dramatically." *Business Owner's Toolkit.* Available online at www.toolkit.cch.com/columns/ people/01-097healthcosts.asp (accessed December 8, 2003).

Seabrook, Jeremy. 2002. *Class, Caste, and Hierarchies.* Toronto: New Internationalist Publications.

Seccombe, Karen. 2002. "Integrating Meaningful Health and Welfare Reforms." In *Work, Welfare, and Politics: Confronting Poverty in the Wake of Wel-*

fare Reform, edited by Frances Fox Piven, Joan Acker, Margaret Hallock, and Sandra Morgen, pp. 289–300. Eugene: University of Oregon Press.

Sharma, Ursula. 1999. *Caste*. Philadelphia: Open University Press.

Short, Pamela Farley, and Deborah R. Graefe. 2003. "Battery-Powered Health Insurance? Stability in Coverage of the Uninsured." *Health Affairs* 22, no. 6 (November/December): 246–255.

Shulman, Beth. 2003a. *The Betrayal of Work: How Low-Wage Jobs Fail 30 Million Americans and Their Families*. New York: The New Press.

———. 2003b. "Four Myths about Low-Wage Work." *Alameda Times-Star*, August 29.

Small Business Administration. 2004. Office of Advocacy. "Small Business by the Numbers." June. Available online at www.sba.gov/advo/stats/sbfaq .html#92 (accessed August 11, 2004).

Sontag, Susan. 1990. *Illness as Metaphor* and *AIDS and Its Metaphors*. New York: Doubleday.

Spannaus, Fred, and Robert Hironimus-Wendt. 2003. *Decatur Impact Project Report*. Decatur, Ill.: Millikin University Press.

Starr, Paul. 1974. *The Discarded Army: Veterans after Vietnam*. New York: Charterhouse.

Stefan, Susan. 2001. *Unequal Rights: Discrimination against People with Mental Disabilities and the Americans with Disabilities Act*. Washington, D.C.: American Psychological Association.

———. 2002. *Hollow Promises: Employment Discrimination against People with Mental Disabilities*. Washington, D.C.: American Psychological Association.

Stewart, W. F., R. B. Lipton, D. D. Celentano, and M. L. Reed. 1992. "Prevalence of Migraine Headaches in the United States: Relation to Age, Income, Race, and Other Sociodemographic Variables." *Journal of the American Medical Association* 267, no.1 (January 1): 64–69.

Stoner, Madeleine R. 1995. *The Civil Rights of Homeless People: Law, Social Policy, and Social Work Practice*. New York: Aldine de Gruyter.

Sullivan, Teresa A., Elizabeth Warren, and Jay Lawrence Westbrook. 2001. *The Fragile Middle Class: Americans in Debt*. New Haven, Conn.: Yale University Press.

Sunley, William T. 1994. "Office Ergonomics and Cumulative Trauma Disorders." *Illinois Municipal Review*. August.

Texas Senate. 2001. "Texas Blue Ribbon Task Force on the Uninsured." Report to the 77th Legislature. February. Available online at www.senate.state.tx.us/ 75r/senate/commit/archive/BR/Blue_Ribbon.pdf (accessed August 30, 2004).

Uchitelle, Louis, and N. R. Kleinfield. 1996. "The Price of Jobs Lost." In *The Downsizing of America. New York Times* Special Report. New York: Times Books.

United Health Foundation. 2002. "State Health Ranking." Available online at www.unitedhealthfoundation.org/shr2002/Findings.html (accessed June 15, 2003).

U.S. Census Bureau. 2002a. *Per Capita Income in 1999 by Race and Hispanic or Latino Origin for the US and All States: 2000 Universe: Total Population.* Available online at www.silo.lib.ia.us/specialized-services/datacenter/datatables/UnitedStates/usstincomepercapbyrace.pdf (accessed June 15, 2003).

———. 2002b. *Percent of People in Poverty by State: 1999, 2000, and 2001.* Current Population Survey. Available online at www.census.gov/hhes/poverty/poverty01/table4.pdf (accessed June 15, 2003).

———. 2003. "Health Insurance Coverage in the United States, 2002." September. Available online at www.census.gov/prod/2003pubs/p60-223.pdf (accessed August 12, 2004).

U.S. Centers for Disease Control and Prevention. 1999. "State-Specific Maternal Mortality among Black and White Women: United States, 1987–1996." *MMWR Weekly* 48, no. 23 (June 18): 492–496.

U.S. Department of Justice. 2003. Bureau of Justice Statistics. "Prison Statistics." June. Available online at www.ojp.usdoj.gov/bjs/prisons/htm (accessed August 30, 2004).

U.S. General Accounting Office. 2001. *Welfare Reform: More Coordinated Federal Effort Could Help States and Localities Move TANF Recipients with Impairments toward Employment.* GAO-02-37. Washington, D.C.: U.S. Government Printing Office.

Verba, Sidney, Bashiruddin Ahmed, and Anil Bhatt. 1971. *Caste, Race, and Politics: A Comparative Study of India and the United States.* Beverly Hills: Sage.

Warr, Peter. 1987. *Work, Unemployment, and Mental Health.* Oxford: Clarendon Press.

Weisman, Andrea. 2000. "Mental Illness Behind Bars." In *Building Violence: How America's Rush to Incarcerate Creates More Violence,* edited by John P. May, pp. 105–110. Thousand Oaks, Calif.: Sage.

Weiss, Julie, and Candice Leonard. 1999. "School Bus Drivers and Repetitive Stress Injuries." National Education Association Report. May. Available online at www.nea.org/esphome/nearesources/repstress.html (accessed July 8, 2004).

Weitzman, Lenore J. 1985. *The Divorce Revolution: The Unexpected Social and Economic Consequences for Women and Children in America.* New York: Free Press.

Whelan, Christopher T., Damian F. Hannan, and Sean Creighton. 1991. *Unemployment, Poverty, and Psychological Distress.* Dublin, Ireland: Economic and Social Research Institute.

Williams, Claudia. 2003. "Tax Subsidies for Private Health Insurance: Who Currently Benefits and What Are the Implications for New Policies?" Synthesis Project, Policy Primer #1. May. Available online at www.rwjf.org/publications/synthesis/reports_and_briefs/pdf/no3_policyprimer.pdf (accessed August 11, 2004).

Willie, Charles Vert. 1989. *The Caste and Class Controversy on Race and Poverty: Round Two of the Willie/Wilson Debate.* New York: General Hall.

Windham C. 2003. "Young Adults Take Gamble Forgoing Insurance." *Wall Street Journal,* August 30.

Woolhandler, Steffie, Terry Campbell, and David U. Himmelstein. 2003. "Costs of Health Care Administration in the United States and Canada." *New England Journal of Medicine* 349 (August 21): 768–775.

Wysocki, Bernard, Jr., and Ann Zimmerman. 2003. "Wal-Mart Cost Cutting Finds Big Target in Health Benefits." *Wall Street Journal,* September 30.

Zedlewski, Sheila R., and Pamela Loprest. 2001. "Will TANF Work for the Most Disadvantaged Families?" In *The New World of Welfare* edited by Rebecca M. Blank and Ron Haskins, pp. 311–334. Washington, D.C.: Brookings Institution Press.

SELECTED WEB SITES FOR FURTHER READING

The following Web sites provide up-to-date and detailed data concerning the uninsured and health care in the United States.

Kaiser Family Foundation, *State Facts Online:* www.statehealthfacts.kff.org

U.S. Census Bureau: www.census.gov

U.S. Census Bureau, Current Population Survey: www.bls.census.gov/cps/cpsmain.htm

U.S. Centers for Disease Control and Prevention, CDC WONDER (Wide-Ranging Online Data for Epidemiologic Research): http://wonder.cdc.gov

U.S. Centers for Disease Control and Prevention, National Center for Health Statistics: www.cdc.gov/nchs

SELECTED BIBLIOGRAPHY FOR THE 2007 EDITION

Cover the Uninsured Week. 2005. "Cover the Uninsured Fact Sheet." May. Available at http://covertheuninsuredweek.org/factsheets/display.php ?FactSheetID=122.

Ditsler, Elaine, Peter Fisher, and Colin Gordon. 2005. *On the Fringe: The Substandard Benefits of Workers in Part-Time, Temporary, and Contract Jobs.* Report, Commonwealth Fund, New York. December.

Hoffman, Catherine, Diane Rowland, and Elizabeth C. Hamel. 2005. *Medical Debt and Access to Health Care.* Report, Kaiser Commission on Medicaid and the Uninsured. September.

Institute for Policy Studies, Northwestern University. July 2002. "Welfare Reform and Health Insurance: How Parents Lose Out." Policy brief 5. Available at www.northwestern.edu/ipr/research/IFS.html (accessed 10 March 2006).

———. September 2005. "Who Gets Ahead: Work Profiles with Former Welfare Recipients in Illinois." Policy brief 9. Available at www.northwestern.edu/ ipr/research/IFS.html (accessed 10 March 2006).

Kaiser Family Foundation. 2005. "Trends and Indicators in the Changing Health Care Marketplace: Section 4. Trends in Health Insurance Benefits." Available at www.kff.org/insurance/7031/print-sec4.cfm (accessed 16 February 2006).

Seifert, Robert. 2005. *Home Sick: How Medical Debt Undermines Housing Security.* Report, Access Project, Boston. November.

INDEX

Page numbers in *italic* refer to figures.

Access Project, 13n
acupuncture, 111
addiction, 176–77; alcoholism, 149–50, 165, 176–77, 181; drug, 149–50, 165, 178, 181
Aetna, profits, 197
African Americans, 152–62; caste, 152–54; diabetes, 82–84, 137–38, 158; Mississippi, 48–49; prisoners, 19, 136–37, 154, 161, 180, 183; underclass, 180; uninsured, 4, 154–62; youth, 136–38, 180
After Marriage Ends: Economic Consequences for Midlife Women (Morgan), 58
age: African American life expectancy, 158; injuries, 130; in manufacturing jobs, 31; uninsured, 4, 7, 129, *130*, 130n; veterans' health care and, 177–78. *See also* children; elders; youth
Agent Orange, 178–79
AIDS/HIV, 164, 165, 174, 181
Aid to Families with Dependent Children (AFDC), 52–53, 55
alcohol use: alcoholism, 149–50, 165,

176–77, 181; Idaho bars, 86–87, 91, 104–6; medicine combined with, 12, 43; prisoners' use, 181, 182; for tooth pain, 166
American Academy of Orthopedic Surgeons, 90n
American dream, xv, 25–26, 39
Americans with Disabilities Act (1990), 150
Archer Daniels Midland (soy processing) plants, 23
arthritis, 80; degenerative/osteoarthritis, 88, 101–2

bankruptcy: health care costs causing, 13, 64, 98; after plant closings, 23
bars, Idaho, 86–87, 91, 104–6. *See also* alcohol use
Bazelon Center for Mental Health Law, 182
Bell Helmet plant, 80
Berlin, New Hampshire, 183
The Betrayal of Work: How Low-Wage Jobs Fail 30 Million Americans and Their Families (Shulman), 45
birth control, xvii–xviii, xxi, 51

Blackford, Mansel, 113, 119
blacks. *See* African Americans
blood cancer, multiple myeloma, 88–89, 95
Blue Cross/Blue Shield, 73, 125, 198
Bluestone, Barry, 25
Bolton, Andrew, 186
Boone, Linda, 177, 178, 180
botanicas, Rio Grande Valley, 142
Boundary Community Health Center, Idaho, 186
breast cancer: 62–65, 111–12, 158–59
Britain: health care costs, 5, 196; Poor Laws, 198
Bush, George W., 1, 190
Butler, Stuart, 195
Byrd, Michael, 153, 154

California, mandating coverage, 186–87
Canada: health care costs, 5, 196; national health insurance, 42, 191–92, 196
cancer, 165; African American, 158–59; blood, 88–89, 95; breast, 62–65, 111–12, 158–59; cervical, 123, 158; and death spiral, 170–71
cardiovascular disease, minorities' treatment for, 158. *See also* heart disease
caregivers. *See* day care center jobs; family caregivers; health care jobs
caste: American ill/infirm/marginally employed, 15–17, 20, 163–73; health care–employment link and, 15–16, 152, 165; mental illness and, 148, 149, 171; physical markers, 15, 44, 165–69; racial, 152–54; ranked by intrinsic worth, 163; welfare reform and, 54, 56; working poor, xvii, xxi–xxiii, 39, 48, 53, 190. *See also* underclass
Caterpillar plant, 25, 159
Catholic Church, 142
cervical cancer, 123, 158
Champaign County Health Care Consumers, Illinois, 13

charity care: clinic, 10, 38; hospital, 1, 2, 13–14, 64, 156, 202–3. *See also* free care
children: Aid to Families with Dependent Children (AFDC), 52–53, 55; child support, 50, 52, 54, 62; with disabilities, 74–75, 76; Medicaid for, xix, 138–39, 200; school health hazards, 20; State Children's Health Insurance Program (SCHIP/Kid-Care), 73–74, 81, 185, 200; Transitional Aid to Families with Dependent Children program, 70; of welfare mothers, 55, 165; women's income with/without, 78n. *See also* infants; mothers
chiropractic, 111, 121
chronic health problems, 9, 20, 29, 116–17, 130, 166, 177–78, 190, 202
churches: African American, 154; clinics, 1, 2, 10; and contraception, xvii–xviii, xxi; as resources, 171; Rio Grande Valley, 142
Civil Rights Act (1964), 154
class: African American mobility, 152; American shift to caste from, 14–15; and weight, 167; youth uninsured and, 135–37. *See also* caste; middle class; poor; underclass; working class
Clayton, Linda, 153, 154
clinics, 1, 2, 203–4; charity cases, 10, 38; church, 1, 2, 10; finding, 206; Mississippi options for poor, 48; sleep, 81; with sliding-scale fees, 1, 83–84, 131, 201–2, 203, 205
CMV (cytomegalovirus), 73, 74
COBRA (Consolidated Omnibus Budget Reconciliation Act), 129, 197
collection agencies, for hospital bills, xx, 13, 202
Collective Home Care, 7n, 112–13, 119–21
colonia, Rio Grande Valley, 142–44, 171
Community Catalyst, 206
Community Health Centers, 186, 205

community mental health services, 176
Congressional Budget Office (CBO), 200
Conilogue, Alan, 92–93, 94, 95
construction jobs: injuries on the job, 86, 97–99, 101–2, 156; self-employed, xv–xxiii, 108–10
contraception, xvii–xviii, xxi, 51
co-payments, 9, 30, 201; with employer-sponsored health insurance, 41, 45, 73, 116, 120, 197
corporations, layoffs, 21–39, 160, 183. *See also* manufacturing jobs
costs: Agent Orange damage award and, 179; caregiver's services, 76–77; divorced women's, 65; domestic violence and, 70; education, 41, 111; food, 31, 35, 45, 167; Mississippi substandard housing, 48; musician's, 131; parents helping youth with, 124–29, 136, 170; for poor, xix, xx, xxi, 40, 46; rent with roommates, 134; unaffordable necessities, 31, 34–35, 44n; Wal-Mart, 34n. *See also* bankruptcy; health care costs; health insurance costs; taxes
counseling and therapy, 36–37, 69, 134, 144, 172
Covering Kids and Families, 205
cowboys, injuries on the job, 104
crime: drug-related, 136, 161, 180–81; juvenile, 136; after plant closings, 23; underclass, 165. *See also* prisoners; violence
Cullen, Lisa, 94, 95, 96

day care center jobs: insured, 72, 74; training, 74; uninsured, 122–24, 137
death rate: homeless, 18, 175; infant, 48, 158; job hazards, 103; minority males, 158; Mississippi, 48; poor, 45–46; war, 178
death spiral, 5–20, 123, 163–83; caregiving, 72, 76, 77, 78n, 85; class, 136; crucial tipping point, 169–70;

dead-end job, 124; divorced uninsured women, 8, 64; domestic violence, 8, 71; final descent, 172–83; health care reform and, 189; homelessness, 18, 35, 106, 170, 173–80; injuries on the job, 102, 103; layoffs, 29; mental illness, 151, 171, 176–77; motherhood, 78n; prisoners, 183; racial discrimination, 152; rate of descent, 169–72; resources as handholds slowing/stopping, 169–72; stress, 47, 171–72; universal coverage and, 20, 190
Decatur, Illinois, 21–39, 154–57, 159–62
Decatur Impact Project Report, 31n
Decatur Memorial Hospital, 37
deductibles, 29–30, 41, 125, 129, 197, 198
dentists: health care reform and, 186; health insurance costs of employer, 117, 118; uninsured employees, 118–19; uninsured not using, 44, 166–67. *See also* teeth
depression, 143; caregivers', 78; divorced women, 62; drugs for, 23, 30–31, 36–37, 62, 134, 172; homeless, 175; men injured on the job, 101–2; plant closings and, 23, 30–31, 36–37; youth, 128, 134, 135
diabetes: African American, 82–84, 137–38, 158; caregivers', 72, 74, 75, 82–84; gestational, 72, 74, 75; public health departments and, 202; tooth problems and, 166, 167; youth, 137–38
dioxin, in Agent Orange, 179
disabilities: caregiving family members with, 55, 73–85; population with chronic, 76; SSDI-defined, 199; welfare mothers, 55. *See also* disability (Social Security benefits); health problems; injuries; mental illness
disability (Social Security benefits), 199; and homeless, 176–77; mentally ill

disability (*continued*)
  and, 144–46, 148, 149–50, 182, 199;
  prisoners and, 182; racism, 148;
  Social Security Disability Insurance
  (SSDI) system, 149–50, 176–77,
  182, 199; Supplemental Security
  Income (SSI), 55, 56, 127, 149–50,
  176–77, 182, 198; for terminally ill,
  17; and workers' comp loss, 89, 95,
  99–100. *See also* Medicare
*The Discarded Army: Veterans after Viet-
  nam* (Starr), 178
discrimination, 16; mental illness,
  148–51, 164, 176–77; obesity, 167;
  race, 148, 152–61, 171. *See also*
  caste; stigma
divorce, 57–64, 66–68; financial losses,
  33, 63–64; health care coverage lost
  by women in, 8, 57–60, 62–64, 65,
  66
The Divorce Revolution (Weitzman), 59
doctors: at clinics, 203–4; costs for visiting, 42, 68, 83–84; drug access for
  uninsured, 11, 68; government
  spending for, 195; Massachusetts
  number of, 135; and Medicaid eligibility, 84; Medicare coverage, 198;
  uninsured treatment by, 10, 42,
  67–68, 82–84; and workers' comp,
  87, 95
Dollard, John, 153
domestic violence, 8, 65–71, 171; health
  problems, 65–70, 181–82; welfare
  reform and, 54, 70, 71; and women's
  health care coverage, 60, 65–67, 70
downsizing, 25, 27–28, 29. *See also* layoffs
drugs, 11–12; addiction, 149–50, 165,
  178, 181; for breast cancer, 64;
  chemical and biological warfare protection, 179; at clinics, 202, 203–4;
  costs, xix, xx–xxi, 64, 67, 82, 195n,
  203–4; crimes, 136, 161, 180–81; for
  depression, 23, 30–31, 36–37, 62,
  134, 172; free samples, 11, 145–46;

from friends and family, 12, 50–51,
  105–6; government spending for,
  195; Gulf War Syndrome, 179; kidney effects of, 132; for laid-off workers, 29–30; low-wage workers'
  needs, 45, 50; Medicare and, 160,
  198, 203–4; for mental illness, 144,
  145–46, 147, 150; from Mexico, 11,
  20, 141; for migraines, 67–68; Mississippi pharmacies, 48; for narcolepsy, 81; over-the-counter,
  xviii–xix, xxi, 11, 12, 43, 48, 81, 90,
  105, 141; prisoners' use, 181, 182;
  for repetitive stress injuries, 97; for
  tooth pain, 166; for ulcers, 68. *See
  also* self-medication

Eagle supermarket, 33
Economic Policy Institute, 44n
education: caste and, 165; costs, 41,
  111; and earnings by race, 157;
  Head Start, 72; health hazards at
  school, 20; public, 191, 194. *See also*
  training, job
elders: home health care, 119–21;
  Medicare/Medicaid, 198; veterans'
  health care, 177–78
Emergency Medical Treatment and
  Active Labor Act (EMTALA), 202
emergency room use, by uninsured, xx,
  10, 12, 17–18, 67, 82, 202–3
Employee Retirement Income Security
  Act (ERISA), 114
employer-sponsored health insurance,
  4–7, 26, 33, 104, 196–97; cash benefit in place of, 189–90; co-pay, 41,
  45, 73, 116, 120, 197; costs, 7, 26,
  34n, 114, 117, 118, 121, 187, 197;
  day care centers, 72; employer
  avoidance measures, 5, 7, 34n,
  43–44, 89–90, 91, 93n, 98–99, 118,
  121, 137, 188–89; firing after use of,
  159; health care reform and, 187,
  188; and injuries on the job, 97, 104,
  156; lumber mill, 107; mandated,

187; Medicare, 198; mental illness and, 150, 151; Mexico, 143–44; self-employed, 108, 111; size of firm and, *114*; small business, 8, 113–17, *114*, 119–20; temporary jobs, 134; welfare reform and, 53. *See also* union jobs

employment: construction, xv–xxiii, 86, 97–99, 101–2, 108–10, 156; family caregivers leaving/returning to, 73–81; globalization, 8, 26–27, 29, 47, 160, 187; health hazards on the job, 32, 41, 49, 80, 86–106, 155–56; layoffs, 21–39, 160, 183; logging, 101, 107; low-wage, 40–56, 113, 155–56, 157, 187, 190; manufacturing, 7, 8, 21–39, 47, 136, 160, 183; nonunion, 28–29; prison, 183; racial discrimination, 154, 155, 157; self-employment/small businesses/entrepreneurs, xv–xxiii, 8, 107–21, 188; temporary, xxii, 7, 8, 43–44, 121, 133–35, 157, 189; training for, 28, 31–32, 37, 41, 111, 160; union, 5, 7, 21–39, 160, 188; without workers' comp, 92, 93n, 98–99, 156. *See also* health care–employment link; health care jobs; unemployability; unemployment; uninsured and employment

entrepreneurs, 107–21. *See also* self-employment; small businesses

environmental health hazards, xix. *See also* pollutants; toxins

European Federation of National Organizations Working with the Homeless (FEANTSA), 176

FabuCuts, 41

families: extended, 59; "family gap," 78n; government programs for, 52–55, 70, 205; nuclear, 59–60. *See also* children; family caregivers; marital status; parents

Families USA, 206

family caregivers, 72–85, 185; burn-out, 75–76, 147–48; health insurance, 8, 72–79, 81, 83, 84; health problems, 72–76, 78, 79–85, 147–48; of mentally ill family members, 142–43, 147–48; uninsured, 72–79, 81; virtues, 75–77; welfare mothers, 54–55; women, 8, 49, 54, 59, 73–85. *See also* health care jobs

farmland, 22, 47

federally qualified health centers (FQHCs), 201–2. *See also* clinics: with sliding-scale fees

Feminist Perspectives on Family Care: Policies for Gender Justice (Hooyman and Gonyea), 76, 77, 78

Firestone tires, plant closings, 22–23, 24–25, 31n

Flat Broke with Children: Women in the Age of Welfare Reform (Hays), 53–55

food: costs, 31, 35, 45, 167; food banks, 22; food industry jobs, 7, 20, 134–35; food stamps, 53; in poor neighborhoods, xix, 46, 48; tooth problems and, 166–67

Francis Nelson Clinic, 83–84

free care, 203; clinics, 206; drug companies offering, 202; hospital, 64, 111–12, 118, 202. *See also* charity care

Freund, Peter, 167

Furstenberg, Frank, 136

Gans, Herbert, 164–65

Garicaparra, Nomar, 100

gay men and women, health insurance, 59

gender, and discrimination, 160; and poverty, 46 *See also* men; sex; women

General Motors, 39

globalization, 8, 26–27, 29, 47, 160, 187

Gonyea, Judith, 76, 77, 78

government programs, 10; African Americans and, 161–62; Aid to Families with Dependent Children

government programs (*continued*)
(AFDC), 52–53, 55; eligibility for
(general), xxiii, 52–53, 200; experience in applying for, 84–85; federally
qualified health centers (FQHCs),
201–2; and homelessness, 176–77;
mental illness, 144–45; prisoner
denial of access, 182; State Children's Health Insurance Program
(SCHIP/KidCare), 73–74, 81, 185,
200; Temporary Assistance to Needy
Families (TANF), 53–55, 70; welfare
reform, 52–56, 70, 71, 154, 165, 180.
See also disability (Social Security
benefits); government spending,
health care; Medicaid; Medicare;
national health insurance; public
health insurance
government regulation, of trusts and
mergers, 27
government requirements, hospital
charity care, 2
government spending, health care:
Massachusetts, 135; U.S., 195–96.
See also government programs
Greenstein, Robert, 53
Gulf War Syndrome, 178–80
"Gulf War Syndrome: The 'Agent
Orange' of the Nineties" (Milano),
178–79
Guyer, Jocelyn, 53

Hadley, Jack, 192
Harrison, Bennett, 25
Harvey, Brian, 176
Hawaii, mandating coverage, 186
Hays, Sharon, 53–55
headaches, xxi; migraine, xx, 66–68, 69,
171
Head Start, 72
health care: acupuncture, 111; counseling and therapy, 36–37, 69, 134, 144,
172; domestic violence and, 60,
65–68, 70; innovation, 193–94; long-
term, 201; Mississippi and Ohio,

49; patchwork, 10–12, 20; prison,
181, 182, 183; reform, 184–94, 206;
resources for, 205–6; welfare mothers, 55, 165; women's family responsibility for, 4. *See also* health care
costs; health care–employment link;
health problems; medical care; nursing homes; scraping by
health care costs, 196; African American uninsured, 156; American vs.
Canadian/British/European, 5, 196;
bankruptcy caused by, 13, 64, 98;
"body attachment" of uninsured, 14;
clinics, 203–4; collection agencies
and, xx, 13, 202; deductibles, 29–30,
41, 125, 129, 197, 198; for divorced
uninsured women, 63–64; doctor
visits, 42, 68, 83–84; domestic violence victims, 67, 68; drugs, xix,
xx–xxi, 64, 67, 82, 195n, 203–4;
emergency room use, xx, 67, 203;
government spending for, 135,
195–96; higher hospital charges
for uninsured, 12–14, 203; infant,
73–74; for low-wage workers, 42,
50; managed-care plans and, 197;
with Medicare, 198; mental illness
stigma and, 149; Pap smears, 123;
parents helping with, 124–26, 136,
170; pregnancy and delivery, 130;
repetitive stress injuries, 90n, 97;
self-employed uninsured, 108–10;
sliding-scale fees, 1, 83–84, 131,
201–2, 203, 205; transportation to
health care, 82; workers' comp and,
88, 93–94. *See also* health insurance
costs
health care–employment link, 4–8,
19–20, 188; American dream, 25;
caste and, 15–16, 152, 165; health
care reform and, 188–89, 194; and
homelessness, 176–77; layoffs and,
29–37; and marital status, 58–60;
market-based approaches to weakening, 189–90; nuclear family

households, 59–60; union health care benefits, 5, 7, 26, 29–30, 39. *See also* employer-sponsored health insurance; health hazards on the job; uninsured and employment

health care jobs, 203; home health aides, 7n, 50, 112–13, 119–21; hospital, 37, 183; nurses, 102–3, 135; nurse's aides, 142, 144, 146–48, 159, 160. *See also* doctors

health hazards: children at school, 20; environmental, xix. *See also* health hazards on the job; pollutants; toxins

health hazards on the job, 86–106; animal feed plant, 155–56; factory, 31–32; haircutting salon, 41, 47; home health aides, 50, 121; injuries, 9, 86–106, 156; occupational variations, 103; repetitive stress, 32, 80, 89–90, 96–97, 103; toxins, 89, 103

health insurance, 10; divorced women's loss of, 8, 57–60, 62–64, 65, 66; experience rating, 114–15; family caregivers', 8, 72–79, 81, 83, 84; HMOs, 196–97; indemnity, 196–97; managed-care plans, 196–97; mandating, 186–88; military, xv, 65–66, 137; not-for-profit, 197–98; parents' coverage for children, 124–26, 128, 129, 137; point-of-service plans (POS plans), 196–97; PPOs, 196–97; same-sex couples, 59; underinsurance, 9–10, 201; universal, 20, 189–94; workers' comp and, 95–96; work-related health problems not covered by, 92, 103–4, 197; wraparound, 198. *See also* employer-sponsored health insurance; health care–employment link; private health insurance; public health insurance; uninsured and employment

health insurance costs, 30, 32; for chronically ill, 190; day care center jobs, 74; deductibles, 29–30, 41, 125,

129, 197, 198; employer-paid, 7, 26, 34n, 114, 117, 118, 121, 187, 197; employer subsidies/tax deductions, 5, 189, 192, 193; exclusions, 197; mandated coverage and, 187; Medicaid percentages, 200; with Medicare, 198; motor vehicle accidents, 197; private, 197; self-pay, 30; tax credit and, 190; universal coverage, 192; for youth, 127, 129. *See also* co-payments

health maintenance organizations (HMOs), 196–97

health problems, 20; arthritis, 80, 88, 101–2; caste marked by, 15, 44, 165–69; chronic, 9, 20, 29, 130, 166, 177–78, 190, 202; from domestic violence, 65–70, 181–82; family caregivers', 72–76, 78, 79–85, 147–48; headaches, xx, xxi, 66–68, 69, 171; hiring influenced by, 116–17, 187; HIV/AIDS, 164, 165, 174, 181; holistic reality of human body and, 96; of homeless, 174–75; low-wage jobs and, 40–47, 49; Mississippi, 48–52; as moral failure, 16, 164, 165; of nurse's aides, 146–48; obesity blamed for, 167–68; of poor, xvi–xxi, 45–52, 55–56, 165–69; of prisoners, 19, 181; racial minorities, 11, 140–48, 153–54, 156–59, 161; stress-caused, 40, 42, 47, 78; ulcers, xxi, 68; unemployment affecting, 23–37; unemployment as punishment for, 165; of veterans, 178, 179; work affected by, 9. *See also* cancer; diabetes; disabilities; health care; health hazards; heart disease; injuries; mental illness; rotten teeth

heart disease, 29; African American, 158; and death spiral, 170; tooth problems and, 166

hiring, discrimination in, 31, 101, 116–17, 151, 154, 157, 161. *See also* employment

Hispanics: health problems among, 11,
140–48, 157, 158, 161; prisoners,
136–37, 161; Rio Grande Valley,
11, 140–48; uninsured, 4, 140–48,
157
HIV/AIDS, 164, 165, 174, 181
HMOs (health maintenance organizations), 196–97
Holahan, John, 192
Holtz-Eakin, Douglas J., 200
Home Depot, 41, 42
home health care: aides, 7n, 50, 112–13,
119–21; government spending for,
196
homelessness, xxiii, 173–80; death spiral, 18, 35, 106, 170, 173–80; mental
illness, 151, 175–77; underclass,
165
homes. See housing
Hooyman, Nancy, 76, 77, 78
hospitals: charity care, 1, 2, 13–14, 64,
156, 202–3; collection agencies used
by, xx, 13, 202; end-stage treatment
wards, 17–19; free care, 64, 111–12,
118, 202; government spending for,
195; jobs at, 37, 183; Massachusetts
uncompensated care pool for, 135;
Medicare coverage, 198; Mississippi
urgent care clinics, 48; Nightingale
on, 184; not-for-profit, 202; provider of last resort, 202; psychiatric,
175–76, 182; and racial discrimination, 153–54; Rio Grande Valley,
140–41; treatment of uninsured,
10n, 11n, 12–14, 17–18, 39, 111–12;
and union health benefits, 39. See
also emergency room use
housing: divorced uninsured woman,
63–64, 65; homeless shelters, 174,
175, 177; homeownership as resource, 169, 170, 171; Mississippi
substandard, 48; after plant closings,
23; racially segregated, 155; with
roommates, 134; self-built, 108; VA
and, 178. See also homelessness

Humana, 129
HumanaOne College Graduate, 129

Idaho, 2, 118; bars, 86–87, 91, 104–6;
Boundary Community Health Center, 186; health hazards on the job,
86–106; Read to Me Coalition, 168;
rugged individualists, 107–10
Illinois, 2; African American uninsured,
154–62; Champaign, 81–82, 83,
137; Champaign County Health
Care Consumers, 13; Chicago, 137,
183; Danville, 28, 38, 172, 183;
Decatur, 21–39, 154–57, 159–62;
family caregivers, 72–85; job
retraining programs, 28, 31–32, 37,
160; plant closings, 22–39, 160;
prison industry, 183; unions, 21–39,
160, 172
illness. See health problems
immigrants, 142–44, 152, 171
incest, 33
income: bar manager, 105; child support, 50, 52, 54, 62; construction
contracting, 98; divorced women,
65, 67; family caregivers', 75–76, 81;
and government program eligibility,
xviii, xix, xxii, 49, 50, 52, 185; Hispanics in Texas, 141; KidCare cut-
offs, 74; low-wage, 41, 45, 47, 49,
187; migraine sufferers, 66n, 67n;
minimum wage, 47, 187; Mississippi, 48, 49; of mothers/women
without children, 78n; musician,
131; poverty line, 1, 44n, 53, 141,
157; prisoners, 161; race and, 157;
self-employed, xvii, 109; sliding-
scale fees based on, 202; Supplemental Security Income (SSI), 55,
56, 127, 149–50, 176–77, 182, 198;
unemployment, 35; uninsured by,
46; welfare, 53; youth, 134, 138. See
also scraping by
indemnity health insurance, 196–97
India, caste, 15, 16, 17

infants: health problems, 72–75; mortality rate, 48, 158
injuries: health insurance not covering, 197; self-employed uninsured, 108–10; war, 178; youth, 130
injuries on the job, 9, 86–106, 156; construction jobs, 86, 97–99, 101–2, 156; cumulative smaller, 96–97; sports, 100; "sucking it up," 100–102; working "short," 103. See also health hazards on the job
Institute of Medicine, 12
insurance: motor vehicle, 197; unemployment, 35. See also health insurance; workers' compensation insurance
Internal Revenue Service, 5. See also taxes
Iraq war, homeless veterans, 180
Israel, national health care program, 1, 191

jackhammer use, injuries from, 97
Jahiel, Rene, 174, 175n
Japan, national health care program, 1
jobs. See employment
A Job to Die For (Cullen), 94, 95, 96
John Deere, layoffs and mergers, 25

Kaiser Family Foundation, 13n
Katz, Michael, 180
Kennedy, John F., 132
KidCare, 73–74, 81, 200
kidney disease, Medicare for, 198
kidney stones, 131–33
Klein, Naomi, 21

labor. See employment; union jobs
layoffs: incremental, 25; manufacturing jobs, 21–39, 160, 183; middle-management workers, 27–28, 29
lead, exposure to, 46
Leigh, J. Paul, 93–94, 103
Lennhoff, Claudia, 13
life expectancy, African American, 158

Lipton, Liz, 182
Little, Grady, 100
logging, 101, 107
Loprest, Pamela, 55
Los Angeles County Jail, 19
low-wage jobs, 40–56; income, 41, 45, 47, 49, 187; mandating coverage and, 187; Mississippi, 47–52; racial minorities, 44–45, 155–56, 157; small businesses, 113; tax credits for insurance, 190; whites, 45, 157; working conditions, 41, 47, 54n, 155–56
lumber mill jobs, 107

Maharidge, Dale, 169
managed-care plans, 196–97
mandating coverage, 186–88
manufacturing jobs: buying American, 32–37, minority males, 136; outside U.S., 8, 27, 29, 47, 160; plant closings, 8, 21–39, 160, 183; temporary, 7; working conditions, 31–32
marital status: job loss affecting marriage chances, 136; loving marriage as resource, 170, 171; same-sex couples' health insurance, 59; uninsured women, 8, 57–60, 5862–64, 65, 66. See also divorce; domestic violence; parents
masculinity, "sucking it up," 100–102. See also men
Massachusetts, 2; doctors, 135; Governor's Commission on Domestic Violence, 70; home health care for elders, 119–21; mental health coverage, 125; middle-class temporary uninsured workers, 133–35; nurses, 135; small business health insurance coverage, 115–16; small vs. large firm coverage requirements, 114; Transitional Aid to Families with Dependent Children program, 70; uninsured percentage, 135
massage therapy, 111

Mauer, Marc, 161
Mays, Mary Helen, 201
McGuire, Meredith, 167
Medicaid, 1–2, 10, 38, 199–200; and
    African Americans, 154; for chil-
    dren, xix, 138–39, 200; dentistry not
    covered by, 166n; elders, 198; eligi-
    bility for, xviii, xix, xxii–xxiii, 10, 49,
    50–53, 66, 84, 138–39, 185, 200;
    homeless and, 173, 174n; hospital
    cases, 39; for injuries on the job, 95;
    and low-wage workers, 49, 50, 51,
    52, 53; for mental illness, 144,
    149–50; Mississippi compared with
    Ohio, 49; during pregnancy, xvi,
    xviii, xxiii, 51, 66, 138–39; prisoners
    and, 182; spend-down, 38; welfare
    reform and, xxii–xxiii, 52–53, 154
MediCal, 174n
medical care. See clinics; drugs; health
    care; health care jobs; hospitals
Medicare, 1, 81, 198; and African
    Americans, 154, 159–60; and clinic
    costs, 203–4; eligibility for, 185, 198;
    and mentally ill, 127, 149–50; for
    terminally ill, 17
medication. See drugs
men: animal images for, 100–102; gay,
    59; injuries on the job, 86–102; mas-
    culine "sucking it up," 100–102;
    minorities in manufacturing jobs,
    136; premature death rate by race,
    158; prisoners, 19, 136, 154, 180;
    veterans, 177–80
mental depression. See depression
mental health therapy, 36–37, 69, 134,
    144, 172
mental illness, 140, 142–48, 165, 201;
    and death spiral, 151, 171, 176–77;
    discrimination against/stigma of,
    148–51, 164, 176–77; health care
    reform and, 186; homeless, 151,
    175–77; prisoners, 19, 151, 180, 182;
    substance abuse, 149–50; veterans,
    177, 178; welfare mothers, 55;

youth, 125–27. See also depression;
    mental health therapy
mergers, 25, 27
Mexican Americans, Rio Grande Valley,
    11, 140–48. See also Hispanics
Mexico: drugs from, 11, 20, 141; med-
    ical documentation from, 145, 148
middle class, 14–15; appearance of, 15,
    18, 170; divorced uninsured women,
    33–35, 65; fear of homelessness, 18,
    35; tax credits for insurance, 190;
    and teeth, 168, 170; and underclass,
    164; and weight, 167; young unin-
    sured, 128–29, 133–35, 136
middle-management workers, layoffs,
    27–28, 29
migraines, xx, 66–68, 69, 171
Milano, Fred, 178–79
military: Gulf War, 178–79; health
    insurance, xv, 65–66, 137; Iraq war,
    180; veterans, 106, 177–80; Vietnam
    war, 178–79
minimum wage, 47, 187
minorities. See racial minorities
miracles, church healing services, 142
Mississippi, 2; construction work,
    98–99; "Mississippi appendec-
    tomies" (tubal ligations), 51; poor,
    xv–xxiii, 47–52, 165–69, 171
morality: caste and, 15, 16, 164; entre-
    preneurial mission based on,
    112–13; health problems as failure
    in, 16, 164, 165; about mental ill-
    ness, 148–51, 164; welfare reform,
    53, 165; work ethic, 22, 100–102,
    103, 165
Morgan, Leslie, 58
Mormons, and contraception, xvii–xviii
mortality. See death rate
mothers: and contraception, xvii–xviii,
    xxi, 51; income with/without chil-
    dren, 78n; teenage, 129–30, 165,
    180; welfare, xxii, 54, 55, 164, 165,
    180. See also children; pregnancy
motor vehicle accidents, 197

multiple myeloma, 88–89, 95
musician, uninsured, 130–33

narcolepsy, 81
National Coalition for Homeless Veterans, 177, 180
National Family Caregivers Association (NFCA), 76–77, 78
National Health Care for the Homeless Council, 176–77
national health insurance, 186, 190–92; Canada, 42, 191–92, 196; Israel, 1, 191; Japan, 1; Sweden, 125, 127. See also public health insurance; universal coverage
necessities, unaffordable, 31, 34–35, 44n
New Hampshire, Berlin, 183
New York, Riker's Island, 19
New York Academy of Medicine, 204
Nightingale, Florence, 184
North American Free Trade Agreement (NAFTA), 27, 47, 171
nurses: injuries on the job, 102–3; Massachusetts number of registered, 135
nurse's aides, 142, 144, 146–48, 159, 160
nursing homes: government spending for, 196; Medicaid for, 200

obesity, 46, 163, 165, 167–68. See also caste; stigma; weight
Ohio, health care, 49
Operation Desert Storm, 179

panhandlers, underclass, 165
parents: government program coverage, 185; helping with youths' costs, 124–29, 136, 170. See also mothers
pediatric care, substandard, 163. See also children
Pentecostal churches, 142, 154
Personal Responsibility Act (1996), 52–53, 54

Philadelphia Department of Public Health, 45
physicians. See doctors
plants: closings, 8, 21–39, 160, 183; Decatur, 21–39, 155–56, 160; injuries, 87. See also manufacturing jobs
point-of-service plans (POS plans), 196–97
pollutant(s): physical illness as, 164; plant closings and, 23; poor exposed to, 46; swamp, xix; at work, 89, 103.
poor, 45–56; costs for, xix, xx, xxi, 40, 46; health problems, xvi–xxi, 45–52, 55–56, 165–69; and individual-based insurance market, 190; Medicaid for, xviii, xix, 66, 199–200; migraines, xx, 66n, 67n; Mississippi, xv–xxiii, 47–52, 165–69, 171; poverty line, 1, 44n, 53, 141, 157; prison population, 161; Texas, 141; underclass, 164–65; welfare reform and, 52–56; women's marital status, 58; working, xvii, xxi–xxiii, 39, 48, 53, 190. See also caste; charity care; low-wage jobs
Poor Laws, Britain, 198
population: caregivers, 77; chronic disabilities, 76; deaths from on-the-job health hazards, 103; domestic violence, 69; health problems on the job, 103; homeless men who are veterans, 177; injured youth, 130; Massachusetts doctors, 135; Massachusetts nurses, 135; Massachusetts uninsured, 135; mentally ill, 175; pregnant youth, 129–30; prison, 161, 180, 183; small business jobs, 113; Troy, Idaho, 86; uninsured, 2–3, 4, 200–201; uninsured by race, 157, 158; uninsured youth, 129; veterans, 177
Post, Patricia, 173
post-traumatic stress syndrome, 179
poverty line, federal, 1, 44n, 53, 141, 157. See also poor

praying, 143
preferred provider organizations (PPOs), 196–97
pregnancy: birth control, xvii–xviii, xxi, 51; deficient care during, 163; Medicaid during, xvi, xviii, xxiii, 51, 66, 138–39; public aid personnel recommending, xxiii, 138–39; youth, 129–30, 138–39, 165, 180. *See also* infants; mothers
prisoners, 19, 180–83; mental illness, 19, 151, 180, 182; population, 161, 180, 183; racial minorities, 19, 136–37, 155, 161, 180, 183; underclass, 165
private health insurance, 1, 197; Blue Cross/Blue Shield, 73, 125, 198; for-profit, 4–5, 96, 197–98; mental illness discrimination, 150; workers' comp part of, 95. *See also* employer-sponsored health insurance
profits: for-profit health insurance, 4–5, 96, 197–98; health insurance industry, 197–98; not-for-profit health insurance, 197–98
Prozac, 23, 134, 172
pryidostigmine bromide, 179
psychiatric hospitals, 175–76, 182
psychotherapy and counseling, 36–37, 69, 134, 144, 172
public education, 191, 194
public health departments, county, 45, 202
public health insurance, universal, 20, 189–94. *See also* Medicaid; Medicare; national health insurance

race. *See* racial minorities; whites
racial minorities, 152–62; American dream, 25n; as caste, 152–54; discrimination experienced by, 148, 152–61, 171; low-wage jobs, 44–45, 155–56, 157; manufacturing job loss, 136; prisoners, 19, 136–37, 154, 161, 180, 183; social service system

racism, 148; uninsured, 4, 140–48, 154–62; women, 45, 158–59. *See also* African Americans; Hispanics
rape, 69, 175n
Read to Me Coalition, Idaho, 168
reform: health care, 184–94, 206; welfare, xxii–xxiii, 52–56, 70, 71, 154, 165, 180
religion. *See* churches; spirituality
repetitive stress injuries, 32, 80, 89–90, 96–97, 103
resources: as handholds, 169–72; for health care, 205–6; homeless and, 175
restructuring, corporate, 25–29
retail sector, low-wage, 44
Riker's Island, New York, 19
Rio Grande Valley, Mexican American uninsured, 11, 140–48
Rome, Cheryl, 38–39
rotten teeth: caste marker, 44, 163, 165, 166, 168–69; homeless, 174; self-extraction, xvi–xvii, 166
Rust Belt, 7, 21–39, 72–75, 170

safety net, 185–86, 195, 201–4; clinics with sliding-scale fees, 1, 83–84, 131, 201–2, 203, 205; emergency room use, xx, 10, 12, 17–18, 67, 82, 202–3; health care resources for uninsured, 205–6; holes in, 52–56, 203–4; homeless and, 174n; welfare reform and, 52–56; working poor, 38–39; youth, 134. *See also* government programs
same-sex couples, health insurance, 59
SCHIP (State Children's Health Insurance Program)/KidCare, 73–74, 81, 185, 200
school. *See* education
scraping by, 10, 17, 147; consequences of, 10–14; family caregivers, 81; with job injuries, 106; low-wage workers, 45, 50–51; poor, xviii–xxi; youth, 129. *See also* caste; uninsured

self-employment, xv–xxiii, 107–21. *See also* small businesses
self-medication, 12; domestic violence and, 182; over-the-counter drugs, xviii–xix, xxi, 11, 12, 43, 48, 81, 90, 105, 141; veterans, 177. *See also* addiction; alcohol use
service sector: food industry jobs, 7, 20, 134–35; low-wage, 44, 47; uninsured, 8, 148. *See also* health care jobs
sex: contact between castes, 164; depression and functioning in, 102; incest, 33; rape, 69–70, 175n; same-sex couples, 59. *See also* marital status; men; women
Sharma, Ursula, 152, 164n
Shulman, Beth, 45
slavery, 153
sleep clinic, 81
sliding-scale fees: clinic, 1, 83–84, 131, 201–2, 203, 205; Community Health Centers, 205
Small Business Administration, Office of Advocacy, 114
Small Business Association, health plan, 118, 125–26, 127
small businesses, 8, 107–21, 188. *See also* entrepreneurs; self-employment
Social Security Act amendment (1996), 149
Social Security Disability Insurance (SSDI) system, 149–50, 176–77, 182, 199. *See also* disability (Social Security benefits)
spend-down, Medicaid, 38
spending, government health care, 135, 195–96. *See also* costs; taxes
spirituality, Rio Grande Valley, 142, 143. *See also* churches
SSDI (Social Security Disability Insurance), 149–50, 176–77, 182, 199
SSI (Supplemental Security Income), 55, 56, 127, 149–50, 176–77, 182, 198. *See also* disability (Social Security benefits)

Starr, Paul, 178
State Children's Health Insurance Program (SCHIP/KidCare), 73–74, 81, 185, 200
Stefan, Susan, 150–51, 199
stigma: mental illness, 148–51, 164; obesity, 167; uninsured, 16. *See also* caste; discrimination
stress: and death spiral, 47, 171–72; of economic changes, 37; family caregivers', 78; health problems caused by, 40, 42, 47, 78; job, 9, 32; and mental illness, 149; migraine sufferers, 67n; plant closings, 31n; post-traumatic stress syndrome, 179; repetitive movements, 80, 89–90, 96–97, 103. *See also* depression
Strickland, Ted, 180
substance abuse, 176–77; drug addiction, 149–50, 165, 178, 181. *See also* alcohol use
Supplemental Security Income (SSI) program, 55, 56, 127, 149–50, 176–77, 182, 198. *See also* disability (Social Security benefits)
Sweden, national health insurance, 125, 127

taxes: employer-sponsored health insurance and, 5, 189, 192, 193; hospital tax-exempt status, 202n; mandated coverage and, 187; universal coverage and, 189, 190, 191
technology: computer, 26; health care, 193–94; transportation, 26
teeth, middle class and, 168, 170. *See also* dentists; rotten teeth
Temporary Assistance to Needy Families (TANF), 53–55, 70
temporary jobs, 7–8; middle-class youth, 133–35; uninsured, xxii, 7, 43–44, 121, 133–35, 157, 189
Texas, 2, 118; uninsured in, 20, 140–48
therapy: massage, 111; mental health, 36–37, 69, 134, 144, 172

toxins: on the job, 89, 103; poor exposed to, 46. *See also* pollutants

training, job, 41, 74, 111; retraining programs, 28, 31–32, 37, 160

Transitional Aid to Families with Dependent Children program, Massachusetts, 70

trauma-related health problems, among homeless, 175n

tubal ligations, xvii–xviii, 51

tuberculosis, prisoner, 181

Tufts insurance company, 126–27

ulcers, xxi, 68

underclass, 164–65, 180. *See also* caste; poor

underemployment, middle-management workers, 28

underinsurance, 9–10, 201

unemployability, 15, 35, 37; disability definition, 55; domestic violence, 70–71, 182; family caregivers, 78; health problems, xxii, 9, 18, 37, 88n; homelessness, 175; mental illness, 143, 150–51; obesity, 167, 168; prisoners, 19, 183; substance abuse, 166

unemployment, 16; insurance payments, 35; mental illness and, 150; middle-management workers, 28; Mississippi, 47; as punishment for poor health, 165; Rust Belt, 22; uninsured, 28; veterans, 178. *See also* layoffs

uninsured, 200–201; African American, 4, 154–62; age, 4, 7, 129, *130*, 130n; class and, 135–37; emergency room use, xx, 10, 12, 17–18, 67, 82, 202–3; family caregivers, 72–79, 81; health care reform for, 184–94, 206; health care resources for, 205–6; homeless, 173–74; hospital treatment of, 10n, 11n, 12–14, 17–18, 39, 111–12; by income, *46*; Massachusetts, 135; mentally ill, 144–48; musician, 131; population, 2–3, 4, 200–201; "prob-lem of the uninsured," 4–5; racial minorities, 4, 140–48, 154–62; rea-sons, *32*, 41; Texas, 140–48; women's marital status, 8, 57–60, *58*, 62–64, 65, 66; youth, 7, 122–39. *See also* caste; health care costs; health prob-lems; poor; safety nets; scraping by; uninsured and employment

uninsured and employment, 5, 6–8, 30, *31*; African American, 155–57; full-time, 30, 33, 137; logging, 101, 107; low-wage, 40–43, 45, 53; mandating coverage and, 187; Mississippi, 165–69; nurse's aides, 147; office manager job, 66–67; self-employed, xvii, 108, 113; small business, 8, 105, 113–14, 118–19, 121; temporary, xxii, 7, 43–44, 121, 133–35, 157, 189; Wal-Mart, 33–34, 34n; without workers' comp, 93n; work time restrictions for, 43–44, 89–90, 91, 98–99, 118, 121, 122, 137, 188–89; youth, 7, 122–27, 130–39. *See also* caste

union jobs, 188; health care benefits, 5, 7, 26, 29–30, 39; job retraining programs, 28, 31–32, 37, 160; lay-offs from plant closings, 21–39, 160

universal coverage, 20, 189–94. *See also* national health insurance

upper class, weight control, 167

Urban Institute, 53, 192

U.S. Department of Agriculture, 47

U.S. General Accounting Office, 55

Vermillion County Clinic, 38

veterans, 106; homeless, 177–80; Viet-nam-era, 178–79

Veterans Administration (VA), 106, 177–78

violence: by mentally ill, 143, 144, 146; murder, 23; in prison, 182; sexual, 69–70, 175n. *See also* domestic vio-lence; wars

wages. *See* income
Walgreens, 137
Wall Street Journal, 202n
Wal-Mart, 33–34, 34n, 48
War Labor Board, 5, 188
wars, 4–5, 188; veterans, 106, 177–80
Washington Post, 19
Washington State University (WSU),
    43–44
Web sites: health care reform, 206;
    health care resources for uninsured,
    205–6
weight, and socioeconomic status, 167,
    170. *See also* obesity
Weisman, Andrea, 182, 183
Weitzman, Lenore, 59
welfare mothers, xxii, 54, 55, 164, 165,
    180
welfare reform, xxii–xxiii, 52–56, 70, 71,
    154, 165, 180
whites: drugs from Mexico, 11; immi-
    grant, 152; low-wage jobs, 45, 157;
    male premature death rate, 158;
    Mississippi incomes, 48; nurse's aide
    certification, 160; prisoners, 180; in
    racial hierarchy, 152; Texas incomes,
    141; uninsured, 4
widows, uninsured, 58, 142, 148, 171
Williamson, Michael, 169
Wilson, Mike, 187
women: American dream, xv, 25n; breast
    cancer, 62–65, 111–12, 158–59; busi-
    nesses formed by, 112; cervical can-
    cer, 123, 158; domestic violence,
    65–71, 181–82; family caregivers, 8,
    49, 54, 59, 73–85; family health care
    responsibilities, 4; gay, 59; income
    with and without children, 78n;
    injuries on the job, 89–90, 102–3;
    low-wage jobs, 44–45; marital status
    of uninsured, 8, 57–60, 58, 62–64,
    65; prisoners, 181; racial minorities'

health problems, 158–59; welfare
    reform and, xxii–xxiii, 54–55, 70, 71,
    154; widows, 58, 142, 148, 171
work, paid. *See* employment
workers' compensation insurance,
    88–96, 104, 197; doctors and, 87,
    95; employer avoidance of, 92, 93n,
    98–99, 156; firewall between health
    insurance and, 95–96; lump sum set-
    tlements, 94; masculinity ethic and,
    101; mental illness and, 149; "starv-
    ing them out," 94; vs. "sucking it
    up," 101; workings of, 92
work ethic, 165; masculine, 100–102;
    Rust Belt, 22; and work-related
    health hazards, 100–102, 103
working class, xv, 39; youth, 135–39. *See
    also* union jobs
working conditions, 54n; animal feed
    plant, 155–56; haircutting salon, 41,
    47; manufacturing jobs, 31–32. *See
    also* health hazards on the job; unin-
    sured and employment
working poor, xvii, xxi–xxiii, 39, 48, 53,
    190
work quality, small business vs. national
    chains, 112
World Series (2003), 100
World Trade Organization, 27
World War II, 4–5, 188
wraparound insurance policies, 198

Yale–New Haven Hospital, 14
yoga, 110–11
youth, 7, 122–39; African American,
    136–38, 180; expanding government
    program coverage for, 185; preg-
    nant/mothers, 129–30, 138–39, 165,
    180; prison, 136, 181. *See also* chil-
    dren

Zedlewski, Sheila, 55

COMPOSITOR: Sheridan Books, Inc.
INDEXER: Barbara Roos
ILLUSTRATOR: Bill Nelson
TEXT: 10/15 Janson
DISPLAY: Interstate
PRINTER AND BINDER: Sheridan Books, Inc.